Designing User Interfaces for an Aging Population

Towards Universal Design

Jeff Johnson

Kate Finn

MORGAN KAUFMANN PUBLISHERS

AN IMPRINT OF ELSEVIER

elsevier.com

Library of Congress Cataloging-in-Publication Data
A catalog record for this book is available from the Library of Congress

British Library Cataloguing-in-Publication Data
A catalogue record for this book is available from the British Library

ISBN: 978-0-12-804467-4

For information on all Morgan Kaufmann publications
visit our website at https://www.elsevier.com/books-and-journals

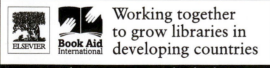

www.elsevier.com • www.bookaid.org

Publisher: Todd Green
Acquisition Editor: Todd Green
Editorial Project Manager: Lindsay Lawrence
Production Project Manager: Punithavathy Govindaradjane
Designer: Matthew Limbert

Typeset by TNQ Books and Journals

Contents

Foreword

My father did his own taxes this year—which might not seem like a huge accomplishment until you realize that he turned 100 last month. He's sharp as a tack, fit, and engaged with the life of his community and his family, just as he always has been, which he attributes to the fact that he's always been a "cock-eyed optimist" in his own words. He uses his computer for emails and online banking and looking up information and listening to music. And let's not forget Skyping—he loves to communicate though Skype with family and friends near and far. Recently, he was even on the cover of *Live Well* magazine as a poster "child" for aging well. He's a good example of, as Jules Renard said, "It's not how old you are, it's how you are old." And he is a great example of someone who is not "old" despite his 100 years.

He is struggling a bit though. See, he didn't grow up with computers. In fact, I gave him his first computer for his 80th birthday. He's now on his 5th one. But learning (and remembering) how to use them hasn't always been so easy, despite his

brilliance (and even though he's using a Mac) and since his tech support (me) lives several time zones away in a different state, so he doesn't have anyone right there to help him out when he hits snags which is frustrating.

I wish this book had been available—and used and applied—*before* he started using computers so they could have been designed to be more accessible for him and folks like him.

There are so many "little" things that make technology so much harder for him— "little" things that are actually arbitrary and don't help anyone. "Little" things that aren't so little when your body has aged and you don't see or hear so well anymore. Or you have a tremor in your hand that interferes with your manual dexterity and eye–hand coordination. Or your memory is not so great anymore. Or your attention wanders sometimes so you're more easily distracted. Or you find it harder to figure out what's the most important thing on visually cluttered screens. Or your joints hurt from arthritis which makes it hard to type. Or all of the above. At the same time. I've seen, for instance, that it's hard to open a pull-down menu and select the right option if it's hard to see and you have trouble controlling the mouse. And then I realize that even I have trouble with that sometimes.

Older adults like my Dad may find that the sum total of all these small "insults" makes them feel stupid and incompetent. For many older adults, this can cause them to shut down altogether, claiming they "don't do computers—that's for kids."

Believe me, I've heard older folks who live around my Dad say exactly these words. Especially because older adults are increasingly segregated from the larger community in many parts of the world, this is tragic because computers can help them stay engaged and informed and entertained. And loved by their far away families and friends.

But it doesn't have to be that way.

There are many ways to design devices, interfaces, and interactions to make them more accessible to older adults—and to all of us for that matter. Remember how curb cuts were originally intended to make sidewalks accessible to people

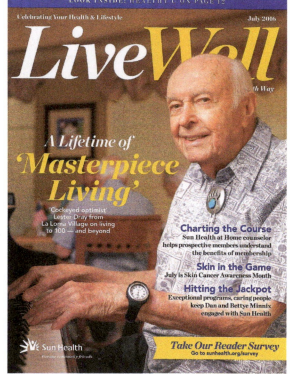

in wheelchairs? And how now they also help when we're wheeling luggage or pushing a cart from pavement to sidewalk? Many "accommodations" actually make things better for all of us.

And let's not forget that we're all aging and that we'll all be elderly—if we are lucky. These things will happen to us—to our bodies—but they don't have to cut us off from life because our technology tools don't work for us, or because the person who designed the very app we most need to use to communicate with our grandchildren was someone who was unaware that not everyone was a twenty-something like they were and that *all* bodies change with time. My Dad likes to remind me of what Doris Lessing said, to wit: "The great secret that all old people share is that you really haven't changed in 70 or 80 years. Your body changes, but you don't change at all."

I hope that you, the reader of this wonderful book, will see ways you can help every older person—even you whether now or in 30 years—to use technology to its fullest because it is designed with everyone in mind. To do this, read and soak up this book and learn it well. Then, get to know some elders. This goes a long way to seeing older people as, well, people which in turn makes it a lot easier to design for them. Then, design and test with older adults. Once you have done this, buy another copy of this book or loan this one to someone else—like your company's engineers and managers—and help them see how designing for older adults is not just "being nice." Show them how designing for older adults can help the bottom line, through better sales, more customer loyalty, and a better reputation. And remind them that they, too, are aging, and that designing for aging might just make their own lives easier in some distant future when they—and you—become Older Adults.

Susan Dray
August, 2016

Acknowledgments

This book is the product of a long-standing passion of both of ours: improving the digital user experience for everyone, including older adults. In looking back at how the book came to exist, we acknowledge that many people played significant roles.

We thank the dedicated staff at Elsevier, especially Lindsay Lawrence and Punitha Govindaradjane, for their diligence and professionalism in guiding this book from inception to publication. We also thank our reviewers, Dan Hawthorn, Stephen Lindsay, Linda Lior, Alan Newell, Frank Vetere, and Chris Wilkinson for their informed, detailed, and timely feedback and willingness to answer follow-up questions. The case study authors (Stefan Carmien, Ana Correia de Barros, Paula Alexandra da Silva, Teresa Gilbertson, Sean Hazaray, Samuli Heinonen, Francisco Nunes, Ana Vasconcelos) were also quite generous and patient with their time, writing several drafts of their works for no compensation other than their dedication to the purpose of making digital technology age-inclusive. We also thank authors who allowed us to reprint parts of their published works, such as tables and images. Finally, we thank Susan Dray for contributing a Foreword.

Over the past 10 years or so, many others—students, friends, and casual acquaintances—have added to our storehouse of anecdotal incidents.

The people who allowed us to use photographs of them for our personas and other images were very gracious and generous. In addition, we appreciate the many older adults who consented to be interviewed or who submitted surveys about their digital experiences, as well as about their health, education, and work backgrounds, all of which went into compiling biographies for the personas.

Jeff's wife, Karen Ande (karenande.com), and Max Keet (Seattle University) provided photos of people used for our personas and other individuals. Max also used his graphic expertise to create most of the original images in the book. Kate's daughter, Fiona Finn Tiene (Seattle University), wrestled the references into shape and provided technical assistance.

AUTHORS' INDIVIDUAL ACKNOWLEDGMENTS

My parents, Jack and Marj Finn, gave me my initial insight into how difficult it can be for older adults to use everyday objects and devices—and how frustrating, demeaning, and draining such interactions can become. My family and friends, who have listened to me go on about this topic for years, deserve thanks for their support. And the book would never have been begun, let alone finished, if not for Jeff Johnson's diligence and work ethic, combined with his vast knowledge and experience, all of which pulled me through some discouraging times.

—Kate Finn

I thank my coauthor and Wiser Usability cofounder, Dr. Kate Finn, for being a fine writer and cooperative spirit, and for helping to keep us focused on the goal of making this book appealing and useful to a broad range of technology designers and developers. I also thank my wife, Karen Ande, for her love, patience, and support during this multiyear project.

—Jeff Johnson

CHAPTER 1

Introduction

Technology is making the world ever smaller: communications are more frequent, transactions are more instantaneous, and reporting is more direct and unfiltered. If you aren't connected, you can be at a real disadvantage. Another disadvantage is being unable to easily and effectively use digital devices and online resources. As designers, developers, and advocates of digital technology, we should be doing our best to make it useful and usable for everyone, so no one will be at a disadvantage.

We know the benefits of staying mentally, socially, and physically active as we age. Digital technology can help with that. So it seems paradoxical that older adults can be particularly susceptible to the ill effects of poorly designed digital devices and user interfaces.

At the highest level, the message of this book can be summarized in these four points:

1. Poor usability detracts from everyone's user experience.
2. Poor usability *tends* (see box **About the Use of Italics in This Chapter**) to affect older adults *more often* and *more seriously* than it affects younger people.
3. Other groups who experience usability issues similar to older adults include people with low tech literacy, second language learners, people with low general literacy, and those with low vision or other impairments.
4. By specifically designing digital user interfaces with these individuals' usability issues in mind, we can improve the user experience for *many* people.

About the Use of Italics in This Chapter

To encourage you to think in terms of tendencies and generalities rather than absolutes, we have italicized words such as *tend (to)*, *some*, *many*, and *often* throughout this chapter. Throughout this book, we emphasize that the number and degree of individual differences increases with age. We all know people whose technical expertise, health, cognition, adaptability, and other relative attributes are exceptionally low or exceptionally high. For every tendency we discuss, there are always exceptions.

Designing User Interfaces for an Aging Population. http://dx.doi.org/10.1016/B978-0-12-804467-4.00001-3

Intended audience

This book should be of value primarily to designers and developers of websites, web apps, desktop apps, mobile apps, and digital appliances. Usability, UI, and UX professionals who are interested in age-friendly user interfaces will also find it valuable. And academics can use it as a course textbook or as a companion to more research-oriented publications.

WHAT DOES "AN AGING WORLD" MEAN?

You've probably heard it said that our world is aging. What does this mean?

Thanks to improvements in sanitation, housing, education, and health care, life expectancy has been increasing since the early 1900s. The World Health Organization (WHO) reports that life expectancy increased by 5 years from 2000 to 2015. In 2015, global life expectancy was 73.8 years for females and 69.1 years for males [WHO, 2016]. As a result, the numbers and percentages of older people in national populations have also grown. And they are continuing to grow.

Consider the number of people currently aged 50+. Figure 1.1 lists the 10 countries with the greatest numbers of people aged 50+ as of 2015. The top three countries, China, India, and the US, also had the largest national populations. There were nearly 400 million people aged 50+ in China alone!

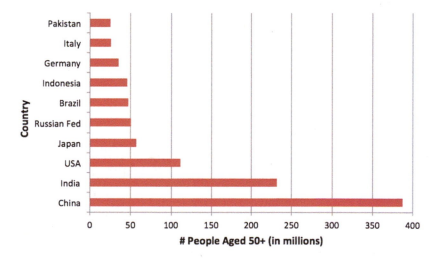

Figure 1.1.
Countries with the greatest populations of people aged 50+ [UNDESA, 2015a].

For another perspective, consider the percentages of people aged 50+. Worldwide, people aged 50+ will make up 28.9% of the population in 2035. In many countries, however, people aged 50+ will constitute an even larger proportion of the general population: nearly 45% of the population in more developed regions will be aged 50+ (see Figure 1.2). Nobody in our field should be ignoring a demographic that comprises 45% of the population.

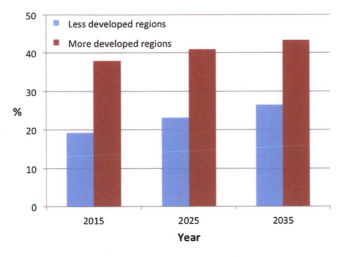

Figure 1.2.
Areas with highest percentage of adults 50+, 2015–35 [UNDESA, 2015a].

Increased life expectancies. More older people. Countries with large populations. Countries with growing numbers and percentages of older people. The data underscore the importance of addressing the needs and desires of a population that is rapidly growing older.

WHY SHOULD THE AGING OF THE WORLD'S POPULATION MATTER TO DESIGNERS?

As usability specialists, we often hear from friends, relatives, and casual acquaintances about their problems with digital devices, websites, or apps. Most of these interactions are with people over the age of 50—as we ourselves are—although *some* are with people much younger. Even when they're not trying to do anything especially complex, people are often frustrated and confused. Our aim with this book is to provide means for lessening their frustration and confusion, thereby enhancing user experience for older adults and their younger counterparts.

Usability studies sometimes directly examine the performance differences between older and younger participants. Compared to younger participants, older ones *tend to*:

- take longer to learn new applications or devices;
- take longer to complete tasks;
- use different search strategies;
- perform worse on tasks relying on memory;
- be more distractible;
- have a harder time dealing with errors;
- make more erratic or accidental movements with the pointer;
- make more input errors;
- have more trouble hitting on-screen targets.

On the plus side, older study participants *tend* to have better vocabularies and can draw from more real-world knowledge and experiences. Perhaps because they *tend* to be less impulsive and more risk-averse, they often use fewer mouse clicks to complete a task.

Believe it or not, there are still people who are not online! In the US as of 2015, 15% of all adults aged 18+ were not online [Perrin and Duggan, 2015]. A much higher percentage of older adults than younger adults are not online (19–42% vs. 4–7%) [Perrin and Duggan, 2015]. Of all off-liners, 32% cited usability issues: "finding it too difficult or frustrating to go online, or saying that they don't know how or are physically unable" [Zickuhr, 2013]. Other reasons included high cost, no perceived benefit, and lack of access or availability.

But *many* other people aged 50+ have used digital technology, in *some* form and to *some* extent, for decades. They may own computers, tablets, smartphones, e-readers, and fitness trackers. *Some* of these older adults are casual users (email, shopping, videos), while others have very high levels of technical expertise. Why do *some* older adults have a hard time with technology?

Maybe their eyesight isn't what it once was. Their hands might not be as steady on touch screens or small targets. It might take longer for them to learn and adapt to something new. Perhaps they don't keep up with social networking trends or understand the latest techno-speak. After all, nobody could have anticipated the frenzied pace of today's tech culture! But like people of any age, we older adults want to be independent, well informed, current, and relevant.

To communicate with friends and associates, shop, make travel arrangements, apply for benefits, conduct financial transactions, access information, and read publications, we are increasingly able—and sometimes forced—to conduct life's affairs online.

Given the general aging of the developed world and the growing expectation that most people are always online, designing age-friendly digital devices and user interfaces is certainly logical. Not only does age-friendly design make sense from the viewpoint of wanting to reach as wide an audience as possible, but it has also taken on an ethical imperative. The universe of digital technology can offer a wealth of information, empowerment, and potential. We cannot justify denying this wealth to any portion of our society.

DO WE REALLY NEED YET ANOTHER SET OF DESIGN GUIDELINES FOR YET ANOTHER SUBGROUP?

A distinguished heritage: other usability guidelines

There are, of course, other sets of guidelines available for designers of digital user interfaces. Perhaps the best-known guidelines are Nielsen's "10 Usability

Heuristics for User Interface Design" [Nielsen, 1995]. Nielsen himself calls them "broad rules of thumb and not specific usability guidelines," but 20+ years later their relevance is still acknowledged, and traces of them can be seen in nearly every other set of guidelines that has been developed since 1995.

There are also guidelines specifically about designing websites for older adults. In 2004–06, AARP sponsored work that resulted in several publications about designing websites for older adults [Chisnell and Redish, 2004; Chisnell and Redish, 2005; Chisnell et al., 2006]. They provided literature reviews, expert reviews of websites, and persona-based assessments to develop "heuristics for understanding older adults as web users."

In 2006, Dan Hawthorn presented his thesis, "Designing Effective Interfaces for Older Users," [Hawthorn, 2006] which contained the most detailed summary of related literature, the design implications of physical and cognitive aging, as well as the results of several programs developed to instruct and support the older adult who is beginning to use computers. Although Hawthorn recommends getting to know older adults by working closely with them, rather than applying a checklist of guidelines to people you don't even know, he nonetheless offers a great deal of insight into designs that do or don't work.

In 2009, the Center for Research and Education on Aging and Technology Enhancement (CREATE) published the second edition of *Designing for Older Adults: Principles and Creative Human Factors Approaches* [Fisk et al., 2009]. That book also covers both the characteristics of aging adults and design methodologies. The authors offer design guidelines for information perception, input/output devices, and instructional programs. They also include a separate chapter on user interface design, listing several well-established guidelines.

In 2013, the Nielsen Norman Group released their second edition of "Senior Citizens (Ages 65 and older) on the Web" [Pernice et al., 2013]. This commercially available report focuses on design guidelines for specific tasks and components of websites.

These publications, as well as countless other efforts, have all contributed to our understanding of older adults as users of digital products and online services: what usability issues they might face; what strategies they might employ to overcome obstacles; what their goals and values are. Most have focused on websites, basing their findings on usability studies and other assessments of existing websites and classroom sessions for teaching basic computer skills.

What about accessibility guidelines?

We are also often asked how designing technology for older adults differs from designing technology to be accessible to people with disabilities.

After all, much of this book describes how certain sensory, motor, and cognitive abilities often decline with age, which means that compared to younger adults, many older adults have disabilities. Some accessibility experts refer to people who lack disabilities as "temporarily able-bodied" [Rae, 1989]. Why isn't it enough for technology designers to just follow accessibility guidelines?

Hopefully, you've heard of WCAG 2.0 (Web Content Accessibility Guidelines 2.0), published in 2008 by the Web Accessibility Initiative (WAI) of the World Wide Web Consortium (W3C) [W3C-WCAG2.0, 2008]. Not as well known, adhered to, or enforced in the US as in some other parts of the world, WCAG 2.0 is the result of a truly herculean and massively democratic effort. However, it is sometimes criticized for being obsolete, inflexible, or overly complex.[1]

The Ageing Education and Harmonisation Project (WAI-AGE), completed in 2010, concluded that WCAG 2.0 was sufficient to ensure web accessibility for older people [W3C-WAI-AGE, 2010; W3C-WAI-older-users, 2010]. WCAG 2.0 has three different success criteria levels, A, AA, and AAA, with AAA being the strictest. Unfortunately, *some* guidelines that we consider necessary for older adults are found only at level AAA. Gilbertson [2015] concurs, as can be seen in her comment:

> While the AAA ranking for link purpose and simple language is likely due to the prescriptive nature of these recommendations to the point where designers would possibly feel constrained...the placement at the AAA level risks rendering such recommendations invisible to designers, developers and project managers – [p. 342, Gilbertson, 2015].

More evidence that WCAG 2.0 is not sufficient to guide designers toward age-friendly design was provided by Gilbertson's survey of industry attitudes toward aging and accessibility [Gilbertson, 2015]. Of the respondents—all from web developer companies in the UK—only about 50% considered aging to be an accessibility issue. And fewer than 20% were aware of how WCAG 2.0 applied to older people. Results were even worse when comparing project managers' responses to front line professionals' responses.

Some additional reasons to look beyond pure accessibility guidelines:
1. Many older adults experience *multiple age-related changes* that affect their ability to use digital technology. The effects of multiple changes can interact with one another, making them even more difficult to overcome. Older adults' multiple-age differences are best addressed together. (Interacting age-related changes are mentioned elsewhere in the book, in particular in the final chapter.)
2. Older adults are prime potential beneficiaries of digital technology, so we want to go beyond making such technology merely *accessible* for

---

1 The word *inaccessible* comes to mind.

them. We also want to make it attractive, easy, productive, and enjoyable to use.

3. Older adults may differ from younger adults in their *knowledge* and *attitudes* about new digital technology (see Chapters 7: Knowledge and 9: Attitude). Accessibility guidelines rarely address such differences, possibly because young people, regardless of ability, typically have very similar knowledge and attitudes about technology—there *tends* to be a greater degree of difference among older adults.

4. Older adults *often* possess greater task-domain knowledge than younger adults. With respect to "know-how," younger adults are *often* at a disadvantage. Where appropriate, design can take advantage of this difference by giving older adults a way to use their domain knowledge.

So, yes, you should be aware of accessibility guidelines, but also be aware that following them may not suffice to provide older adults with positive user experiences.

What makes this book's guidelines different?

None of us wants to design completely different versions of devices, apps, and online services for different age groups. But we also don't want to design technology exclusively for one age group and risk alienating all the other age groups. So, what's a designer to do?

Many of the guidelines we present are not exclusive to older users; in fact, you may look at them and think, "But this is just plain old good UI design!" (or just common sense). But remember, older people will *tend* to have *more frequent* and *more serious* usability issues with user interfaces that don't observe age-friendly guidelines.

Our view is that user interfaces designed for older adults are often better for a lot of other people. Take, for example, this recommendation from Chapter 3: Vision (Figure 1.3).

Make controls prominent.

- Ensure that main elements – links, menus, buttons, etc. – stand out. Distinguish interactive controls from non-interactive text and graphics. Make clickable elements look quite different from non-clickable ones by using different colors (not just a different hue).

Figure 1.3.
An example guideline from Chapter 3: Vision.

That's not unreasonable, is it? After all, who wants to hunt around on a screen trying to figure out which bits are active and which bits are just decorative?

And here's another example taken from Chapter 4: Motor Control (Figure 1.4).

Provide big tap targets.

- Tap targets on touchscreens should be larger than click targets on desktop and laptop computers, because fingers are larger than cursors. For high accuracy (90%+), tap targets should be at least 16.5mm diagonally (11.7mm square).
- Smaller targets will result in decreased accuracy. For example, with tap targets only 9.9mm diagonally, seniors' accuracy dropped to 67%, and task-completion time increased by 50%.

Figure 1.4.
An example guideline from Chapter 4: Motor Control.

Our guidelines for sizing and spacing of targets maximize the odds that someone will be able to hit their intended target instead of the one next to it. Shouldn't that prove beneficial for just about everyone?

Think of These Guidelines as Curb Cuts and OXO Designs for Digital Technology

Curb Cut – [Photo by Jeff Johnson].

Curb cuts (also known as kerb ramps or dropped kerbs) are inclined planes that provide a gradual change from one height to another. They are typically used at curbs or staircases. They were originally intended to improve access for people using wheelchairs, but have proven to be helpful for people using other mobility aids (e.g., canes, rolling walkers, crutches, motorized scooters). Curb cuts also benefit users of shopping carts, baby strollers, wheeled suitcases, skateboards, bicycles, roller-blades, etc.

Similarly, the US-based manufacturer OXO originated when its founder, Sam Farber, noticed the difficulties his wife Betsey had using a kitchen peeler. Sam promised Betsey, who suffered from arthritis in her hands, that he would invent a more comfortable peeler for her. The first 15 OXO kitchen tools—including a peeler—were introduced in 1990. The product line has since grown to include over 1000 items for the kitchen, office, and home. OXO products are famous for their ergonomic design and are enjoyed by people of all ages and abilities [OXO, 2016].

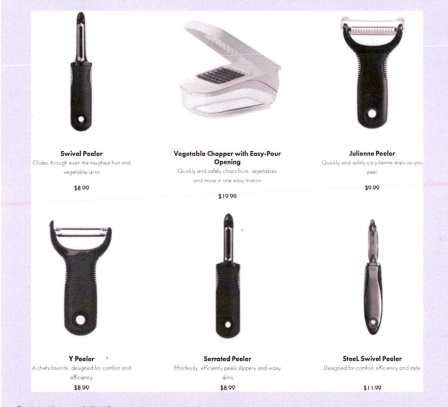

Swivel Peeler
Glides through even the toughest fruit and vegetable skins
$8.99

Vegetable Chopper with Easy-Pour Opening
Quickly and safely chops fruits, vegetables and more in one easy motion
$19.99

Julienne Peeler
Quickly and safely cut julienne strips as you peel
$9.99

Y Peeler
A chefs favorite, designed for comfort and efficiency
$8.99

Serrated Peeler
Effortlessly, efficiently peels slippery and waxy skins
$8.99

Steel Swivel Peeler
Designed for comfort, efficiency and style
$11.99

Selection of OXO peelers and choppers.

Both of these are cases where a design intended to provide an improvement for one demographic had the unforeseen consequences of providing improvements for many other people.

Following such guidelines can make digital products and services more usable for *many* people, not just older adults. There are people of *all* ages with visual impairments, hearing loss, low literacy, limited motor ability, poor technical experience, and memory loss.

Moreover, consider instances of situational impairment. People who, due to temporary medical conditions, aren't functioning at full capacity. Sleep-deprived students, workers, or parents. Individuals in dimly lit, noisy, or bumpy environments. Drivers of nondriverless cars who can't use their hands. People struggling to focus under distracting conditions. Anyone moving from a dark to a bright environment, whose eyes need time to adjust, and whose digital display is no longer sufficiently contrastive. People with cold, damp, or gloved fingers, whose touch-screen devices won't recognize their attempts at interactions.

MOVING FORWARD

The designer's maxim "Know your user" still applies. But in our experience, *many* designers have not had the opportunity to actually work closely with older adults. As a result, they may be operating from misconceptions and stereotypes. They may not have much background in cognitive science or human aging. The chapters in this book are intended to provide our readers with a practical and sufficient—but not overwhelming—amount of background information on older adults and user experience. But you should still get to know some real users!

We readily acknowledge that there's more to creating a great user experience than merely complying with a checklist of guidelines. Guidelines, of course, are simply recommendations. How applicable and how appropriate they are depend on many factors, such as the user population, the purpose of an application or device, the circumstances of use, and the technical specifications.

That's why, instead of just listing guidelines, we give you contextual information that you can use in deciding how, when, and whether to apply a particular guideline. We describe the general sensory, cognitive, knowledge, and experiential changes or circumstances of older adults which, if properly addressed, can provide better user experiences. The guidelines we suggest are all derived from the publications we reference. The authors of those publications were all motivated to provide improved user experiences for older adults in light of age-related changes, differences, and trends.

It would be lovely if, one day, user interfaces were so smart that they adapted to each user's individual needs and preferences, whether long-term or situational. Maybe, one day, we won't think in terms of *interfaces* because everything in the entire world will be so interconnected.

And it might be possible for you to create age-friendly digital designs just based on a list of guidelines—possible, but not likely. It really helps to understand what lies beneath the guidelines.

Still, please don't just take our word(s) for any of the information in the following chapters. If you yourself are not an older adult, we strongly encourage you to get to know some of them. And if you are an older adult, get to know members of your age group who are outside your typical social and business circles. Expand your horizons; empathize!

ORGANIZATION OF BOOK

Most of this book is organized into categories of the major age-related sensory, cognitive, and behavioral changes and characteristics that can potentially impact people's use of technology.

Since you will probably want to focus on the guidelines, we minimized the background noise. On the other hand, we don't expect you to just accept the guidelines at face value without knowing what motivates them. So we prefaced each chapter's guidelines with information about age-related changes and how these changes can affect our use of digital devices.

Chapter 2. Meet Some Older Adults

In Chapter 2, we paint a very broad picture of older adults. We describe them in terms of their relative online percentages, device ownership, and birth or technology generations. We then present six personas representing typical technology-using older adults in the developed world.

Chapter 3. Vision

Chapter 4. Motor Control

Chapter 5. Hearing and Speech

Chapter 6. Cognition—Attention, Learning, and Memory

Chapter 7. Knowledge

Chapter 8. Search

Chapter 9. Attitude

In Chapters 3–9, we describe age-related changes and characteristics with data on the prevalence of these changes and characteristics. We focus on the age-related characteristics that are most likely to impact user experience. We believe that giving this background information will help you understand the motivation for the guidelines. Realistic simulations, and real-life positive and negative examples (marked with green √s or red Xs), show how these characteristics impact user experience, and illustrate the chapters' guidelines.

Isn't Mobile Design Different From Desktop/ Laptop Design?

We are often asked if designing mobile technology requires different guidelines than designing desktop/laptop technology. Don't we need separate guidelines for the two platforms?

Fortunately for designers, researchers who investigated this concluded that mobile user interface guidelines, including guidelines for designing for older adults, are mostly the same as guidelines for desktop user interfaces. They simply need to be combined with guidelines for touch screen–based user interfaces [Strengers, 2012], as we have done in our chapters.

Chapter 10. Working With Older Adults

In Chapter 10, we describe what you may encounter when working with older adults as design or usability study participants. We discuss aspects of selecting a design protocol as well as practical considerations for conducting your design or evaluation sessions.

Chapter 11. Case Studies

Chapter 11 contains descriptions of five different projects, written by their respective researchers. Several of the projects describe participatory design processes and iterations of age-friendly technology interfaces. One is a summary of a dissertation detailing the development of an instructional third-age simulator, intended to build empathy among designers.

Chapter 12. Summary

Chapter 12 summarizes the major points of the book, linking them back to the purposes we have identified in this introductory chapter.

Appendix—Design Guidelines

The Appendix presents all the guidelines from all the chapters, combined into one location. The guidelines are organized by chapter title.

Why Does That Guideline Look So Familiar?

We have tried to be as precise as possible with the wording of our guidelines. In cases where research related to only one type, or version, or generation of a device, we generalized the findings to arrive at more broadly applicable guidelines.

Some guidelines relate to topics that span multiple chapters, so you will see them repeated in each chapter. This results in a certain amount of redundancy among the guidelines shown in chapters.

Our guidelines about designing to accommodate older adults are meant to be used along with your favorite other user interface design guidelines, not instead of them. Conflicts will inevitably occur, and you will need to resolve them using your own best judgment for the circumstances at hand.

References

The References section includes all sources cited throughout the book.

NOTE

Left-to-right languages

For brevity, our discussions on displaying and reading text assume languages that are read left to right. For languages read in other directions, we assume that you can adjust the guidelines appropriately.

CHAPTER 2

Meet Some Older Adults

The ironic thing is that aging is the one thing we have in common, if we're lucky. – Barbara Beskind (90+-year old employee at the design firm IDEO) [Tsui, 2015]

WHO ARE WE TALKING ABOUT?

There's no universal agreement on the age at which people are considered "older." One humorous definition of "old" is "at least 10 years older than I am now." An AARP study [AARP, 2014] produced an infographic, *You're Old, I'm Not*. When 1800 people were asked when they thought "old age" begins, they responded as shown in Table 2.1. Interestingly, everyone described themselves as young "for their age."

In the US, age 65 has commonly been associated with old age, because that is the age at which one becomes eligible for Social Security and many senior discounts.[1] But these days, due to financial circumstances and increasing life expectancies, people retire at many different ages. Some individuals retire multiple times, or not at all. For example, Dr. Ephraim Engleman continued seeing patients, conducting research, and writing books at University of California San Francisco Medical Center until the day he died, at age 104 [Whiting, 2015]. There just doesn't seem to be that much significance to age 65 anymore.

AARP, with 40 million members, was formerly known as the American Association for Retired Persons. It just goes by AARP now and uses "real possibilities" as its motto. AARP starts sending membership information to people approaching their 50th birthdays. Anyone age 50 or older can join.

There's fun in impersonating old age—I mean real old age. – Ian McKellen, 76, on playing the character of 93-year-old Sherlock Holmes [Zeitchik, 2015].

---

1 In 1935, when US President Franklin Roosevelt signed the Social Security Act, retirement age was 65. The average life expectancy of people turning 65 in 1940 was 77.7 years for men and 79.7 years for women [www.ssa.gov/history/lifeexpect.html].

Table 2.1	Average Responses to "At What Age Is a Person 'Old'?" – (Source: based on AARP [2014])
Responder's age	**When they think "old age" starts**
40s	63
50s	68
60s	73
70s	75

For this book, we chose age 50 as the starting point for "older-hood." While most 50-year-olds are still healthy, active, and full of life, they are also likely to have begun experiencing some age-related changes:

■ People most commonly start noticing farsightedness (presbyopia) between the ages of 42 and 44 [Bonilla-Warford, 2012].

■ Nearly one in five people of age 12 and older has unilateral or bilateral hearing loss; the prevalence increases with every age decade [Lin et al., 2011].

■ The process of losing memory making and cognitive abilities is well under way by age 40, after which it accelerates [Oregon State University, 2013].

Perhaps most significantly, people now aged 50+ did not experience the current, latest generation of technology during their formative years. They belong to a different technology generation than younger people. The concept of technology generations is discussed in more detail later in this chapter and also in Chapter 7: Knowledge. Keep in mind that what is referred to as "the current, latest generation of technology" is constantly changing.

THE NAMING OF THINGS IS A DIFFICULT MATTER

How should we refer to people who are "older"? There is not much agreement on what term to use. There isn't even agreement on whether there should *be* a term.

Responding to criticism about The New Old Age Blog's title, the author interviewed a number of prominent individuals from relevant fields [Graham, 2012]. Among other suggested terms for old age, the interviewees suggested *older people*; *young-old* and *old-old*; *aging past youth*, or *aging into the middle years*, or *aging toward old age*; and *aging*.

Over 300 readers, most of whom were probably over 50, commented. Many offered their own ideas, which included *mature, senior, old elders*, the *long-lived, platinum, geezer* and *geezerette, wrinklers, boomers* (shortened from "baby boomers"), *retired persons*; decade identifications such as *septuagenarian* and *octogenarian*; *silver surfers, vintage, spring bats* (combining "spring chickens" with "old bats"), *elderly*, and *golden agers*.

The terms they offered were variously earnest, humorous, rude, and creative. Some commenters' preferred terms were considered insulting by others. *Boomers* is US centric and captures only the one generation of people born between 1945 and 1964 and thus isn't inclusive of all current or future older adults. Some terms, such as *elder* or *pensioner*, apply in some cultures or countries but not all. So, there is basically no agreement about terminology.

Many people don't want to consider themselves old, older, aged, or aging. Still, we need a common language for talking about it.

> What's going on is we have a problem with the subject itself. Everyone wants to live longer, but no one wants to be old… Personally, I tend to use the term "older people" because it's the least problematic. Everyone is older than someone else. – Harry Moody, quoted in [Graham, 2012].

Taking a tip from this, we're going with the term *older adults*. While no term will meet with everyone's approval, we hope the term *older adults* doesn't offend anyone.

You Can't Be Talking About Me!

We sometimes give presentations about how to design technology that doesn't exclude older adults. These presentations include examples of design flaws that cause older adults to struggle with websites, mobile apps, and digital devices. Many audience members at our presentations appear to be our age (60s) or older. Occasionally, one of them will approach us and say, "You know, it's not only old people. Even **I** have trouble with that!" Our usual response is to just nod silently.

SOMETIMES, AGE REALLY *IS* JUST A NUMBER

> Thank goodness we have evolved to where we are now, where 'ageless' really means just transcending your number. We're not the total sum of our years. We're so much more. – Barbara Hannah Grufferman, author and AARP Bulletin Contributor [Bowen, 2015].

We've probably all heard people say something like, "60 is the new 40!" In early 2016, there was a flurry of newspaper articles in the UK making the case for 85 being "old age" (for examples, see [Sayid, 2016; Spencer, 2016]). The articles were based on a survey by the Royal Voluntary Service, which found that more than 10% of people aged 60+ considered "old age" to begin around 90. Respondents drew inspiration from active older celebrities such as Dame Helen Mirren. For one perspective on this attitude, see Figure 2.1.

Figure 2.1.
Old is the new black [used by permission, Judith Boyd, StyleCrone.com; photo credit Daniel Nolan; shirt design by Ari Seth Cohen of AdvancedStyle.com and Fannie Karst].

Within any given age range, there is variation in the ability, aptitude, and attitude of users regarding digital technology. Individuals can differ in:

- whether or not they experience any given age-related change;
- the age of onset of any change;
- the extent of the change;
- how successfully they compensate for each change.

And often, aging affects an individual in multiple ways. While the effects of a single age-related change might be mild, the cumulative effects of multiple changes can have a profound impact on a person.

The bottom line is that age alone doesn't determine someone's success in texting on a smartphone or navigating a website. In this book, however, we **do** focus on certain "age-related" characteristics precisely because they **are** so closely correlated with age.

As one looks at increasingly older age groups, averages become less accurate, ranges of abilities become broader, and individual variation becomes more pronounced [Hawthorn, 2006]. The variability among individuals within an age group only increases with age.

Because of this variability, nobody can truly be summed up by a list of labels or expressed by a single data point in a graph. Age, by itself, reveals little about the characteristics and abilities of any given individual. In their seminal work on designing usable websites for older adults, Chisnell and Redish [2005] recommended characterizing technology users along three additional dimensions:

- Ability: degrees of physical and cognitive limitations or restrictions requiring little remediation, up to needing assisted living.
- Aptitude: expertise with computers and the Web (being more relevant than straight measures of experience).
- Attitude: positive (forward-looking, risk-taking, and experimental) or negative (fearful or diffident) confidence levels and emotional need for support from another human being.

CHARACTERISTICS OF *SOME* OLDER ADULTS

We want our products to appeal to older people as well as to younger ones. But what do we really know about older people? Are they just like everyone else, but…older? In the introduction, we listed some ways in which older adults differ from younger ones in the context of usability studies. What about a more general picture of who older adults are?

Online versus offline

Internet use has grown steadily due to increased access, but also due to the growing perception of the Internet as useful and desirable. As shown in Figure 2.2, the percentage of every age group of US adults who go online has grown since 2000. The steepest increase in people going online has been in the 65+ age group. This represents an enormous potential market.

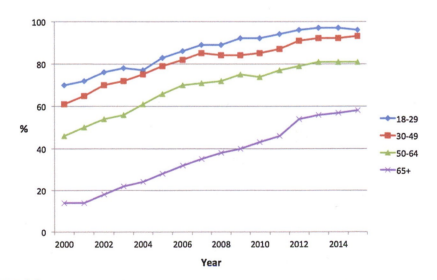

Figure 2.2.
Percentage of US adults who use the Internet, from 2000 to 2015, by age [Perrin and Duggan, 2015].

As of 2013, however, 15% of all US adults were *not* going online. That includes 19% of those aged 50–64 and 42% of those aged 65+. That's a lot of people!

As with the rates of people going online, these data depict US adults only, but may also be representative of people in countries with similar development, literacy, education, and income levels. In the report "Smartphone Ownership and Internet Usage Continues to Climb in Emerging Economies" [Poushter, 2016], two particularly interesting points emerge:

1. Most adults in advanced economies use the Internet.
2. The majority of Internet users in most countries are daily users.

Unfortunately (for our purposes), the report only breaks the data into two age groups: younger people (18–34) and older generations (35+).

The difference between online and offline populations is known as the digital gap or digital divide.

Digital device ownership

In the US, as of 2015, 92% of all adults own some kind of mobile phone, 68% own smartphones, 73% own a desktop or laptop computer, 45% own tablet computers, and 19% own e-readers [Anderson, 2015].

Older US adults have been acquiring digital devices and increasing their online presence. As shown in Figure 2.3, in 2015 most people aged 65+ still preferred simple mobile phones (feature phones) to smartphones, and a majority also owned desktop or laptop computers.

As before, these figures represent data from the US only, but can be considered representative of other developed countries. Some countries (e.g., South Korea, Australia, and Israel) have even higher rates of smartphone ownership than the

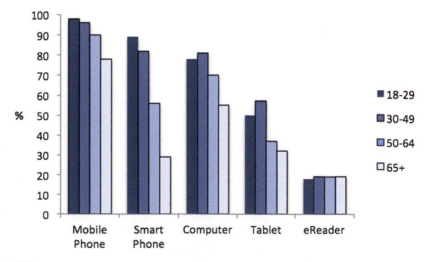

Figure 2.3.
Percent of US adults who own digital devices, by age and device type [Anderson, 2015].

US. But of course, many people of all ages worldwide can't afford such devices and are not computer literate.

In countries with large populations, the absolute number of older adults using digital technology can be large even if there is a digital divide between younger and older people. For example, India has a population of 1 billion people, of which 890 million (89%) use the Internet or own a smartphone. Poushtar [2015] found a clear digital divide between people aged less than 35 years and people aged 35 years and above. Despite that gap, there are millions of people aged 50+ in India who use the Internet and smartphones. All of them are potential beneficiaries of age-friendly technology design!

A generation gap, or something else?

We made the case above that age alone is not an indicator of technical proficiency. In this section, we discuss a different aspect of age—birth generations—and how it may predict older adults' ability to use digital technology.

Birth generations

In the US, the end of World War II brought the return of military personnel, a booming economy, and an unprecedented upsurge in the number of babies being born that continued for nearly 20 years. Babies born between 1945 and 1964 came to be known as the Baby Boom Generation, Baby Boomers, or just Boomers.

Apart from the social impact of the Boomers, this phenomenon gave rise to a trend in designating generations. The preceding generation was variously named the Silent Generation, the GI Generation, or the Greatest Generation. Subsequent generations were somewhat unimaginatively called Gen X, Gen Y, and Gen Z (other names exist as well). The Baby Boom Generation had a definitive starting event (the end of World War II), and generations are usually considered to be about 20 years long, but the generations since the Baby Boomer Generation have been less clearly delineated.

Then, academicians got involved and made something of a science out of it. In Figure 2.4, we present the US generations born since about 1900. Our generations are loosely based on those defined by Neil Howe and William Strauss [Howe and Strauss, 2007]. Note that we use "Gen Y" for people born since 2005 (no final cutoff year yet). Several other names have been suggested for Gen Y, but nothing has been agreed.

As we readily admit, these generation names are US specific. Other countries and cultures use other names or denote these generations with other dates.

Digital natives and digital immigrants

In 2001, Marc Prensky coined the terms *digital natives* and *digital immigrants*. He wrote that people born after 1980 were "all 'native speakers' of the digital language of computers, video games, and the Internet" [Prensky, 2001]. Since 2001, the terms have made their way into common speech (in some circles anyway), and some people seem to think that anyone born after 1980 is a digital native.

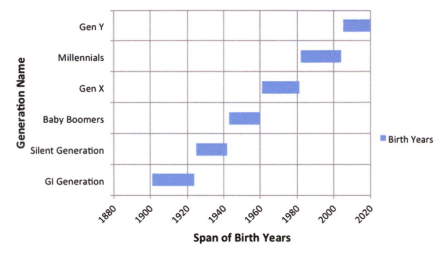

Figure 2.4.
Birth generations [Howe and Strauss, 2007].

But such a generalization does not hold up under examination. Within any group of individuals, there is considerable variation. Yes, younger adults, *as a group, tend* to be more comfortable with living a connected and digital existence than older adults *as a group*, but they're not born that way (see Figure 2.5).

Figure 2.5.
Digital Natives: Just born that way? [Source: www.dreamstime.com].

Variations on a Theme

Consider these quotes from people who have worked with older adults in design and evaluation settings:

There is a huge diversity of OLDER ADULTS as a group—in education, work experience, health, age-related issues, life stage....And unlike other "groups," they can span anywhere from 50 (or 55, 60, 65...) on up—a much broader age range than most other groups include.... Diversity can mean that techniques that work for some may not work for others. – [Dickinson et al., 2007].

One methodological size does not fit all especially when it comes to usability evaluations with older adults. – [Franz et al., 2015].

The [participatory design] process also forced us to try to respect the diversity of our participants and drives home the fact that these participants are not, by any means, a homogeneous group. – [Lindsay et al., 2012].

The process is made even more challenging by the fact that "older adults" are very diverse. While improved usability helps everyone, there are times when a change intended to improve usability may benefit one portion of an audience and hinder another. – [Ostergren and Karras, 2007].

Many young people now in the work force aren't particularly computer literate, and they aren't gaining technical experience or competencies at school or work. External factors such as socioeconomic status, education, culture, and location, plus internal factors such as health, motivation, intelligence, and memory all contribute to the making of a so-called digital native. The same external and internal factors apply to older people, in determining how readily they'll be able to use digital technology. But for older adults, there is another factor: what *technology generation* they belong to.

Technology generations

As with birth generations, researchers have identified several different technology generations. Most of us are most comfortable using whatever form of technology was current during our formative period: ages 10–25 [Lim, 2010]. We belong to the technology generation that was dominant during those years. As we age beyond 25 (approximately), and technology advances, we may have trouble learning or remembering how to use products or services we did not grow up with [Wilkinson, 2011]. It's not impossible...it's just not as easy.

The effects of technology generations are discussed in more detail in Chapter 7: Knowledge, but for now, just keep in mind that technology generations exist. The technology generations that we are concerned with are shown in Figure 2.6.

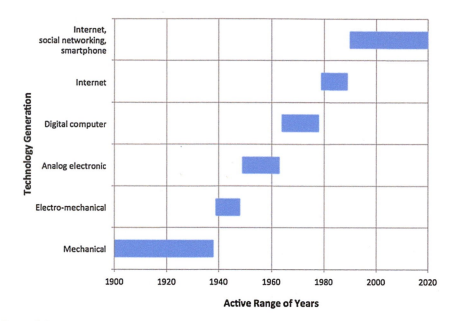

Figure 2.6.
Technology Generations (adapted from Docampo Rama et al. [2001]; Lim [2010]; Sackmann and Winkler [2013]).

Don't Forget About All Those Caregivers

A rapidly increasing older population means a greater need for caregivers. In the US, 29% of the adult population provides care for someone. Women make up 66% of family caregivers. A family caregiver might be responsible for researching treatments, arranging medical care, and contacting support systems. The typical caregiver is a 49-year-old woman who works full time outside the home; in addition, she spends 24.4 h per week on caregiving. For care recipients 65+, the average caregiver is 63 years old. One-third of these older caregivers are themselves in fair or poor health [Family Caregiver Alliance, 2012]. Caregivers and care recipients are likely to experience negative effects when a caregiver is stressed, in poor health, and not technically skilled.

PERSONAS FOR THIS BOOK

To illustrate the diversity among older adults and to provide examples for this book's discussions and guidelines, we developed six personas—fictional people—representing older adults. Details of our personas were derived from many sources, including publications of the United Nations [UNESCO, 2013; UNDESA, 2015b], the US Department of Health and Human Services [Blackwell et al., 2014], the US Census Bureau [Werner, 2011], and informal surveys of family, friends, and colleagues from around the world. Throughout this book, we illustrate the guidelines with quotes and anecdotes attributed to these six personas.

Carolina

Carolina, 52, works as a music therapist for a veterans' hospital in the US. She also teaches folk dance at her local community center. Carolina moved to the US from Latin America when she was a young adult. Although English is not her first language, she obtained her master's degree in art therapy from a US university. Carolina must use digital technology at work, but all too often she struggles with its complexity. She sometimes has to ask for help from her coworkers and even from some of her clients. Still, she finds that she knows more than some of her clients, whom she helps with relatively simple things such as making online appointments, finding and downloading items from the Web, and interpreting health information.

Hana

Hana, 68, is a retired business manager in Japan. She and her husband have two children and four grandchildren. Their daughter and her family live nearby; their son and his family live in the US. Hana enjoys spending time with her grandchildren, and she has taken up *ikebana* (Japanese flower arranging). She uses a tablet computer mostly for games and social media and a smartphone mostly for making calls. She's currently being treated for cancer and has noticed that her medications affect her memory and concentration. These days, she is completely reliant on her family for technical help, such as finding apps on her devices, remembering passwords, and changing settings.

John

John, a retired 80-year-old teacher, lives by himself in London. John currently donates his services to a migrant education centre. He loves to travel and visit his children and grandchildren. Staying in touch with family and colleagues means that John spends a great deal of time online. John has impaired vision; as a result, he makes extensive use of the visual magnification properties and audio capabilities of his digital devices. He recently purchased a tablet computer and hopes to make good use of it, instead of his smartphone, when he travels.

Monika

Monika is a 63-year-old retired banker in Germany. She now manages the small apartment building where she lives. She and her brother devote a lot of time taking care of their mother, who has multiple health conditions. These days, it seems, much of Monika's time online is spent looking for medical information, arranging for care, and making doctors' appointments for her mother. While generally in good health herself, Monika takes a medication that induces hand tremor. This makes it difficult for her to accurately hit keyboard keys, select small onscreen targets, or make touch gestures. She increasingly relies on voice input to interact with her devices.

Stefano

Stefano and his wife own an automobile repair shop in Italy. They have a large extended family nearby. Stefano, 58, is physically active: he bikes, and he and his wife take hiking tours around Europe. His only concern is that, as a result of noise exposure during military service, he has lost quite a bit of hearing; this makes it difficult for him to hear audio alerts or the sound on videos. As a business owner and fitness enthusiast, Stefano welcomes technology for contacting customers, keeping financial records, ordering parts, and planning bike routes. But he struggles to keep up with his customers' expectations that he is using the most current technology.

Wong

Wong, 70, and his wife live in a small apartment near their son, daughter-in-law, and grandson in a small city in China. He enjoys playing *Xiang qi* (Chinese chess), practicing *Qigong*, and spending time with his family. Wong uses a desktop computer to keep track of his appointments, reports, news, and financial transactions. He uses his smartphone mostly for phone calls but also for weather, transportation, and some social networking. He tried to use a *Xiang qi* app on his smartphone but had trouble seeing and manipulating the very small objects on the screen.

CHAPTER 3

Vision

When we talk about age-friendly technology, a common first response is "Oh, you mean bigger fonts?"

"Use bigger fonts" is indeed an important guideline for making digital technology more accessible to older adults, because vision tends to get worse as people age. However, as with all age-related changes, there is great variability between individuals in both the extent of changes and the age of onset. More importantly, "declining vision" is complex: vision has many different aspects that can decline. Bigger fonts only help for some of them.

The problem of older adults having difficulty seeing details is of course not limited to digital technology. Printed materials—books, magazines, brochures, package labeling and ingredients, drug usage directions, legal documents, and so forth—have for centuries been plagued by designs that don't work for older adults. This continues despite laws requiring that materials be accessible to people with poor vision, such as the US's Americans with Disabilities Act (ADA, passed in 1990) and the UK's Disability Discrimination Act (DDA, passed in 1995).

The persistence of senior-unfriendly printed materials is due at least partly to poor communication between companies and the designers who work for them. Companies assume that their designers know the accessibility requirements and will design accordingly, but designers assume that if their client companies wanted designs that were highly visually accessible they would specify that in their requirements [Cornish et al., 2015]. The result: poor visual accessibility.

Sadly, design that works poorly for visually impaired people, including many older adults, has spread into the realm of digital products and services. Again, this is despite international standards such as the World Wide Web Consortium's Web Content Accessibility Guidelines (WCAG 1.0, published in 1999, and WCAG 2.0, published in 2008), which were adopted by the International Standards Organization (ISO) in 2012.

In this chapter, we describe the most common vision changes that occur as people age. Then we offer design guidelines to help you ensure that your digital products and services work for older people. Following these guidelines will generally improve the visual experience for people of all ages.

Designing User Interfaces for an Aging Population. http://dx.doi.org/10.1016/B978-0-12-804467-4.00003-7

CHARACTERISTICS OF VISION IN OLDER ADULTS

Reduced visual acuity

Human visual acuity—our ability to see fine details—normally peaks between our late teens and early twenties, and then begins to decline. As explained earlier, the age at which this decline starts and the rate of decline vary, but most of us have the best acuity when we are young adults (see Figure 3.1). At some point above age 50, visual acuity typically begins to decline faster [Hawthorn, 2006; Mitzner et al., 2015], but again, when this occurs and the degree to which it occurs vary from person to person.

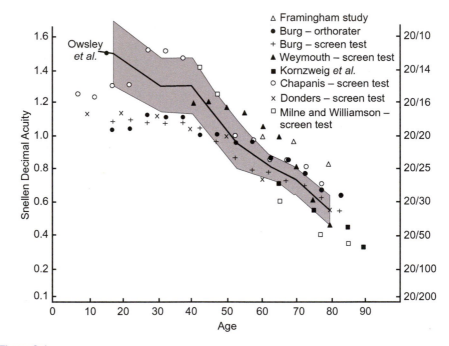

Figure 3.1.
Mean visual acuity as a function of age (source: Owsley et al. [1983], reprinted with permission).

People who experience this decline in acuity have difficulty seeing information on displays and trouble hitting their intended targets [Mitzner et al., 2015]. For example, research has shown that small text fonts reduce reading speed in everyone, but they reduce it more in older adults than in younger ones [Charness and Dijkstra, 1999]. Mobile devices can exacerbate these problems if designers don't design carefully for the smaller screen size.

Farsightedness

People of all ages—even children—vary in whether they are nearsighted, farsighted, or have "normal" vision. *Normal* vision means the lenses of the eye can focus on objects both near (e.g., a few inches or centimeters beyond the nose) and far (e.g., across the street). Each of our eyes has a tiny muscle, called the *ciliary* muscle, that adjusts the lens to focus at different distances.

People who are *nearsighted* can focus their eyes on nearby objects but have difficulty focusing on distant objects. *Farsighted* people have the opposite problem: their eyes can focus on distant objects but have trouble focusing on nearby objects.

I need reading glasses to use my computer or mobile phone. Even then, the text on many screens is small and blurry. – Wong

Beginning around age 40, the lenses begin to harden and the ciliary muscles weaken, making it harder to focus on nearby objects (see Figure 3.2). This is

Figure 3.2.
Normal vision and farsightedness, simulated using CoveredCA.com.

known as age-related farsightedness—the fancy medical name is *presbyopia*. Age-related farsightedness is nearly universal in people over the age of 65, so it is considered a normal part of aging. We all know people who have to start using reading glasses at some point in their lives—many of us *are* such people.

To allow users to compensate for poor visual acuity and farsightedness, most computers, tablets, and mobile phones these days allow users to increase text font sizes and general screen magnification. However, some older adults have not learned how to make such adjustments, especially if the controls to do so are hidden.

Narrowing of peripheral vision

Peripheral vision is the ability to see things where you are not directly looking—"out of the corner of your eye." Even in young people with normal vision, peripheral vision is poor [Johnson, 2014]. It's just how human eyes are: we have high-resolution vision only in a small area in the very center of each eye's visual field—an area called the "fovea" that is about 1% of the total visual field (see box **Human Vision Is Mostly Low Resolution**). Most of our visual field—the other 99%—has very low resolution: it sees the world as if through frosted glass [Eagleman, 2011] (see Figure 3.3).

Figure 3.3.
Only the very center of our visual field has high resolution; the periphery has low resolution.

Human Vision Is Mostly Low Resolution

The fovea—the 1% of your visual field at the center that has high resolution—is small. To see how small, hold your arm out, stick up your thumb, and focus on your thumbnail. At arm's length, your thumbnail is about the size of your fovea. The rest of your visual field can be considered peripheral vision, with significantly lower resolution [Johnson, 2014].

As bad as peripheral vision is in young adults with normal vision, it gets worse with age. Our field of useful vision gradually narrows, so we can't take in as much in one glance as we used to [Mitzner et al., 2015]. How much worse? It varies, but on the average, we lose about 1–3 degrees from the edges of our visual field every 10 years. By 70–80 years of age, most of us have lost 20–30 degrees from the edges of our visual field. Like age-related farsightedness, this gradual narrowing of our field of vision is common and considered normal.

Sometimes, I don't even notice things on the edges of the screen. – Carolina

Obviously, peripheral vision is needed to notice on-screen content that is not where our gaze is focused. Reduced peripheral vision increases the chance of people missing error messages, warnings, or other information that appears away from where they are looking [Hawthorn, 2006]. It also reduces peoples' ability to detect motion at the edges of their vision.

Age-related narrowing of peripheral vision also has a negative effect on reading. As we read, our eyes focus on one group of words, take them in, and then jump[1] ahead several words to take in the next group [Johnson, 2014]. Our peripheral vision prescans text ahead of our point of focus, providing information to our brain about what lies ahead, how far ahead to jump, which words to skip over, and where to pause. As our peripheral vision narrows, the scanning becomes less effective, which slows our reading [Legge et al., 2007].

Glaucoma is a medical condition that can cause sudden and/or drastic loss of peripheral vision, sometimes called "tunnel vision" (see Figure 3.4) [Haddrill

Figure 3.4.
CoverCA.com viewed with peripheral vision reduced by glaucoma.

and Heiting, 2014]. The greater your age, the greater your risk of developing glaucoma [National Eye Institute (NIH), n.d.]. It afflicts just under 1% of the population, or about 80 million people by 2020 [Quigley, 2006].

Loss of central vision

A vision ailment that is even more common than glaucoma in older adults is macular degeneration. In contrast to glaucoma, which reduces peripheral vision and narrows the visual field, macular degeneration damages the most important

---

1 The jumps are called "saccadic eye movements" or "saccades."

Figure 3.5.
CoveredCA.com, with simulated age-related macular degeneration and gaze focused on the middle of the page. The obscured area moves as the person moves their gaze around the page.

part of the visual field: the central medium-to-high resolution area that includes the fovea, which is called the *macula* (see Figure 3.5).

Macular degeneration is so strongly associated with age that the medical name for it is "age-related macular degeneration," abbreviated ARMD or AMD. It is the leading cause of vision loss and blindness among older adults [National Eye Institute (NIH), 2015]. Since this age group is increasing as a percentage of the population, the incidence of AMD is increasing. Studies of US adults find that among people aged 66–74 years, about 10% have some form of AMD; among adults aged 75–85 years, the percentage rises to 30%. Currently about 1.75 million US residents have advanced AMD, with that number expected to grow to almost 3 million by 2020 [Haddrill and Heiting, 2014]. Extrapolating worldwide, this suggests that hundreds of millions of people live with AMD.

Diminished light perception

The amount of light our eyes take in and register decreases with age [Mitzner et al., 2015]. This is due to:
- the pupil growing smaller;
- yellowing of the lens from exposure to sunlight;
- clouding of the lens from cataracts;
- increasing porousness of the retina—the layer of light-sensitive cells at the back of the eye;
- scratching of the cornea—the eye's front cover.

The more of these problems a person has, the less light gets through to their retina. Therefore, to see and read well, they need brighter light. For example, the average 60-year-old needs three times as much light as a 20-year-old to perceive the same subjective brightness [Besdine, 2015] (see Figure 3.6).

Figure 3.6.
Older adults typically receive less light at their retina than younger people do.

It's like I'm looking at everything through sunglasses. I need more light and more contrast. – Wong

Decreased contrast sensitivity

Those websites with gray text on a white background are impossible! – Stefano

Above age 50, many people notice a decline in their ability to see subtle differences in shades of gray—or shades of any color. Contrast sensitivity continues to decline, usually becoming acute by age 80 [Hawthorn, 2006; Mitzner et al., 2015]. This suggests that information that contrasts poorly with its background will be hard for older adults to see (see Figures 3.7 and 3.8).

Closely related to contrast sensitivity is people's ability to distinguish objects or read text that is displayed over a pattern or an image. Older adults have more trouble with that than younger adults do.

Diminished ability to discriminate colors

Lower contrast sensitivity (discussed in the previous section) also decreases our ability to distinguish similar colors.

With age, constant exposure to ultraviolet light causes the lens and cornea of our eyes to take on a yellowish tint. This yellowing affects how we perceive colors, particularly differences between colors. Imagine yourself viewing the world

Figure 3.7.
iOS weather app with white, gray, and blue text on gray background. It is hard to read the daily low temperatures and the percentage chance of rain, and nearly impossible to see the rain drops under the cloud symbols.

Figure 3.8.
Wall thermostat with low-contrast display, making it difficult to read the temperature.

through yellow-tinted glasses. Obviously it would be hard to tell which items are yellow versus white (see Figure 3.9).

Other colors would be tinted toward yellow, making certain pairs of colors harder to distinguish, especially greens, blues, and violets [Mitzner et al., 2015] (see Figure 3.10).

Color discrimination is also affected by older adults' diminished sensitivity to light. As discussed above, everything tends to look darker to older adults, so they have a harder time distinguishing dark colors, such as navy blue and black, or red and purple (see Figure 3.11).

Figure 3.9.
Buzzfeed mobile site viewed normally and through simulated yellowed cornea and lens. Ads are marked in yellow. Users who have a yellowed cornea or lens may not see the marking.

Figure 3.10.
CoveredCA.com viewed normally and through simulated yellowed cornea and lens. Users who have a yellowed cornea or lens may have trouble distinguishing blues from greens.

The incidence of hereditary—i.e., non–age-related—color blindness in the general population is 8% of males and 0.5% of females [Johnson, 2014]. The yellowing and darkening of older adults' vision gives them a form of color blindness—diminished ability to distinguish certain colors—thereby increasing the percentage of the population afflicted with some form of color blindness.

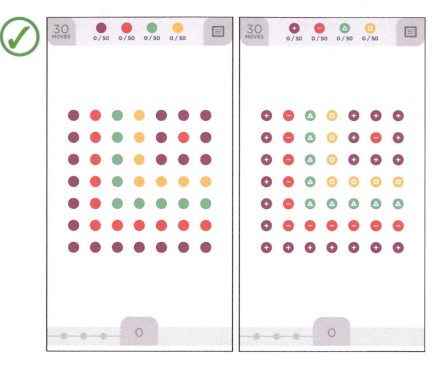

Figure 3.11.
Two Dots smartphone game, popular in a retirement community. Many residents have trouble distinguishing red versus purple dots (left). To accommodate them, the game offers a Color Blind setting that adds distinctive symbols to the dots.

 I discovered the text links on my news website purely on accident. They look just like the regular text, except they are dark blue instead of black. Very difficult to distinguish!
– John

Finally, our gaze is unconsciously attracted to areas of highly saturated color (see Figure 3.12) [Bera, 2016]. Therefore, gratuitous use of color in a display can be distracting, time-consuming, visually straining, and otherwise detrimental [NASA, 2015], especially to older adults.

Figure 3.12.
Highly saturated colors attract our gaze more than less saturated colors do.

Increased glare sensitivity

Accumulated scratches, cataracts, and other deformities on the cornea and lens don't only decrease the total amount of light transmitted to the retina. They also cause increased sensitivity to glare, as light passes through the scratched and misshapen areas and is scattered in all directions. This is why many older adults have difficulty driving at night. The glare from approaching headlights can be nearly blinding. Similarly, glare from external light sources, such as sunlight on a computer or smartphone screen, can cause more difficulty for older adults than for younger ones [Mitzner et al., 2015] (see Figure 3.13).

Figure 3.13.
CoveredCA.com viewed with simulated glare.

 I keep the screen brightness turned up high so I can read it, and I need good ambient light to see what I'm doing. But then reflections and glare often make it hard to see details on the screen. – Monika

Sensitivity to glare also means that it is possible for a display's contrast to be *too* high for some older adults. Some researchers have found that reading black text on pure white backgrounds for long periods can cause eyestrain in older adults, suggesting that off-white backgrounds are better for older adults than pure white ones [Dickinson et al., 2007; Dunn, 2006].

Slower adaptation to changes in brightness

Our visual system is most effective within a narrow range of brightness. To keep the amount of light that reaches the retina within its optimal range, the iris adjusts the size of the pupil—the opening in the center of the iris. In low light or darkness, the pupil opens wide (dilates) to let in as much light as possible; in bright light, it closes down (contracts) to a tiny hole.

When we are young, our eyes adjust rapidly to changes in brightness. As we grow older, our eyes adjust more slowly. If an older person goes from a brightly lit area into a darker room, or vice versa, they might find themselves temporarily unable to see information on a screen until their eyes adjust—information that younger people have no trouble seeing.

If I am working on the computer and then go outside, the light is just blinding. And then when I go back inside, it takes quite some time before I can see well enough to read the computer screen again. – Stefano

Diminished ability to detect subtle visual indicators and distinctions

As we grow older, our vision problems grow, combine, and compound each other to cause higher-level problems. For example, narrowed peripheral vision combined with reduced ability to distinguish colors can cause older people to not be able to see small, subtle elements or button labels, even when they know where to look (see Figure 3.14).

Figure 3.14.
The Mac OS Dock marks running apps with small black dots—too subtle for many older adults!

The young man at the Apple Store told me that on my Mac, apps that are running have little black dots beneath them. Who can see those? I certainly cannot! – John

Increased susceptibility to eyestrain

Even if a person can, with careful scrutiny, see details or read text on a screen at one point in time, they may not be able to do so at another time. The vision problems described earlier can increase or decrease over the course of an hour, a day, or a week.

Regardless of one's age, prolonged reading or viewing can cause eyestrain, especially with poor displays or under poor conditions, such as glare or contrast that is too low or too high. Our vision also varies depending on our level of physical or mental exhaustion, stress, and illness. However, older adults are more susceptible to eyestrain than younger ones [Zajicek, 2001].

Continued use of one form of output mode can lead to tiredness. Eyestrain can affect levels of visual impairment where older adults may be able to read text at the beginning of the session, but start later on to rely on voice output – [Zajicek, 2001a]

Therefore, making information just visible is not enough. Information must be *highly* visible to avoid causing eyestrain, especially in older adults.

Slower visual processing and increased sensitivity to visual distractions

In addition to the age-related declines in vision discussed earlier, the *speed* at which people process visually presented information declines with advancing age. This is due to several factors, some visual, some cognitive, and some attitudinal.

The cognitive factors, explained more fully in Chapter 6: Cognition, are declining short-term memory, greater difficulty storing and recalling memories, and declining ability to focus attention and ignore visual elements unrelated to our goal.

Any application window, app screen, or web page has one or more reasons for existing—the main things users can do there. What users can do on a page or screen is represented by interactive elements such as text input fields, buttons, and other controls. In user interface design parlance, these interactive elements are called "calls to action." The older we grow, the more we are slowed down by extraneous calls to action and other distracting visual elements.

The attitudinal factors involved with processing speed are explained more fully in Chapter 9: Attitude. As we age, our scanning of screens tends to be slowed by our increased aversion to risk and greater fear of making mistakes. Older adults are more likely than younger adults to carefully read or scrutinize most of the content of a page before choosing what action to take [Carmien and Garzo, 2014]. Risk aversion also makes older adults less likely to try to make adjustments in the display or web browser that could improve their reading and scanning rate [Hawthorn, personal communication, 2016].

Taken together, these factors can cause older adults to take significantly longer than younger people to read or scan information on electronic displays. This slowdown varies greatly between individuals, but study after study of people of different ages using websites and software applications has found this difference [Hawthorn, 2006; Kerber, 2012]. A Scandinavian study found that visual processing speed decreased approximately linearly with age and was, on average, reduced by *half* between 70 and 85 years of age [Habeskot et al., 2012].

 I like to read everything on the page before I decide what to click on. – Hana

Slower visual processing means that older adults have more trouble reading text that moves across a marquee display, especially if it moves quickly or the window is short (see Figure 3.15).

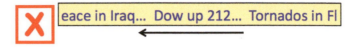

Figure 3.15.
Moving (marquee) text can be hard for older adults to read if it moves quickly.

If there's text scrolling across the screen, I usually can't read it fast enough. And I don't know how to stop it or slow it down. – Carolina

Slower visual search

One type of visual processing with potentially distracting items is visual search. When you search for a specific item among many very similar items, your eyes focus on the items, one by one, until you spot the target item (see Figure 3.16). In such a situation, we say that visual search time is "linear": the time to find

```
L Q R B T J P L F B M R W S
F R N Q  S P D C H K U T
 G T H U  J L U 9 J  V Y I  A
E X C F T Y N H T D O L L 8
G V N  G R Y J G Z S  T 6 S
3 L C  T V B H U S E M U K
W Q E L  F G H U Y I K D 9
```

Figure 3.16.
Linear visual search. Find the Z.

the target item increases roughly linearly with the number of nontarget items the person must scan before arriving at the target, which in turn depends on how many other items there are and where the target is among them.

However, if the target looks quite different from the nontarget items—e.g., the target is a **boldface** letter amid a field of nonbold letters—there is no need to scan through the items. If we have normal eyesight, we can spot the target in our peripheral vision and move our eye straight there (see Figure 3.17). In such cases, where the target "pops" in the periphery, we say that visual search time is *not* linear; the time to find the target is independent of the number of other items and the target's position in them.

I often lose track of my cursor on the screen. – John

```
G T H U  J L U 9  J V Y I  A
L Q R B  T J  P L F  B M R W  S
3 L C T V B H U S E M U K
F R N Q  S P D  C H K  U T
W Q E L  F G H  B Y I K D 9
G V N  G R Y  J G Z S  T 6 S
E X C F T Y N H T D O L L 8
```

Figure 3.17.
Nonlinear visual search. Find the bold letter.

Figure 3.18.
Mac OS X application folder has items that are distinctive but some that are similar. Finding one of the similar items takes more time than finding one of the distinctive ones, especially for older adults.

The older we get, our diminished peripheral vision means that fewer target items "pop" in our periphery, causing more of our visual search to be linear and therefore more time-consuming. The more cluttered a display or screen, the more it slows older people down, especially if the items on the screen are similar (see Figure 3.18).

I sometimes have trouble finding something on a page, even when I **know** it's there somewhere. – Hana

Faster reading!

One interesting research finding is that even though older adults are slower than younger adults at visual search tasks, they are often *faster* at reading [Koyani et al., 2002]. This indicates that visual search and reading are quite different tasks, involving different visual and cognitive mechanisms.

DESIGN GUIDELINES THAT HELP OLDER ADULTS (AND OTHERS!)

To ensure that adults of any age can notice, see, scan, and read what your application or website displays, follow the design guidelines in this section.

We said earlier that using large fonts is the first guideline most people think of when talking about how to design for older people, and it really *is* important, so we start with that.

3.1 Maximize legibility of essential text

Use large fonts *[Campbell, 2015; Carmien and Garzo, 2014; Chisnell et al., 2006; Czaja and Lee, 2007; Hawkins, 2011; Hawthorn, 2006; Kascak and Sanford, 2015; Kurniawan and Zaphiris, 2005; Ligons et al., 2011; Miño, 2013; Nielsen, 2013; National Institute on Aging (NIH), 2009; Nunes et al., 2012; Pernice et al., 2013; Phiriyapokanon, 2011; Wirtz et al., 2009]*

- For computers with large screens, we recommend a minimum of 12 point (4.2 mm tall on the display); but 14 point (5 mm tall) is even safer.

- On high-resolution smartphone screens, use fonts *larger* than 12–14 points to make the text legible for more people (see Figure 3.19, left).

Figure 3.19.
AMD.org uses large fonts and provides a font enlarger (left), but does not display well on mobile phones (right).

- For websites, simply making them mobile-enabled goes a long way toward ensuring that text is displayed at a size suitable for small screens. When viewed on a smartphone, websites that are *not* mobile-enabled usually display text that is too small to read (see Figure 3.19, right), requiring users to zoom in to view a small part of the page.

- *Note: following this guideline may conflict with guidelines about minimizing the need for scrolling (see Guideline 3.7).*

Use plain fonts *[Carmien and Garzo, 2014; Chisnell et al., 2006; Kurniawan and Zaphiris, 2005; Ligons et al., 2011; Miño, 2013; National Institute on Aging (NIH), 2009; Nunes et al., 2012; Pernice et al., 2013; Phiriyapokanon, 2011; Silva et al., 2015; Weinschenk, 2011]*

- Use simple font families, such as Arial, Frutiger, Helvetica, Lucida, Universe, Verdana, or Tiresias.[2]

- Avoid fancy font styles, such as italics or condensed.

- Avoid light-weight (i.e., thin) fonts, such as Avenir Light, Arial Narrow, or Lato Thin.

- Some experts say that on today's high-resolution screens, serif fonts (e.g., Times Roman) are OK. Most published guidelines still recommend using only sans-serif fonts, especially for body text, so that is what we recommend.

Use mixed case *[Carmien and Garzo, 2014; Kurniawan and Zaphiris, 2005; National Institute on Aging (NIH), 2009; Weinschenk, 2011]*

- Display body text in mixed case; avoid using all caps for body text. IT IS HARDER FOR MOST PEOPLE TO READ TEXT IN ALL CAPS BECAUSE SEEING TEXT PRESENTED THAT WAY IS LESS FAMILIAR.

Make text enlargeable *[Campbell, 2015; Chisnell et al., 2006; Dunn, 2013; Hawkins, 2011; Hawthorn, 2006; Miño, 2013; National Institute on Aging (NIH), 2009; Nielsen, 2013; Nunes et al., 2012; Pernice et al., 2013; Silva et al., 2015; Wirtz et al., 2009]*

- Make it easy for users to enlarge important text by providing a highly visible control to do so.

- In smartphone apps and websites, providing a visible control for adjusting the font size is often impractical, so just use large enough fonts that users need not enlarge them.

- Don't embed text in images, as it cannot be enlarged separately from the image. If text must be overlaid on an image (but see "Use plain backgrounds"), actually overlay it, don't embed it.

---

2 The Tiresias font family was designed in the UK for people with impaired vision [Wikipedia, 2015].

Make information easy to scan *[Chisnell et al., 2006; Hawthorn, 2006; Kurniawan and Zaphiris, 2005; Ligons et al., 2011; National Institute on Aging (NIH), 2009; Pernice et al., 2013; Silva et al., 2015]*

- Make information easy for users to scan. Divide information into small chunks.

- Label information with clearly visible, understandable headings and descriptions.

- Bulletize or number lists.

- Make headings stand out by increasing the font size or weight or by using a different color.

Use plain backgrounds *[Ligons et al., 2011; National Institute on Aging (NIH), 2009; Pernice et al., 2013]*

- Avoid displaying text over patterned or image backgrounds (see Figure 3.20).

Figure 3.20.
Text displayed over a patterned background can be hard to read, especially for older adults.

Use static text *[Chisnell et al., 2006; Hawthorn, 2006; Kurniawan and Zaphiris, 2005; National Institute on Aging (NIH), 2009; Phiriyapokanon, 2011; Strengers, 2012]*

- Avoid text that automatically moves, rolls, or scrolls.

Leave plenty of space *[Carmien and Garzo, 2014; Gilbertson, 2015; Kurniawan and Zaphiris, 2005; National Institute on Aging (NIH), 2009; WCAG 2.0, 2008]*

- Use line spacing of at least 1.5.

- Put more space between paragraphs than between lines: a minimum of 1.5 times the line spacing.

3.2 Simplify: Remove unnecessary visual elements

Present few calls to action *[Chisnell et al., 2006; Hawthorn, 2006; Miño, 2013; Kurniawan and Zaphiris, 2005; Romano-Bergstrom et al., 2013; Silva et al., 2015; Strengers, 2012]*

- Help users focus. Limit the number of calls-to-action to one or two per screen or page (see Figures 3.21 and 3.22).

Figure 3.21.
Arngren.net's home page is cluttered with so many options—navigation and products—it is overwhelming.

Figure 3.22.
Google's main search page is uncluttered and has one main call-to-action: enter search terms.

- Other interactive elements may be present, but they should represent rarely used auxiliary functions.

Keep graphics relevant *[National Institute on Aging (NIH), 2009]*

- Graphics and multimedia content should be task relevant, not just for decoration.

Don't distract *[Chisnell et al., 2006; Hawthorn, 2006; Miño, 2013; Kurniawan and Zaphiris, 2005; Romano-Bergstrom et al., 2013; Silva et al., 2015; Strengers, 2012]*

- Eliminate potentially distracting visual elements. Keep the path to users' goals free of distractions, such as contextual advertising and animations.

- If your app or website displays banner or pop-up advertisements as a source of revenue, make sure the ads don't distract users away from doing what they came to the app or website to do; otherwise the ads may be counterproductive.

Minimize clutter *[Chisnell et al., 2006; National Institute on Aging (NIH), 2009; Romano-Bergstrom et al., 2013; Silva et al., 2015]*

- Use grouping and white space to ensure a clean and uncluttered layout (see Figure 3.23).

Figure 3.23.
Bank of the West's home page is clean, uncluttered, and uses white space effectively.

3.3 Visual language: Create an effective graphical language and use it consistently

Maintain visual consistency *[Miño, 2013; Nunes, 2012; Or and Tao, 2012; Phiriyapokanon, 2011; Russell, 2009; Silva et al., 2015; Subasi et al., 2011; Wirtz, 2009]*

- Use fonts, icons, and color consistently.

Make controls prominent *[Affonso de Lara et al., 2010; Chisnell et al., 2006; Correia de Barros, 2014; Dunn, 2006; Kurniawan and Zaphiris, 2005; National Institute on Aging (NIH), 2009; Pernice et al., 2013; Silva et al., 2015]*

- Ensure that main elements—links, menus, buttons, etc.—stand out. Distinguish interactive controls from noninteractive text and graphics. Make clickable elements look quite different from nonclickable ones by using different colors (not just a different hue).

- Provide prominent, bold navigation cues. If links in a website are underlined, don't underline nonlink items.

Indicate strongly, not subtly *[Czaja and Lee, 2007; Nunes et al., 2012]*

- Use boldface, font size, and/or color to emphasize information users should not miss.

- Status markers and indicators should not be subtle. They should be highly visible and prominent.

- Clearly indicate the input focus and the current content selection.

Change links on hover *[Chisnell et al., 2006]*

- In websites designed for desktop or laptop computers, links and most other clickable items should change noticeably when users point at them.

Mark visited links or not? *[Affonso de Lara et al., 2010; Dunn, 2006; Kurniawan and Zaphiris, 2005; Nielsen, 2013; National Institute on Aging (NIH), 2009; Pernice et al., 2013]*

- Many web usability experts recommend marking visited text links to remind users—especially users with diminished short-term memory—of where they've been and not been. When the linked-to content remains unchanged for long periods, such as health information sites, marking visited links is helpful. It is also helpful in search results. The most common way to mark text links as visited is to change their color.

- However, it makes little sense to mark links as visited when the linked-to content changes often, such as product categories in e-commerce sites or topics in online discussion forums. It also makes no sense to mark links that are *meant* to be visited repeatedly, such as primary navigation links or links to functions such as "Print," "Search," or "Checkout."

Label redundantly *[Correia de Barros, 2014; Leung, 2009; Nunes et al., 2012; Or and Tao, 2012; Phiriyapokanon, 2011; Williams et al., 2013]*

- When possible, label buttons and keys with both text and symbols.

- If space is limited, provide text labels in tooltips.

3.4 Use color judiciously

Use color sparingly *[Kurniawan and Zaphiris, 2005]*

- Use colors for functional purposes, such as to convey information or to distinguish areas of the screen.

- Use bright or saturated colors only where you want people to look.

- Avoid gratuitous colors, overly saturated colors, or too many different colors (see Figure 3.24).

Figure 3.24.
AlzheimersSpeaks.com uses overly saturated colors and more colors than necessary.

Mix colors carefully *[Campbell, 2015; Carmien and Garzo, 2014; Czaja and Lee, 2007; Kurniawan and Zaphiris, 2005; Ligons et al., 2011; NASA, 2015; National Institute on Aging (NIH), 2009; Silva et al., 2015]*

- Avoid requiring users to discriminate blue from green tones.

- Avoid placing highly saturated color opposites, such as bright blue, yellow, and green next to each other.

Use distinguishable link colors *[Nielsen, 2013; National Institute on Aging (NIH), 2009; Pernice et al., 2013]*

- If "unvisited," "visited," and "hover" links are marked by color, ensure that older adults can distinguish the colors (see Figure 3.25).

Figure 3.25.
At KP.org, links turn orange and are underlined on hover (mouseover).

- Avoid using link colors that are too dark or too similar for older adults to distinguish.

- Test your link colors on older adults to ensure that they are distinguishable.

Combine color with other indicators *[Carmien and Garzo, 2014; Kurniawan and Zaphiris, 2005; Silva et al., 2015]*

- Color should not be used as the sole indicator of meaning. It should be used redundantly with other cues.

High contrast *[Campbell, 2015; Carmien and Garzo, 2014; Chisnell et al., 2006; Czaja and Lee, 2007; Dickinson, 2007; Dunn, 2006; Hawthorn, 2006; Kascak and Sanford, 2015; Kurniawan and Zaphiris, 2005; National Institute on Aging (NIH), 2009; Nunes et al., 2012; Pernice et al., 2013; Phiriyapokanon, 2011; Silva et al., 2015; Wirtz et al., 2009]*

- Ensure that color contrast between important elements—such as text and background—is high: the brightness ratio between light and dark should be at least 50:1.

- Display dark text against a light background (compare Figures 3.26 and 3.27), but off-white backgrounds are better than pure white ones because sustained reading of dark text on pure white backgrounds can cause eyestrain in older adults.

- Use online contrast checkers (e.g., webaim.org/resources/contrastchecker/) to check that colors contrast sufficiently.

Adjustable contrast *[Pernice et al., 2013]*

- Provide a way for users to change the contrast of the display. Two websites that do (at the time we are writing this) are AMD.org and CNIB.ca.

- Alternatively, if the platform (device or browser) on which the app or website runs provides contrast adjustment capability, design your app or website to use it and make it easy for users to find and use.

Figure 3.26.
DW.com, the website of German broadcaster Deutsche Welle, displays text (on the right) that contrasts poorly with the background.

Figure 3.27.
Encore.org displays text that contrasts well with its background.

3.5 Position important content where users will start looking

Lay elements out consistently *[Kurniawan and Zaphiris, 2005; National Institute on Aging (NIH), 2009; Nunes, 2012]*

- Web pages, application screens, and appliance displays should be laid out consistently. A control or piece of information should be in the same position on every page where it appears. That way, people can learn where it is and won't have to search for it.

Place important information front and center *[Affonso de Lara et al., 2010; Carmien and Garzo, 2014; Chisnell et al., 2006; Kurniawan and Zaphiris, 2005; National Institute on Aging (NIH), 2009; Nunes et al., 2012; Patsoule and Koutsabasis, 2014; Phiriyapokanon, 2011]*

- The most important content on any screen should be immediately visible without scrolling.

- Concentrate the most important content near the center of the screen.

- *Note: following this guideline may conflict with guidelines about using large fonts (see Guideline 3.1).*

Make error messages obvious *[Nielsen, 2013; Nunes et al., 2012]*

- Make error messages prominent: place them where users won't miss them, such as centrally or near the screen pointer or text insertion point, and highlight or flag them boldly.

3.6 Group related content visually

Group related items *[Chisnell et al., 2006; Czaja and Lee, 2007; Hawthorn, 2006; Johnson, 2014; National Institute on Aging (NIH), 2009; Silva et al., 2015]*

- Place important related items near each other.
- Indicate groupings using spacing, borders, color, etc. Make use of Gestalt principles of visual grouping.

3.7 Take care when relying on scrolling

Minimize vertical scrolling *[Chisnell et al., 2006; Dunn, 2006; National Institute on Aging (NIH), 2009; Nunes et al., 2012; Pernice et al., 2013; Silva et al., 2015]*

- Minimize the need for vertical scrolling. Frequently accessed content should be visible with little or no scrolling. *Note: following this guideline may conflict with guidelines about using large fonts (see Guideline 3.1).*
- On smartphones, scrolling is often necessary due to small screen sizes, but very long pages should be split up into multiple pages.
- On long pages or screens, clearly indicate that the content continues below, so users know to scroll down.
- Avoid horizontal graphics or elements that may falsely indicate the bottom of a page.

Don't require horizontal scrolling *[Chisnell et al., 2006; National Institute on Aging (NIH), 2009]*

- Don't require users to scroll horizontally to access information. Most won't, so they will miss that content.

3.8 Provide text alternatives for nontext content

Supplement images and videos with text *[Arch, 2008; Campbell, 2015; Patsoule and Koutsabasis, 2014; Kurniawan and Zaphiris, 2005; National Institute on Aging (NIH), 2009]*

- Provide content in text as well as in other media, so it can be rendered in other forms people need, such as text, large print, Braille, speech, symbols, or simpler language.
- Videos should have transcripts or closed captioning.
- In websites, images should have alt tags, for example, <img src=Jeff. jpg" alt=Jeff Johnson">.

Summary of Vision Guidelines

3.1 Maximize legibility of essential text	■ Use large fonts. ■ Use plain fonts. ■ Use mixed case. ■ Make text enlargeable. ■ Make information easy to scan. ■ Use plain backgrounds. ■ Use static text. ■ Leave plenty of space.
3.2 Simplify: Remove unnecessary visual elements	■ Present few calls to action. ■ Keep graphics relevant. ■ Don't distract. ■ Minimize clutter.
3.3 Visual language: Create an effective graphical language and use it consistently	■ Maintain visual consistency. ■ Make controls prominent. ■ Indicate strongly, not subtly. ■ Change links on hover. ■ Mark visited links or not? ■ Label redundantly.
3.4 Use color judiciously	■ Use color sparingly. ■ Mix colors carefully. ■ Use distinguishable link colors. ■ Combine color with other indicators. ■ High contrast. ■ Adjustable contrast.
3.5 Position important content where users will start looking	■ Lay elements out consistently. ■ Place important info front and center. ■ Make error messages obvious.
3.6 Group-related content visually	■ Group related items.
3.7 Take care when relying on scrolling	■ Minimize vertical scrolling. ■ Don't require horizontal scrolling.
3.8 Provide text alternatives for nontext content	■ Supplement images and videos with text.

CHAPTER 4
Motor Control

Perceiving what a device displays is only half of interacting with it. Interaction requires that we *act* on the device, i.e., manipulate or operate it in some way. The most obvious way to manipulate or operate a device is manually, using our hands to interact with physical knobs, buttons, sliders, pointing devices, keyboards, touch screens, and motion-activated game controllers.

As we age, our ability to manipulate things with our arms, hands, and fingers tends to decline. Most digital devices aren't designed for limited manipulation abilities. This makes them very difficult for some older adults to use.

Even young people can experience diminished motor control, due to afflictions unrelated to aging such as cerebral palsy, muscular dystrophy, multiple sclerosis, or amyotrophic lateral sclerosis. In addition, temporary conditions such as tendonitis, drug side effects, or riding on a bumpy bus, plane, train, or horse can reduce peoples' motor control (see Figure 4.1).

This chapter begins by describing the most common ways in which manual abilities decline with age. We then present design guidelines that allow people to use digital devices confidently, reliably, and effectively, regardless of their age and the bumpiness of their usage environment.

Figure 4.1.
Bumpy transportation can cause temporary loss of motor control in people of all ages.

Designing User Interfaces for an Aging Population. http://dx.doi.org/10.1016/B978-0-12-804467-4.00004-9

MOTOR CONTROL IN OLDER ADULTS

With age, most people experience declines in their sensorimotor abilities.

Reduced manual dexterity (fine motor control)

After the age of 50, most people's fine motor control begins to decline—slowly at first, more rapidly in later decades. Arthritis, Parkinson's disease, strokes, and other illnesses hasten the decline. Frequent, careful practice can slow the age-related decline of specific movements, such as playing a musical instrument or knitting. But eventually, the precision of our arm, hand, and finger movements decreases noticeably.

This decline in manual dexterity means that in our later years, we experience greater difficulty grasping and manipulating small objects. We also have more trouble executing *coordinated* gestures. These include pinch, spread, and other multi-finger gestures used on many touch-screen devices.

 I find it very frustrating to try to use the small letter keys on my smartphone. Because of a medication I must take, my hands tremble very slightly. Even that slight movement means I often have to try several times before I can type the right letter. – Monika

Reduced hand–eye coordination

Closely related to fine motor control, and exhibiting a similar age-related decline, is hand–eye coordination. In hand–eye coordination, we use our vision to guide our hands. With declining hand–eye coordination, we experience increased difficulty hitting small targets or keeping a pointing device within a narrow path.

Hand–eye coordination has two components: the *hand* part and the *eye* part. First, we will discuss the *eye* part. Chapter 3 described some of the ways in which vision can decline with age. If your vision is poor, your hand–eye coordination suffers: it's hard to point at or drag something you can't see clearly.

In desktop computers that use a mouse or touch pad and a screen pointer (cursor), an additional problem is that the screen pointer itself can be hard to see. Even when users can see the cursor, they may not notice that only a small part of it is the "hot spot" that can click on targets [Worden et al., 1997].

 While using an actual keyboard, I have no trouble writing articles or filling out forms. But when I have to use a mouse or touch the screen with my finger – then I run into difficulties. – John

Now, let's consider the *hand* component of hand–eye coordination. To better understand how it works, we'll deconstruct one example task: pointing at targets.

Since the 1950s, we've known that pointing at objects on a display follows Fitts' law, and moving pointers along constrained paths follows the Steering law.[1]

- **Fitts' law**: The larger our target is on a surface or screen, and the nearer it is to our starting point, the faster we can point to it (with size being much more important than distance).
- **Steering law**: If we have to keep a pointer within a confined path while moving it to a target, then the wider the path, the faster we can move the pointer to the target.

Fitts' law and the Steering law apply to *all* pointers, including mouse, trackball, and trackpads. They even apply to a finger on a touch screen.

For an intuitive grasp of Fitts' law, think about pointing at something on a screen. A target appears and you decide to point to it. The decision takes time, your muscles take time to react to signals from your brain, and your hands and the pointing device have inertia. After a moment, your movement toward the target starts, accelerating rapidly to a peak speed. The initial phase of the movement is gross and ballistic: a barely controlled shot in the target's general direction. As the pointer nears the target, the movement slows as your hand–eye feedback loops take control. The movement ends slowly, with finer and finer corrections until your pointer arrives at the target (see Figure 4.2). The larger the target, the fewer adjustments are needed at the end.

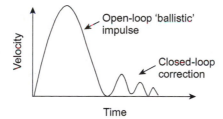

Figure 4.2.
Pointing movement predicted by Fitts' law and observed (used with permission from Johnson [2014]).

Now let's examine how aging affects pointing (see Figure 4.3). Compared to younger adults' pointer movements, those of older adults:

- start more slowly due to slower perceptual and motor processing (although this varies greatly between people),
- accelerate more gradually and peak at a lower top speed, and so have a less pronounced ballistic phase,
- decelerate more slowly, and
- include a greater number of slow, controlled adjustments as the pointer reaches the target [Ketcham and Stelmach, 2002].

Thus, in contrast to younger adults, for whom a significant portion of a pointing movement is fast and ballistic, an older adult's pointing movements have

---

1 For details of Fitts' law and the Steering law see [Johnson, 2014], Chapter 13.

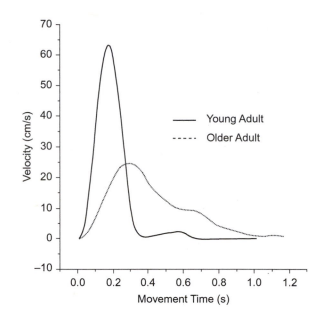

Figure 4.3.
Pointing movement observed for younger and older adults [from Encyclopedia of Aging, 1E. © 2002 Gale, a part of Cengage Learning, Inc. Reproduced by permission. www.cengage.com/permissions].

a smaller ballistic component and a slower, more deliberate movement. The result is that small targets reduce pointing speed more for older adults than for younger ones.

Interestingly, some researchers find that pointing *accuracy* is not lower for older adults than for younger ones; in some cases, it is *higher* [Bakaev, 2008].

> On average, it took elder participants twice as much time to complete movement tasks, but their accuracy was two times higher. – [Bakaev, 2008]

One explanation is that older adults are *aware* that their hand–eye coordination is waning, so they compensate by moving more slowly and deliberately.

Regarding the Steering law, research indicates that our ability to keep a pointer inside a narrow channel or twisty path while moving it to a target is subject to age-related declines. Young adults tend to move a pointer more quickly and less carefully along a narrow path. Older adults tend to move the pointer more slowly and carefully along the path to the target. Widening the path makes the task easier for people of all ages, but it helps older adults more.

Drawing on a screen and tracing complex shapes, either with a pointing device or with a finger, involves both moving to target locations and moving along constrained paths, so both Fitts' law and the Steering law are relevant. Drawing and tracing on a digital screen tend to get harder as we age.

Slower movement

As we mentioned, older adults tend to execute movements more slowly than younger people do. This could be due to slower mental processing, a tendency to execute movements deliberately and consciously, or stiffness or pain that inhibits movement.

Experiments comparing pointer movement speed between younger and older users of digital devices have found that movement for older adults, across a variety of pointing devices and tasks, is slower by factors ranging from 1.3 to 3 [Bohan and Scarlett, 2003; Stößel, 2012].

As we said above, slower movement doesn't necessarily mean reduced accuracy. In general, the *accuracy* of pointing and shape-tracing gestures is often unaffected by age unless a person suffers from hand tremors (discussed later in this chapter):

> The results showed generally an influence of age on the execution speed, but not on error rate or the accuracy of gesture performance. ... [O]lder users have no more problems than younger users in performing accurate gestures, even for more complex gesture patterns and even on very small screen devices. – [Stößel, 2012]

Increased *variance* in movements

As we reach ages above 50, most of us find it harder to reliably execute hand and arm movements the same way every time. Causes include increases in "noisy" neural activity, incidence of transitory muscle spasms, and likelihood of hand tremors.

Hand tremors are a common cause of variability in gestures. If your hands shake as you execute a gesture, the gesture will likely be different each time you do it. Tremors can be caused by chronic conditions, such as Parkinson's disease or other degenerative neural diseases. They can also result from temporary conditions, such as too much coffee, medication side effects, or withdrawal symptoms. A common test of hand tremors is to ask a person to draw a spiral on paper, freehand. People without hand tremors can do it easily, but people with tremors cannot (see Figure 4.4).

Imagine that you have hand tremors and are trying to sign your name or trace a complex "unlock my phone" pattern on a device's screen, either with a pointing device or with your finger (see Figure 4.5). You would become very frustrated or discouraged, very quickly.

If a person can't execute hand movements reliably, they are more likely to miss their intended targets or make unintended gestures. The risk of such errors increases when targets are too small or too close to each other and when different gestures are too similar to each other. And compared to younger people, it often takes older adults longer to recover from unintended link clicks, button presses, menu choices, and gestures.

Figure 4.4.
Spiral drawings by a person with no hand tremors (left) and a person with tremors (right).

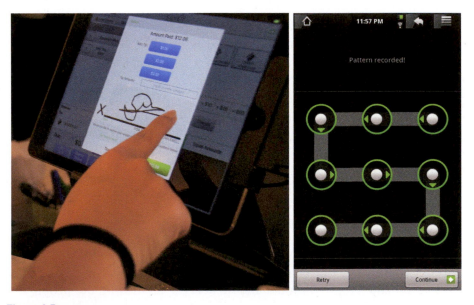

Figure 4.5.
Signing one's name or tracing an unlock pattern may be hard for older adults.

Buttons and links are just so very small! It is not easy for me to select the correct one. – Wong

To understand how variance between different executions of the same movement can be a problem, let's consider a pointing-device gesture that is common in desktop and laptop computers: double clicking. It is a quick way to open documents and start applications; an alternative to selecting and invoking an

Open command from a menu. Double clicking by older adults can easily fail in several ways:

- **Clicks too slow**: The interval between clicks is too long, causing the computer to time-out and register two single clicks rather than a double click. The file or app does not open. Most operating systems allow users to adjust the double-click time-out, but many older adults don't know how to do that and may not even realize that adjusting the time-out would help them.
- **Clicks too shaky**: The effort of clicking causes the user's hand to move off the target, so the target receives only one click or no clicks. The file or app does not open. Sometimes a shaky second click is interpreted as a drag motion, causing the object to be moved unintentionally. These mishaps are common in users who have hand tremors.
- **Overgeneralized**: The user overgeneralizes double click, using it not only to open files and apps, but also to select links and buttons, menu items, and checkboxes and radio buttons. This can cause unwanted or unexpected results, such as opening something they meant only to select, or getting two results instead of one. Once this overgeneralization has been burned into a person's muscle memory, it is very hard to unlearn.

Increased variance of movement can make it difficult to maintain steady pressure on a mouse button, touch pad, or touch screen long enough for the device to register. If an intended click or tap includes unintended sideward movement, the target may move rather than open. With diminishing motor control, it also becomes more difficult to execute continuous movements, such as dragging a slider control, operating a scrollbar, moving through a menu to the desired item (see Figure 4.6), or dragging an on-screen object to a new position.

Reduced strength and stamina

Finally, as we age, our hand and arm muscles tend to weaken, reducing our strength. This means we apply less force to physical buttons, knobs, keyboard keys, trackpad

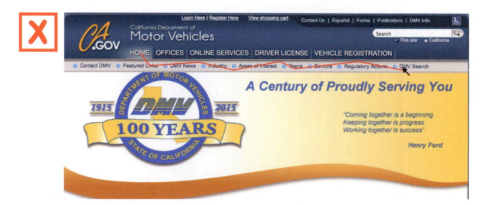

Figure 4.6.
Calif. DMV multilevel menu. Users must move over HOME to open its submenu, then down and rightward to select DMV Search. If the cursor goes outside the narrow gray strip, the submenu vanishes.

clickers, variable-pressure touch screens, and other input devices. A physical switch or slider may be too hard to move. A physical knob may be too stiff to turn.

Diminishing strength brings with it diminishing stamina, the length of time a person can maintain a sustained force. Older adults are more susceptible than younger adults to fatigue and strain. This includes simply holding our arms and hands in any non-neutral position.

 I asked my daughter to get me a stand for my tablet. Holding it while scrolling through Facebook postings tires me out. – Hana

For example, research indicates that targets at the upper left of a touch screen are harder for right-handed older adults to hit accurately (top-right for left-handed ones) [Leitão and Silva, 2012]. Why? Because hitting targets requires stretching the arm farther across the display. The farther the stretch (see Figure 4.7), the more strain on the arm and the less accurate the hand movements are.

Figure 4.7.
Tapping the top-left icon requires right-handed users to stretch their arm farther than does tapping the bottom-right icon.

DESIGN GUIDELINES THAT HELP OLDER ADULTS (AND OTHERS!)

The following are research-based guidelines that can help you design digital technology that takes into account the motor control requirements of older users. In most cases, following these guidelines helps users of all ages, just as curb cuts help not only people in wheelchairs, but also people with baby carriages, roller suitcases, shopping carts, and skateboards (see box **Think of These Guidelines as Curb Cuts and OXO Designs for Digital Technology** in Chapter 1).

Most of the guidelines in this book are the same regardless of whether the digital device being designed is controlled mainly by touch screen, as in smartphones and tablet computers, or by a pointing device separate from the screen, as in desktop or laptop computers. However, this chapter is about motor control. The guidelines for touch-screen devices, while similar to guidelines for other devices, often differ in details. Therefore, we separate the guidelines about the two types of devices and we use different terminology. In guidelines for desktop or laptop computers, we use the term "click target." For touch-screen devices, we use the terms "tap target" and "swipe target."

4.1a Make sure users can hit targets (desktop and laptop computers)

Big click targets *[Campbell, 2015; Chisnell et al., 2006; Czaja and Lee, 2007; Hawthorn, 2006; Kascak and Sanford, 2015; National Institute on Aging (NIH), 2009; Nielsen, 2013; Pernice et al., 2013; Wirtz et al., 2009]*

- On desktop and laptop computers, where users point with a mouse, trackpad, or similar device, make click targets big enough for users to hit. We recommend that click targets (such as buttons and text boxes) should accept clicks in an area spanning at least 11 mm diagonally (see Figure 4.8).

Figure 4.8.
Click targets that are too small (left) and big enough (right) for older adults to hit easily.

Maximize clickable area *[Affonso de Lara et al., 2010; Pernice et al., 2013]*

- When links have graphics and text, make both part of the link to increase the target's area.

- Avoid "buttons" that accept clicks only on their labels (see Figure 4.9).

Figure 4.9.
Navigation bar "Buttons" at ChicagoFed.org accept clicks *only* on their text labels.

Put space between click targets *[Affonso de Lara et al., 2010; Arch et al., 2008; Campbell, 2015; Chisnell et al., 2006; Hawthorn, 2006; Kurniawan and Zaphiris, 2005; National Institute on Aging (NIH), 2009; Nielsen, 2013; Pernice et al., 2013; Wirtz et al., 2009]*

- Provide blank space around clickable targets. This allows users to easily hit their desired targets and avoid hitting other targets unintentionally.

- In web forms, provide extra space between questions and answer boxes.

Make the cursor big *[Koyani et al., 2002; Worden et al., 1997]*

- If possible, give users a screen pointer (cursor) that is larger than the usual size.

- Alternatively, make the pointer's effective "hot spot" larger than the actual cursor is.

4.1b Make sure users can hit targets (touch-screen devices)

Big tap targets *[Carmien and Garzo, 2014; Gao and Sun, 2015; Kobayashi et al., 2011; Kurniawan and Zaphiris, 2005; Leitão, 2012; Phiriyapokanon, 2011; Stößel, 2012; Wroblewski, 2010]*

- Tap targets on touch screens should be larger than click targets on desktop and laptop computers, because fingers are larger than cursors. For high accuracy (90%+), tap targets should be at least 16.5 mm diagonally (11.7 mm square) (see Figure 4.10).

- Smaller targets will result in decreased accuracy. For example, with tap targets only 9.9 mm diagonally, older adults' accuracy dropped to 67%, and task completion time increased by 50%.

Tap Targets Too Small   Big Enough

Figure 4.10.
Tap targets that are too small (left) and big enough (right) for older adults to hit easily.

Maximize tap target *[Affonso de Lara et al., 2010]*

- When graphical links have a text label, make both part of the link to increase the target's area. Don't limit the target to one small symbol (see Figure 4.11).

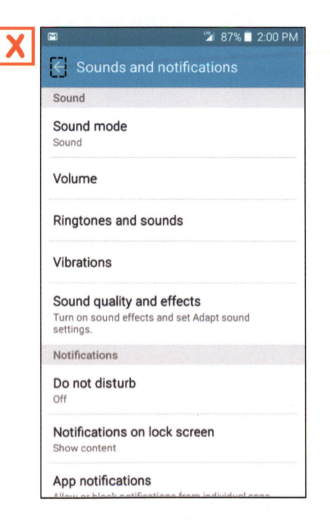

Figure 4.11.
In Android 5.1.1, the control at the top to go back one level only accepts taps on the arrow, not on the text label.

Big swipe targets *[Leitão, 2012]*

- Swipe targets are targets that users must hit at the end of a finger swipe, such as a trash can into which users drag apps they wish to remove (see Figure 4.12), or a folder into which a file is to be dropped. Swipe targets should be larger than tap targets.

- For high accuracy and speed, make them at least 17.5mm square. Smaller sizes can be used, but accuracy and task completion times will suffer.

Figure 4.12.
Example of a swipe target: the trash can for deleting apps from a smartphone desktop.

Put space between tap targets? Maybe *[Carmien and Garzo, 2014; Correia de Barros et al., 2014; Gao and Sun, 2015; Kobayashi et al., 2011; Leitão and Silva, 2012; Phiriyapokanon, 2011; Wroblewski, 2010]*

- The spacing needed between touch targets depends on the size of the targets. If the targets are large enough that users can't miss them, spacing between them can even be zero (see Figure 4.13). If targets are small, make the spacing between them visible, e.g., 3mm.

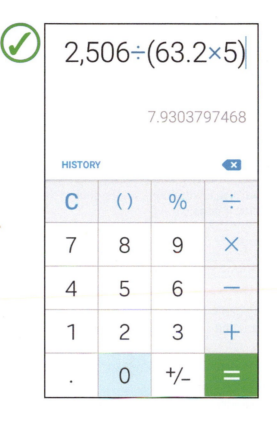

Figure 4.13.
In Android's calculator app, the number and function keys are big enough that they don't need space between them, but the auxiliary controls (History and Backspace) are smaller and do need space separating them from other controls.

Place important tap targets near users' hand *[Leitão and Silva, 2012]*

- On touch-screen devices with large or medium-sized screens such as tablets, place tap targets near the center or the bottom of the screen to minimize the distance users must extend their arms (see Figure 4.7, above). On small screen devices such as smartphones, stretching distance is not much of an issue.

Place swipe targets bottom or right *[Leitão and Silva, 2012]*

- Swipe targets that require high accuracy should be placed differently, depending on whether they require vertical or horizontal swiping. *Horizontal* swipe targets should be in the bottom half of the screen. *Vertical* swipe targets should be in the right half of the screen.

4.2a Keep input gestures simple (desktop and laptop computers)

Avoid double click *[Carmien and Garzo, 2014; Hawthorn, 2006; Kurniawan and Zaphiris, 2006; National Institute on Aging (NIH), 2009]*

- The primary way to open files or applications should require only single clicks: click on item to select, open File menu, select Open menu item. Double click should only be a shortcut alternative method.

- If users double click in situations where double click isn't needed, ignore the second click if possible.

Avoid drag *[Affonso de Lara et al., 2010; Chisnell et al., 2006; Gao and Sun, 2015; Hawthorn, 2006; Kurniawan and Zaphiris, 2005; National Institute on Aging (NIH), 2009; Nielsen, 2013; Pernice et al., 2013; Phiriyapokanon, 2011; Silva et al., 2015; Wirtz et al., 2009]*

- Avoid requiring users to click-drag. Make menus open and close on click, instead of requiring users to click to open, drag to desired item, and release.

- For tasks that require lengthy dragging (>310 mm), provide alternative controls, e.g., a button.

- Avoid having scrollbars be the only means of scrolling.

Leave menus open *[Affonso de Lara et al., 2010]*

- However menus are opened—mouseover, click, tap—they should remain open until the user either selects a menu item or clicks or taps elsewhere.

Multilevel menus: avoid or design carefully *[Finn and Johnson, 2013]*

- Try to avoid multilevel menus.

- If that's not possible, don't require users to keep the pointer within a narrow path while moving to the submenu (see Figure 4.14). Make the path for the pointer wide (i.e., tall), or allow the pointer to move outside the current menu item briefly without closing the menu item's submenu. This can be done either by allowing a brief "grace period" during which the current menu item remains open even if the pointer goes briefly outside of it, or by requiring a click outside of the current menu item to change to a new menu item and submenu.

Figure 4.14.
Road Scholar menus, 2011 versus 2015. Users had to move the pointer strictly horizontally or the country menus disappeared (left). Increasing the height of menu items (right) made the menus easier to use.

4.2b Keep input gestures simple (touch-screen and touch pad)

Avoid multi-finger gestures *[Gao and Sun, 2015; Leitão and Silva, 2012; Stößel, 2012]*

- If possible, make touch-screen apps and websites work using simple one-finger gestures, e.g., **tap** and **swipe**.

- It is OK to *allow* multitouch gestures such as pinch, spread, tap-and-hold, and double-tap for people who can use them reliably, but simpler gestures should also be available for the same functions. For example, if two-finger pinch and spread gestures invoke **zoom in** and **zoom out**, provide + and − buttons also (see Figure 4.15).

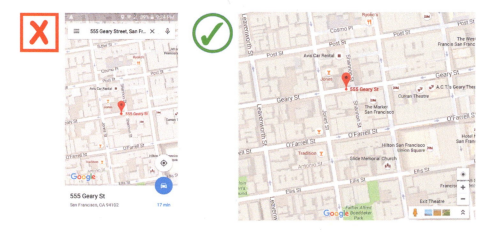

Figure 4.15.
Mobile phone Google Maps requires two-finger spread/pinch gestures for zoom, but the desktop version allows zoom by two fingers or +/− buttons.

4.3 Make it obvious when a target has been selected

Make feedback obvious *[Carmien and Garzo, 2014; Hawthorn, 2006; Kurniawan and Zaphiris, 2005; Silva et al., 2015]*

Figure 4.16.
On the Mac OS desktop, selecting a folder (Cats in this example) highlights it and its name.

- Provide obvious feedback (visual, audio, tactile) when a target is selected by highlighting the target in some way (see Figure 4.16).

Provide feedback immediately *[Chisnell et al., 2006; Johnson, 2014]*

- Feedback should be immediate (less than 0.1 s) upon selection of a target. Otherwise users won't perceive a cause–effect relationship between their action and the feedback.

4.4 Minimize the need to use the keyboard

Gesture input preferred *[Carmien and Garzo, 2014; Correia de Barros et al., 2014; Stößel, 2012]*

- On mobile touch-screen devices, wherever possible allow users to input data via gestures rather than by typing on a keyboard.

Structure user input *[Affonso de Lara et al., 2010]*

- In desktop applications, allow users to enter structured data such as dates, times, and quantities without using the keyboard, by providing defaults, menus, radio buttons, sliders, etc.

4.5 For touch-screen devices, provide within-app training on gestures, if possible

Provide in-app demos *[Leitão, 2012; Stößel, 2012]*

- Demonstrate an app's control gestures within the context of the app itself, rather than in separate documents or videos.

- Demonstrations can be video or animation.

4.6 Allow users plenty of time to complete operations

Avoid time-out *[Miño, 2013; Stößel, 2012]*

- Don't time-out interactions after a short, fixed amount of time. Allow great flexibility in user response and gesture execution times.

4.7 Avoid causing physical strain

Keep user's body position neutral *[Kascak and Sanford, 2015]*

- Allow users to maintain a neutral body position. Don't require users to hold their bodies in uncomfortable positions. For example, don't require them to hold their hands up for long periods, or to tilt their head to see content.

Minimize repetition *[Kascak and Sanford, 2015]*

- Minimize repetitive actions and sustained physical effort to avoid over-taxing users' stamina or causing repetitive stress injuries.

Minimize movement *[Campbell, 2015; Miño, 2013]*

- Cluster related controls near each other, but not so close as to violate spacing guidelines.

Summary of Motor Control Guidelines

4.1 Make sure users can hit targets	Desktop/Laptop Computers	Touch-Screen Devices
	■ Big click targets. ■ Maximize clickable area. ■ Put space between click targets. ■ Big tap targets. ■ Maximize tap target.	■ Big swipe targets. ■ Put space between tap targets? Maybe. ■ Place important tap targets near users' hand. ■ Place swipe targets bottom or right.
4.2 Keep input gestures simple	■ Avoid double click. ■ Avoid drag. ■ Leave menus open. ■ Multilevel menus: avoid or design carefully.	■ Avoid multi-finger gestures.
4.3 Make it obvious when a target has been selected	■ Make feedback obvious. ■ Provide feedback immediately.	
4.4 Minimize the need to use the keyboard	■ Gesture input preferred. ■ Structure user input.	
4.5 For touch-screen devices, provide within-app training on gestures, if possible	■ Provide in-app demos.	
4.6 Allow users plenty of time to complete operations	■ Avoid time-out.	
4.7 Avoid causing physical strain	■ Keep user's body position neutral. ■ Minimize repetition. ■ Minimize movement.	

CHAPTER 5

Hearing and Speech

In the early days of personal computers—the 1970s and 1980s—audio output was limited to beeps and start-up chimes. Audio input, mainly speech, did not exist outside of research labs. Even with the meteoric rise of the Internet and Web in the 1990s, audio output remained limited—confined largely to games—and audio input was practically nonexistent. The early Web was mainly visual for output and keyboard-and-pointer controlled for input.

Things have certainly changed! The new millennium saw a huge increase in the importance of audio: music and video sharing and playing, videophone services, and social media networks. Mobile phones feature many alert and ring tones. Public transit systems and elevators announce arrivals and upcoming stops to us with synthetic voices.

Control via speech input also proliferated, starting with voice-controlled telephone systems that recognized numbers and simple spoken responses such as "yes," "no," "3," and "reservation." As the accuracy and vocabulary of speech recognition improved and systems became able to handle more complex utterances, such as "Find Italian restaurants near me," voice control spread into mobile phones, search engines, and computers.

This proliferation has made it more important for audio output and speech input to work for all potential users.

This chapter describes how the ability to hear and speak changes with age. Based on those changes, we provide guidelines that can help you create digital products and online services that work for people of all ages.

AGE-RELATED CHANGES IN HEARING

As we age, most of us gradually lose our hearing. It's a fact of life.

Age-related hearing loss has a medical name: *presbycusis*, from ancient Greek words meaning "elder hearing." It is the second most common age-related malady, after arthritis. It is caused by a combination of factors:
- loss of hair cells in the inner ear,
- wearing out of the cochlea and sound-transmitting physical parts of the inner ear,
- degeneration of auditory neurons, and
- faulty recruitment of neurons into auditory recognition patterns.

Designing User Interfaces for an Aging Population. http://dx.doi.org/10.1016/B978-0-12-804467-4.00005-0

The rate at which people lose their hearing and the degree of loss vary widely from person to person, but generally speaking, human hearing grows worse with increasing age. Most hearing loss occurs after age 50, but certain losses start in early adulthood.

One way to understand how much of their hearing people lose as they age is to consider the results of a study in which people in several age groups listened to recorded speech and indicated the volume that was most comfortable for them to understand the speech [Cohen, 1994]. People's comfort level depended on their age: older people needed speech to be louder to consider it comfortable (see Table 5.1). How much louder? An increase of 10 decibels (10 dB) makes a sound

Table 5.1	Average Audio Volume for "Comfortable" Understanding of Recorded Speech, for Different Age Groups (Source: Cohen [1994])	
Age (years)	**Volume (dB)**
15	54
25	57
35	61
45	65
55	69
65	74
75	79
85	85

about twice as loud to human ears, so the 31 dB difference in average comfort level between 15-year-olds and 85-year-olds means that the 85-year-olds needed speech to be about eight times louder than 15-year-olds did to hear it comfortably.

How common is age-related hearing loss? About 10% of people aged 45–59 have hearing loss significant enough to affect interactions with others. By age 60–65, the percentage is 33%, by age 75–80 it is up to 55% (see Figure 5.1), and above age 80 it rises to 89% [Arch et al., 2009; Mitzner et al., 2016; O'Hara, 2004; Stevens et al., 2013].

Presbycusis has an assortment of causes, and therefore a variety of symptoms. The primary ones, which are discussed in more detail later in this chapter, are reductions in:
- ability to hear low-volume sounds,
- sensitivity to high-frequency sounds,
- ability to localize sounds,
- ability to filter out background noise,
- ability to understand fast speech.

We don't discuss the less common symptoms of presbycusis, but you should know about them:
- *over*sensitivity to certain sound frequencies,
- tinnitis: ringing, buzzing, hissing, or other perceived sounds when no sound is present.

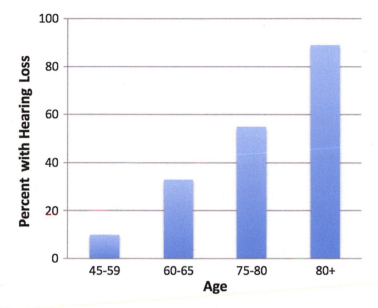

Figure 5.1.
Percent of people with hearing loss sufficient to affect everyday interactions, by age.

In addition to suffering the symptoms of presbycusis, older adults also suffer from negative stereotypes of people who hear poorly. This causes some people to deny that they have hearing loss and avoid remedies that could help them, such as hearing aids and enhanced-volume phones [Nunes, 2010; Wilkinson and De Angeli, 2014]. However, now that it is common for people with normal hearing to wear bluetooth earphones, it should be possible to make hearing aids that are less embarrassing to wear.

Reduced ability to hear low-volume sounds

If you have "perfect" hearing, you can detect sounds as quiet as 10–15 dB[1]—the sound of gently rustling leaves or someone breathing near you. Few people have such perfect hearing—at least not for long. With age and exposure to loud music and noisy environments, our ability to hear soft sounds diminishes, so sounds must be louder—30, 40, 50 dB—before we hear them. A person who cannot hear sounds below 35 dB—such as quiet conversation with a person across a room, or mail falling through a mail slot in a different room—is considered to have "severe" hearing loss [Fisk et al., 2009].

Diminished ability to hear low-volume sounds has these real-world effects:
- Sounds or speech are muffled, making it harder to hear details and extract meaning.
- Audio sources—TVs, radios, music players, telephones, video players, and videophone services—must be turned up to louder volumes.

---

1 An increase of 10 dB is about twice as loud to the human ear, so a 60-dB humming refrigerator sounds to most people about twice as loud as a 50 dB one.

- Audible alerts, such as ring tones, turn signal indicators, and appointment reminders, may be missed [Mitzner et al., 2016].
- If a sound is barely heard, its source or direction is also hard to identify.
- People with this problem often prefer reading transcripts over listening to video and audio recordings.

Reduced sensitivity to high-frequency sounds

Hearing loss usually begins in our late 20s with diminished ability to hear very high-frequency sounds. The highest frequencies go first. As we age further, we become even less able to hear high-frequency sounds. The higher the frequency, the louder the sound must be for us to hear it. Above age 55, our threshold for hearing high-frequency sounds increases by about 1 dB/year, on average [Stößel, 2012]. Thus, for every decade we live, high-frequency sounds become about half as loud to our ears, until they drop below our ability to hear them at all.

Teenagers and adults up to about 30 years old can typically hear high-pitched sounds up to 16,000 vibrations per second (16 kHz) played at moderate loudness. The average person of 31–50 years old can hear high-pitched sounds up to about 12 kHz. Most adults over 50 cannot hear sounds above 8 kHz [Fisk et al., 2009; Nunes, 2010] unless those sounds are very loud (see Figure 5.2). These are just average population values; people vary in what frequencies they can hear.[2] For example, males tend to lose more high-frequency hearing than females do.

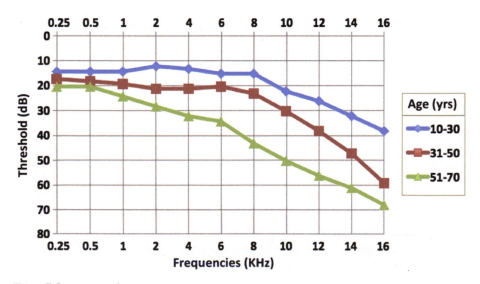

Figure 5.2.
Loudness thresholds for hearing of sounds across the frequency spectrum, by age group (data source Singh et al. [2008]).

---

2 Test your hearing at various frequencies by searching the Web for "hearing frequency test" and trying a test.

The Mosquito/Teen Buzz

The 16 kHz whine is known as *mosquito tone*. Few people over 20 years of age can hear it. Mosquito tone is used both *by* teenagers and *against* them. Some teenagers use Teen Buzz as a ringtone on their mobile phones; they can hear it ring but their parents and teachers usually cannot. On the other hand, there is the Mosquito, an electronic product that emits the mosquito tone. Used by business owners to discourage young people from loitering, it doesn't bother most other customers.

Critical components of speech, such as consonants, are high-frequency sounds. Diminished ability to hear high-pitched sounds can therefore make it harder for us to understand speech, especially speakers with higher voices, or whose faces we can't see[3] [Charness and Boot, 2009; Mitzner et al., 2016; Nunes, 2010]. For example, if you don't hear consonants well, you might mis-hear "the rain in Spain" as "the drain's in pain."

Inability to hear high frequencies causes additional problems as we age [Pak and McLaughlin, 2011]:

- reduced understanding of artificial speech;
- inability to hear all the frequencies that comprise the tonality of a musical instrument;
- inability to hear high-pitched beeps and chimes from home appliances such as doorbells, coffee machines, microwave ovens, and washing machines;
- inability to hear high-frequency alerts that many mobile devices emit (often exacerbated by not knowing how to change the alert sounds);
- reduced ability to discern the direction or source of sounds (discussed next).

Reduced ability to localize sounds

Our auditory system determines the direction of sounds by comparing the time and phase of sound waves arriving at our two ears. The differences are

---

3 Reading a speaker's lips helps people understand speech, even when they have not explicitly learned to read lips. This is made clear by the McGurk effect [see www.youtube.com/watch?v=G-lN8vWm3m0].

measured in thousandths and ten-thousandths of a second. Thus, our ability to localize sounds is closely connected to our ability to hear and distinguish high-frequency sounds. As our hearing for high-frequency sounds declines, so does our ability to pinpoint the source and direction of sounds [Stößel, 2012].

My mobile chirps when I get a text. But, unless I am carrying it, I cannot tell where it is. – Stefano

The higher the pitch of a sound, the harder it is to localize the sound. Also, the briefer a sound, the harder it is to localize. Increasing the duration of sounds gives our auditory system more time to localize them (Nunes, 2010).

Reduced ability to filter out background noise

You may have heard of the "cocktail party effect": our ability to talk with another person when other conversations are going on all around us (see Figure 5.3). Usually, people with normal hearing can filter out most of the background chatter and focus on their own conversation.

Figure 5.3.
Cocktail party effect: our ability to listen to one person in the midst of other conversations and noise.

However, as we age, we gradually lose the ability to understand speech in the presence of background noise [Nunes, 2010; Mitzner et al., 2015; Stößel, 2012]. This decline is caused by changes in both our auditory system (described above) and in our attention mechanisms (described in Chapter 6: Cognition).

Diminished ability to filter out background noise has several undesirable consequences:

- Holding a simple conversation in noisy environments can require intense concentration. Being in noisy places, such as bars and restaurants, can be exasperating and confusing [O'Hara, 2004].
- Websites and apps that automatically play music or sound effects can be quite distracting and annoying [Fisk et al., 2009; Nunes, 2010].
- Understanding spoken instructions while driving can be difficult, especially if the voice is artificial [Mitzner et al., 2015].
- Hearing aids provide limited help. Most modern hearing aids include directional microphones and noise-reduction algorithms to try to filter out irrelevant noise, but research indicates that their effectiveness is limited and variable [Desjardins and Doherty, 2014; McCreery et al., 2012].

These consequences are experienced by younger people as well as older ones. Therefore, minimizing noise that is unrelated to what technology users are trying to do will help older adults and make things more pleasant for younger ones too.

Reduced ability to understand fast speech

Age-related hearing loss is often accompanied by a diminished ability to understand speech that is unusual or abnormal [Mitzner et al., 2015], such as:

- spoken very fast,
- spoken with a strong, unfamiliar accent,
- spoken by an artificial voice that violates conventions of pronunciation, inflection, and rhythm.

The loss of ability to understand fast speech can start as early as age 30 [Heingartner, 2003].

Poor hearing + other deficits = double trouble!

Many older adults experience losses in more than one sensory system. For example, it is common for older people to have declining vision as well as declining hearing. This complicates efforts to design technology to overcome the losses.

For example, if someone cannot hear the audio in a movie very well, they may appreciate having text captions. However, captions that are too small or contrast poorly with the movie background won't help someone who also has poor vision.

AGE-RELATED CHANGES IN SPEECH

In addition to slowly losing our hearing, as we age we often find ourselves less and less able to speak quickly and clearly. Specifically, three age-related changes in our speech affect our ability to control devices and enter data by voice.

Slower, more hesitant speech

With increased age, our speech tends to slow down, due to slower articulation of words and because it includes more pauses, interruptions, false starts, and filler utterances such as "um," "uh," "er." Pauses often result from situations where a speaker cannot recall the precise word they intended. Controlled studies have measured older adults' speaking rate at about 14% slower than that of younger adults [Hawthorn, 2006; Koyani et al., 2002].

Higher pitched voice

With age, the pitch of many people's voice rises, which can cause difficulty for some automatic speech recognition systems [Koyani et al., 2002].

Reduced articulation

As we grow older, so do the parts of our body that control and affect our speech: larynx, throat, palate, tongue, teeth, diaphragm, and lungs. Muscles grow weaker with age, neural control diminishes, and scars accumulate, all of which affect our ability to articulate words. Stroke or Alzheimer's disease may accelerate this process [Hawthorn, 2006; O'Hara, 2004].

In addition, with increasing age, human voices tend to become more "breathy" and more prone to hoarseness, and breathing often becomes more audible [Alexenko et al., 2013; Hawthorn, 2006; Vipperla, 2011].

These factors combine to make older adult voices harder for speech recognition systems to understand.

DESIGN GUIDELINES THAT HELP OLDER ADULTS (AND OTHERS!)

If your application, website, or device produces audio output or accepts speech input, follow these guidelines to help ensure that people of all ages can use it.

5.1 Ensure that audio output is audible

Avoid high-frequency sounds *[Carmien and Garzo, 2014; Hawthorn, 2006; Nunes, 2010; Silva et al., 2015]*

- Alerts and confirmation tones should be mainly in the 500–1000 Hz range.
- Use lower frequency voices for important information.

Ensure that sounds are loud enough *[Carmien and Garzo, 2014; Nunes, 2010; Strengers, 2012]*

- Default audio volume should be loud enough to be heard by older adults, at least 50–60 dB.

Make auditory signals long *[Nunes, 2010]*

- If users need to locate sounds, avoid very short chirps and beeps. Make audible alerts and other signals last long enough to allow users to localize them, e.g., several seconds or longer.

5.2 Minimize background noise

Avoid distracting sounds *[Fisk et al., 2009; Nunes, 2010]*

- Don't play sounds that are not related to the users' task, such as background music or autoplaying videos.

- If the hardware platform makes noise (e.g., with cooling fans), minimize it.

5.3 Convey important information in multiple ways

Supplement images with text *[Chisnell et al., 2006; Hawthorn, 2006; Kascak and Sanford, 2015; Miño, 2013; National Institute on Aging (NIH), 2009; Pernice et al., 2014; Phiriyapokanon, 2011; Silva et al., 2015]*

- Augment images with captions and alt text.

- Augment video and audio playback with transcripts or closed captions (see Figure 5.4), and ensure that the text is easy for older adults to read.

- Use videos and audios to supplement text, not to replace it. Older adults benefit from redundancy.

Make alerts multimodal *[Carmien and Garzo, 2014; Gilbertson, 2014; Williams et al., 2013]*

- Provide alert signals in multiple forms: audible, visual, and if possible, tactile (e.g., vibration). Beware, however, of overwhelming users with too many different alerts for the same event.

Provide text-to-speech *[Affonso de Lara et al., 2010; National Institute on Aging (NIH), 2009]*

- Ensure that a text-to-speech function is available, either in your software or in the underlying platform, so users can hear the text being read out loud. Test the speech output to make sure users of all ages can understand it.

Figure 5.4.
Provide captioning for video and audio recordings. A dark background for the captions helps ensure that older adults can read it. [Used with permission from 3Play Media: 3playmedia.com].

5.4 Allow users to adjust device output

Make volume adjustable *[Nunes, 2010]*

- Applications with audio output should allow users to easily adjust the volume.

Let users replay audio *[Nunes, 2010]*

- Provide an easy way for users to replay audio messages.

Make play speed adjustable *[Affonso de Lara et al., 2010; Nunes, 2010]*

- Give users an easy way to adjust the play speed of multimedia content. Adjusting speech speed should not affect the pitch.

Let users select alert sounds *[Hawthorn, 2006]*

- Allow users to choose alert sounds, and make finding the controls and setting them easy.

Provide alternative voices *[Almeida et al., 2015]*

- For devices that provide speech output, provide several alternative voices and an easy way for users to choose one.

5.5 Make speech output as normal as possible

Not too fast *[Carmien and Garzo, 2014; Fisk et al., 2009]*

- Play speech at a consistent pace, no faster than 140 words per minute.

Avoid robot speech *[Nunes, 2010]*

- Ensure that synthetic speech closely emulates normal human speech. Avoid speech output that sounds heavily artificial.

5.6 Provide an alternative data entry method for people who cannot use the main one

Allow speech input *[Hawthorn, 2006; Strengers, 2012]*

- In systems that are controlled mainly manually, provide a way to enter text and commands via speech recognition if possible. Note that speech recognition software may have more trouble understanding the voices of older adults.

But don't require speech input *[Strengers, 2012]*

- In systems in which speech is the main input method, provide a way for users to enter data and commands manually—using a keyboard or other controls.

Summary of Hearing and Speech Guidelines

5.1 Ensure that audio output is audible	■ Avoid high-frequency sounds. ■ Ensure that sounds are loud enough. ■ Make auditory signals long.
5.2 Minimize background noise	■ Avoid distracting sounds.
5.3 Convey important information in multiple ways	■ Supplement images with text. ■ Make alerts multimodal. ■ Provide text-to-speech.
5.4 Allow users to adjust device output	■ Make volume adjustable. ■ Let users replay audio. ■ Make play speed adjustable. ■ Let users select alert sounds. ■ Provide alternative voices.
5.5 Make speech output as normal as possible	■ Not too fast. ■ Avoid robot speech.
5.6 Provide an alternative data entry method for people who cannot use the main one	■ Allow speech input. ■ But don't require speech input.

CHAPTER 6

Cognition

Age-related declines in people's sensory and motor abilities (discussed in Chapters 3–5) are fairly straightforward to detect and measure. Although they interact, sensory channels are clearly separate from each other and from motor control channels. The mechanisms of human perception and motor action, including their decline with age, are well understood, at least in enough detail for developing user interface design guidelines.

Declining cognitive capabilities, in contrast, are not as straightforward to detect and measure. Human cognition is not yet well understood. Its mechanisms and components are not as clear-cut and distinct as are those of perception and motor control. In the research literature, the components of cognition vary depending on which tasks are studied and which theory is used to predict and explain how people perform those tasks. Furthermore, theories of human cognition continue to be developed and refined as more experiments are conducted and more data are collected and analyzed.

However, for our purposes—designing digital information and communications technology (ICT) for people of all ages—we need not concern ourselves with fine distinctions between different theories of cognition, with their slightly different component breakdowns. We have simply chosen a commonly accepted component breakdown and describe the effects of age on each component of cognition.

COGNITION IN OLDER ADULTS

Cognitive scientists generally agree that most cognitive abilities decline with age. However, people vary enormously in *which* abilities decline, *when* they start declining, and *how rapidly* and how *much* they decline [Hart et al., 2008; Reddy et al., 2014]. Some of this variability is due to genetics, and some results from each person's life experiences. However, there are common patterns.

For example, cognitive decline begins earlier than "old age" (age 50+, by this book's definition). Aging is a lifelong process, starting when we are born. Just as hearing usually peaks when a person reaches young adulthood and begins to decline soon after (see Chapter 5: Hearing and Speech), some aspects of cognition start to decline when we are still fairly young—in our 30s and 40s [Stößel, 2012]. Other aspects of cognition hardly decline at all as we age, and may even improve.

Designing User Interfaces for an Aging Population. http://dx.doi.org/10.1016/B978-0-12-804467-4.00006-2

Let's now examine the components of cognition to see how age affects them. This will provide insight into how to design information/communications technology so as not to exclude people who experience normal, mild forms of cognitive decline.

Reduced short-term (working) memory capacity

A simple view of human memory is that it consists of two main components: short-term memory and long-term memory. Short-term memory holds information for periods ranging from a fraction of a second to many minutes, while long-term memory retains information for longer intervals, all the way up to a lifetime.

Of course, the human mind is more complicated than that. It has several types of short-term and long-term memory, each with different characteristics. For example, each perceptual channel has its own brief short-term memory caused by neural activity that continues briefly after a stimulus ends, like a bell that rings briefly after it is struck [Johnson, 2014].

However, the main thing psychologists mean—and what we mean—by "short-term memory" is *working memory*: a mechanism for holding items of information in our awareness, allowing us to evaluate, combine, compare, and manipulate them. Don't think of working memory as a storage *place*. It is not located in any specific part of the brain. Instead, working memory consists of those few items from our perception and long-term memory that we are attending to at any given time—the combined focus of our attention. The capacity of working memory—the number of items we can keep in mind at one time—is pretty low: between three and five information "chunks."[1]

The capacity of human working memory typically rises as we develop from babies into adults and begins to decline when we are in our 30s. The peak capacity of working memory varies somewhat among people, but the rate at which the capacity declines and the ages at which the decline accelerates vary *greatly* from one person to another. On average, however, the working memory capacity of older adults is lower than that of younger adults [Salthouse and Babcock, 1991].

When so many steps are required, I often lose track of what I was trying to do. – Hana

Declining working memory capacity has powerful effects on our ability to think, reason, and make sense of the world. It diminishes our ability to combine concepts, compare ideas and objects, multitask, keep track of what we have done and not done, and more [Campbell, 2015; Carmien and Garzo, 2014; Charness

---

1 The capacity of human working memory used to be estimated at 7 plus or minus 2 chunks, but later research found that to be an overestimate [Johnson, 2014].

and Boot, 2009; Czaja and Lee, 2008; Fairweather, 2008; Hawthorn, 2006; Newell, 2011; Pernice et al., 2013; Stößel, 2012; Wirtz et al., 2009].

Research with older adults has shown:

- A complex task with many things to keep track of can exceed working memory capacity and overwhelm older adults unless they can break the task into simple steps and write down intermediate steps. When overwhelmed, older adults often start over or give up [Fairweather, 2008].
- A complex sentence—such as one containing many negatives or clauses—can strain working memory, making it hard to understand (see Figure 6.1) [Arch, 2008].

ADOBE
Personal Computer Software License Agreement

1. WARRANTY DISCLAIMER, BINDING AGREEMENT AND ADDITIONAL TERMS AND AGREEMENTS.

1.1 WARRANTY DISCLAIMER. THE SOFTWARE AND OTHER INFORMATION IS DELIVERED TO YOU "AS IS" AND WITH ALL FAULTS. ADOBE, ITS SUPPLIERS, AND CERTIFICATION AUTHORITIES DO NOT AND CANNOT WARRANT THE PERFORMANCE OR RESULTS YOU MAY OBTAIN BY USING THE SOFTWARE, CERTIFICATE AUTHORITY SERVICES, OR OTHER THIRD PARTY OFFERINGS. EXCEPT TO THE EXTENT THAT ANY WARRANTY, CONDITION, REPRESENTATION, OR TERM CANNOT OR MAY NOT BE EXCLUDED OR LIMITED BY LAW APPLICABLE TO YOU IN YOUR JURISDICTION, ADOBE AND ITS SUPPLIERS AND CERTIFICATION AUTHORITIES MAKE NO WARRANTIES, CONDITIONS, REPRESENTATIONS, OR TERMS (EXPRESS OR IMPLIED, WHETHER BY STATUTE, COMMON LAW, CUSTOM, USAGE, OR OTHERWISE) AS TO ANY MATTER, INCLUDING WITHOUT LIMITATION NON-INFRINGEMENT OF THIRD-PARTY RIGHTS, MERCHANTABILITY, INTEGRATION, SATISFACTORY QUALITY, OR FITNESS FOR ANY PARTICULAR PURPOSE. THE PROVISIONS OF SECTIONS 1.1 AND 10 SHALL SURVIVE THE TERMINATION OF THIS AGREEMENT, HOWSOEVER CAUSED, BUT THIS SHALL NOT IMPLY OR CREATE ANY CONTINUED RIGHT TO USE THE SOFTWARE AFTER TERMINATION OF THIS AGREEMENT.

Figure 6.1.
Adobe's Software License Agreement contains many negations and complex clauses, straining working memory. This makes the agreement difficult for people, especially older adults, to understand.

- Older adults have more trouble than younger adults do remembering what they have already searched. They revisit pages and screens more often than younger adults do when browsing and searching [Boechler et al., 2012; Czaja and Lee, 2008].
- In many computer tasks, older adults are as accurate or successful as younger adults. They achieve this through a speed/accuracy trade off: they perform tasks more slowly and carefully than younger adults do. However, when the number of details to keep track of increases to the point where it exceeds older adults' working memory capacity, their accuracy decreases [Docampo Rama et al., 2001].
- Some applications, websites, and devices have "modes" of operation, meaning that controls or user actions change their effect based on what mode the system is in. For example, a car's accelerator makes the car go forward or backward, depending on what mode (gear) the transmission is in. Similarly a digital camera's shutter button either snaps a photo or starts a video, depending on whether the camera is in photo or video

mode. Unless moded systems display the current operational mode prominently, users must use their working memory to know what mode the system is in. If users lose track of the mode, they make mode errors, like driving backward when they mean to drive forward, or starting a video when they want to take a photo, or drawing a line in a drawing app when they intend to draw a circle.

The Guidelines section of this chapter includes guidelines for minimizing the demands your application or online service places on its users' working memory. For example, with practice, an activity can become automatic, so it consumes little working memory and requires little or no conscious monitoring and control. Therefore, designs and training that encourage repetition and practice can help older adults overcome short-term memory deficits [Fairweather, 2008].

Less effective long-term memory storage and retrieval (i.e., learning)

Long-term memory is obviously required for learning. Studies show that older adults typically learn new technical skills more slowly than younger adults do and, during learning, require more help, repetition, and hands-on practice [Czaja and Lee, 2008; Hart et al., 2008; Plaza et al., 2011].

I learn things more slowly now. To learn something new, I must do it over and over, many times. – Wong

The theory behind this slower learning rate is that, as we age, our brain's ability to store new memories in long-term memory declines [Arch et al., 2008]. Specifically, neurological evidence suggests that as we age, our brains store information with less and less appropriate metadata, making new memories harder and harder to retrieve later [Boechler et al., 2012]. The result is that older adults are worse than younger adults at recalling new memories of events or facts, but just as good at recalling old memories that were stored when their long-term memory encoding still worked well [Boechler et al., 2012; Czaja and Lee, 2008; Fairweather, 2008; Hawthorn, 2006; Nielsen, 2013].

In addition, conscious recall of events or facts declines with age. This is at least partly because conscious thought uses working memory, which, as described in the previous section, declines in capacity with age [Boechler et al., 2012].

As we age, our diminished ability to store and recall details and attributes makes it harder for us to remember specifics of how to operate information and communications technology from one usage to the next [Arch et al., 2008; Arch and Abou-Zhara, 2008]. As we learn our way around in any space—whether it is a physical space or an information space—we build in our mind a *mental map* of how the space is organized: a representation of what places are near each other, what places are far from each other, and how to get from place to place. Similarly, as we learn to use devices, software, or websites, we build in our mind a *mental model* of how they work, to help us remember how to operate them [Wilkinson, 2011]. Well-designed applications or information spaces make it easier for users to develop mental maps and models than poorly designed ones do [Johnson and Henderson, 2011]. As we age, declining memory reduces our ability to develop mental maps and models of apps, devices, and websites, making efficient navigation and operation difficult. For example, researchers find that older adults are generally less successful at retracing a route than younger adults are [Zajicek, 2001].

A lack of effective mental maps and models is often cited as explaining older adults' tendency to want detailed lists of steps to follow in using digital technology. If you need to use a device, software application, or service, but don't understand how it works, you probably will want step-by-step instructions on how to obtain your desired results.

These facts about age-related declines in memory may be depressing, but the truth isn't all bad. Not all aspects of long-term memory decline with age. We mentioned earlier that people have several types of long-term memory. Psychologists distinguish these types:

- *Semantic memory*: the ability to store and recall concepts, ideas, facts, and the relationships between them. Examples include knowing that dropped objects usually fall, ducks are birds, most birds fly, cows don't fly, and smartphones can receive calls, text messages, and email.
- *Episodic memory*: the ability to remember events in the past, such as your college graduation, your last argument with your spouse, or your last vacation.
- *Prospective memory*: the ability to remember planned future tasks and events. Planned future tasks could include taking medicines before going to bed, attending next week's doctor appointment, or buying flowers for your partner on your anniversary.
- *Procedural memory*: the ability to remember and apply previously learned skills, such as riding a bicycle, baking a cake, adding a contact to your mobile phone, or booking a flight online.

The encouraging news is this: some types of long-term memory decline less than others, and some types normally don't decline at all. Procedural and semantic memory typically decline less than episodic and prospective memory do, except when a person suffers from a dementia condition such as Alzheimer's disease [Campbell, 2015; Stößel, 2012].

Within each of the above types of long-term memory, psychologists also distinguish *recognition* from *recall*, based on the theory that they require different cognitive resources [Johnson, 2014]. Recognition is knowing—or believing—that you have experienced the current situation before, as in recognizing a face, an odor, or a chess game position. Recall is bringing something back into your awareness even though the thing is not currently present, as in recalling a poem, a phone number, or where you left your wallet.

Research has found that older adults tend to perform worse on *recall* tasks than younger adults do, but just as well as younger adults on *recognition* tasks. This suggests that recognition typically does not decline—again, except in clear cases of dementia. The explanation is that recall requires more processing resources than does recognition, and those resources are depleted with age [Boechler et al., 2012]. The implication for designing for older adults, expressed in guidelines presented later in this chapter, is that user interfaces should rely more on users' recognition memory and less on users' ability to recall information.

Many older adults realize that their memory isn't as good as it once was, and adopt compensatory strategies. They write appointments in calendars and datebooks, and check them daily. They place notes around their homes. They ask friends and relatives to call and remind them of things. They use gadgets and adopt daily habits to help them remember when to take medications. They make notes on how to use equipment, software, and websites. In the latter case, changes in a user interface that users have carefully documented for themselves can really set older adults back [Pernice et al., 2013].

The good news for us as technology designers is that augmenting people's memory is something digital technology can help with by providing alarms, calendar event reminders, location-based reminders, and connections to family and friends. However, that means we must design digital technology, so people with poor memories—which includes many older adults—can learn it and use it.

Less generalization (skill transfer) between situations

In addition to having trouble recalling details and therefore with learning new skills, older adults typically show less transfer of skills between situations than their younger counterparts do. For example, older adults in self-paced learning situations take about *twice* as long as younger adults to learn a new word processing application, even when they and their younger counterparts have had the same amount of prior experience with other word processing applications [Charness and Boot, 2009].

My nephew rolled his eyes and told me 'it's like what I just **showed** you', but to me this seems quite different.
– Stefano

Diminished ability to ignore distractions and focus attention

If a website has lots of stuff moving around, I leave. I can't concentrate. – Carolina

Anyone who has watched older adults using digital technology knows that "too much going on," "too many distractions," and "too many ways to get off-track" are common complaints they make [Arch et al., 2009]. Such complaints are common because as people age, their ability to filter out distractions and focus on their goals decreases. Many apps, websites, and electronic appliances are not designed to take this into account.

Research has made it pretty clear that as we age, we are more easily distracted by off-task navigation links, graphics, advertisements, and other screen elements (see Figure 6.2). We are less able to ignore irrelevant information or prevent our eyes from glancing at extraneous elements on the display [Carmien and Garzo, 2014; Charness and Boot, 2009; Czaja and Lee, 2008; Fairweather, 2008; Hanson et al., 2001; Hart et al., 2008; Hawthorn, 2006; Newell, 2011; Stößel, 2012].

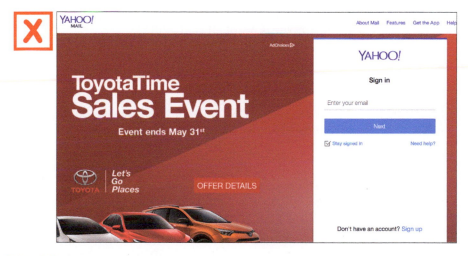

Figure 6.2.
The login page for Yahoo mail displays an advertisement more prominently than the login form, possibly distracting users from their main task.

I find many websites overwhelming...too many things to click on. Just show me what I want. – Monika

Many websites and some apps collect revenue by advertising. How can companies include advertising while not distracting older users from achieving their goals in using the app or website? A hint might come from the difference between banner ads and goal-sensitive ads. If ads have little or nothing to do with the users' goal, they are potential distractions that can divert users from achieving not only what they want, but also what the company that created the website or app wants. In contrast, if ads are alternative suggestions to the user for achieving the users' indicated goal, they need not be considered distractions.

My phone has too many settings. I have no idea what most of them do. – Hana

A final source of distractions is our own wandering minds. As we grow older, our own thoughts and recollections are more likely to intrude and distract us from tasks we are trying to do, or disrupt our attempts to understand events and recall memories. To test this, researchers conducted a study in which the brain activity of younger and older adults was monitored as they watched a movie. Younger adults all showed very similar patterns of brain activity, presumably because they were all focused on the movie. In contrast, the brain activity of older adults varied greatly, suggesting that different individuals were thinking about different things as they watched the movie [Campbell et al., 2015].

Reduced ability to multitask

I used to be able to manage two or three tasks, but nowadays I do one thing at a time. – Monika

Closely related to the ability to concentrate on one task is the ability to divide one's attention between two or more different tasks. It is difficult for people of all ages, but gets more difficult as we grow older.

True multitasking—doing more than one thing at once—is really only possible with activities that are highly practiced and automatic to the point where they don't require conscious monitoring or control, such as walking while listening to a radio show in your native language, or beating an egg while humming a familiar tune [Johnson, 2014]. Multitasking such activities doesn't require dividing your attention, because neither task requires attention [Kahneman, 2011]. As far as researchers know, the ability to multitask automatic activities does not diminish with age.

In contrast, tasks that require conscious attention and control, such as planning a vacation, booking a hotel room, reading, driving an unfamiliar route, or talking on the phone *cannot* be multitasked. Some people *believe* they can multitask such activities, but they are wrong. What they are really doing is rapidly switching their attention back and forth—"juggling" tasks. Juggling conscious tasks makes heavy use of working memory and requires strong control of attention. Because both working memory and control of attention decline with advancing age, the ability to juggle conscious activities *is* diminished by age in most people [Campbell, 2015; Czaja and Lee, 2008; Hawthorn, 2006; Miño, 2013].

Declining spatial memory and control of attention affect ability to navigate

Spatial memory, a type of semantic memory, is the ability to navigate in real or virtual spaces by consulting a mental map representing spatial and connectivity relationships between places (see Figure 6.3). Researchers have found that spatial memory declines as people age, and with it, the ability to navigate easily in menu hierarchies, websites, apps, and other abstract spaces [Boechler et al., 2012; Czaja and Lee, 2008; Docampo Rama et al., 2001; Stößel, 2012; Wirtz et al., 2009].

Figure 6.3.
Most smartphones have multiple home screens to allow quick access to users' favorite apps. Android has four, indicated by dots near the bottom. Navigating between screens uses spatial memory.

 I don't expect to remember what I find by exploring, so I rarely explore. – Wong

Navigation is not the only task that requires spatial reasoning. Manipulating documents, images, and other objects on a computer—for example, moving photos from one folder into another—requires people to mentally model and predict the result of the manipulation. That involves something that researchers call *visual–spatial working memory*. When researchers ask people of different ages to perform visual–spatial manipulation and comparison tasks, they find that older adults are slower and less accurate than younger ones [Leung et al., 2010; Stößel, 2012].

Diminished ability to focus attention is another factor in older adults' reduced ability to find a path to their goal when faced with numerous choices along the way. Choosing your next step in an unfamiliar website or app often requires you to focus and maintain attention on the different options and compare those options in your working memory. As we have explained, working memory capacity and control of attention are cognitive attributes that decline with age [Jahn and Krems, 2013]. Most websites and apps display many possible user actions on every page or screen, but many, through poor labeling, fail to show users the way toward their goal. The result is that older adults often have trouble navigating in websites and apps, are more likely than younger adults to get "lost in cyberspace" and to have more difficulty recovering from being lost [Arch et al., 2009; Hawthorn, 2006; Koyani et al., 2002; NIH/NIA, 2009].

Part of knowing the way to your goal is knowing where you are at steps along the way. Not only do indicators of current status or location help you get to your goal, they also help you build a mental map or model of the information space. Unfortunately, many websites and software applications provide insufficient cues about the user's current status or location [Johnson, 2007]. Some even provide *misleading* cues. As we age, decreasing ability to focus attention on the cues about our location (if any), combined with reduced ability to form and use mental maps, allows us to be distracted and disoriented by irrelevant features on the page or screen. For example, if a prominent image or color on a web page changes automatically, some users, especially older adults, may mistakenly believe they are on a different page [Finn and Johnson, 2013] (see Figure 6.4).

Figure 6.4.
GrandCircleTravel.com's homepage has large images that change automatically, causing some older adults to think they are on a different page.

It is of course easier to construct and remember a mental map of an information space if the space is well marked with indicators of where you are in the space and where each path leads. This is the basis for the guidelines presented later in this chapter about navigation structure, status and progress indicators, labeling, consistency of terminology, etc.

Increased risk of cognitive "blindness"

I don't always notice when something on the screen changes. – John

When our mind is occupied with a task, perception, or strong emotion, we may fail to see objects and events that are in plain view. It is a temporary "blindness" caused by the operation of our perception and attention. Psychological researchers have identified three variations:

- *Attentional blink*: not noticing something that occurs immediately after we see something else that grabs our attention.
- *Inattentional blindness*: not noticing objects or events that don't match our interests.
- *Change blindness*: not noticing changes in our visual field that are unrelated to our goals.

Attentional blink occurs when two or more important events happen in front of our eyes in rapid succession. For example, if you are looking at your phone and a calendar reminder pops up, it probably grabs your attention. If in the next half second a text arrives from a close friend, you might not notice it immediately because your mind is busy processing the calendar reminder.

Inattentional blindness is pretty common. Adults—young and old—tend to only notice things that are relevant to what they are trying to do [Johnson, 2014]. If you are seeking specific information on a screen or in a website, you probably will not notice other important information that appears there, because you weren't looking for it.

Change blindness is when an information display changes and you don't notice the change. For example, if you are trying to book a boat cruise, you might choose a different departure date and not notice that doing so caused the price to go up (see Figure 6.5). Or you might choose a different ship cabin to see how it affects the price and fail to notice that the departure date also changed.

Older technology users are more likely than younger users to miss information or changes that are not the direct focus of their attention [Arch and Abou-Zhara, 2008; Veiel et al., 2006].

Fortunately, through age-sensitive design, designers of digital technology can increase the likelihood that users, even older ones, will not miss important changes.

Slower responses; slower processing speed

When I try to get money out of the cashpoint machines, they don't always give me enough time to put in my numbers! – John

Before date change

After date change

Figure 6.5.
Compare upper and lower screens. Users of RoadScholar.com may not notice that if they change the Date Selected (bottom center of screen), the price (middle right of screen) may have changed.

One of the most common findings about older adults performing tasks using digital technology is that they are slower at it than younger users are. Some of this slower performance is due to declining motor abilities: slower movement and more corrections to movements (see Chapter 4: Motor Control). However, even when older adults' slower movement is taken into account, they are still slower to react and to complete tasks than younger adults are [Charness and Boot, 2009; Fairweather, 2008; Stößel, 2012; Wirtz et al., 2009]. For example:

- When using the Web, older adults, on average, are more methodical than young adults. They take more time to read text and to complete tasks. They visit fewer pages. They are less likely to leave a site due to page-loading delays [Hart et al., 2008; Pernice et al., 2013].
- The same is seen with software apps and digital devices, such as smartphones [Campbell, 2015].
- The more complex the task, the greater the difference in the task completion times of older versus younger adults. Older adults are slowed more by complexity than younger adults are [Wirtz et al., 2009].
- Older adults show slower reaction times than young adults [Fairweather, 2008; Hart et al., 2008; Leung et al., 2010].
- Eye-tracking studies show that older adults look longer at interactive elements before taking action than younger adults do [Hanson, 2009].

Many researchers attribute at least some of this age-related slowing down in task performance to a slowing of perceptual and cognitive processing speed. The speed of perceptual and cognitive processing cannot yet be measured directly. However, it can be inferred from the observation that older adults tend to perform tasks even more slowly than would be predicted from all the various physical slowdowns that they exhibit.

Keep in mind that researchers see great *variability* between older adults in the speed at which they do things. The greater the age of the people being studied, the greater the variability [Campbell et al., 2015; Czaja and Lee 2008; Hart et al., 2008; Hawthorn, 2006; Pak and McLaughlin, 2011; Stößel, 2012]. For our purposes as technology designers (and perhaps as technology trainers), it is enough to note that at least *some* older adults react more slowly and take more time— sometimes much more time—to complete tasks. We must take this into account if we want all older adults to be able to use what we design.

Cognitive interactions

We have been discussing the aspects of human cognition as if they were separate, but of course they aren't. They interact and overlap in many ways. For example:

- Slower task completion times and diminishing ability to filter distractions can result from declining working memory capacity [Fairweather, 2008].
- In information processing tasks, researchers see a speed/accuracy trade-off among older adults. They perform as accurately as younger adults when allowed to take more time, but when older adults are rushed their performance drops significantly [Olmsted-Hawala et al., 2013].

- Performance on problem-solving, deductive reasoning, inference formation, and conscious choice tasks typically decline together as people age, suggesting that these tasks share underlying mechanisms [Campbell et al., 2015; Czaja and Lee, 2008].

Psychologists often use the term "fluid intelligence" to cover several interrelated cognitive attributes: working memory capacity, control of attention, problem-solving, spatial and logical reasoning, processing speed, perceptual response time, and learning ability. They have developed tests of fluid intelligence that assess the above-mentioned cognitive attributes. Fluid intelligence generally rises until early adulthood and then begins to diminish, although this varies greatly between people [Charness and Boot, 2009; Hanson, 2009; Wirtz et al., 2009].

However, fluid intelligence is not the only type of intelligence people have. A person's ability to operate successfully in the world also relies upon knowledge, experience, wisdom, judgment, vocabulary, and verbal ability. Psychologists often combine these attributes under the term "crystallized intelligence." Unless a person suffers from serious dementia, researchers find that crystallized intelligence typically does not decline much with age, if at all. Indeed, it may *grow*, as people accumulate more experience and knowledge [Pak and McLaughlin, 2011; Stößel, 2012]. Crystallized intelligence and knowledge as factors in older adults' ability to use digital technology are discussed more in Chapter 7: Knowledge.

DESIGN GUIDELINES THAT HELP OLDER ADULTS (AND OTHERS!)

Following these guidelines will help you ensure that adults of all ages can learn, understand, and remember how to use your application, website, or device and can process the information it provides.

6.1 Design for simplicity

Minimize stimuli *[Carmien and Garzo, 2014; Chisnell et al., 2006; Czaja and Lee, 2008; Hawthorn, 2006; Kurniawan and Zaphiris, 2005; NIH/NIA, 2009; Phiriyapokanon, 2011; Romano-Bergstrom et al., 2013; Silva et al., 2015; Strengers, 2012]*

- Users focus on what is important by eliminating nonessential functions, choices, and visual elements.

- Provide the fewest possible choices, calls to action, and interaction elements. Don't overwhelm users with many competing calls to action (see Figure 6.6). Limit interactive items to three to seven per page.

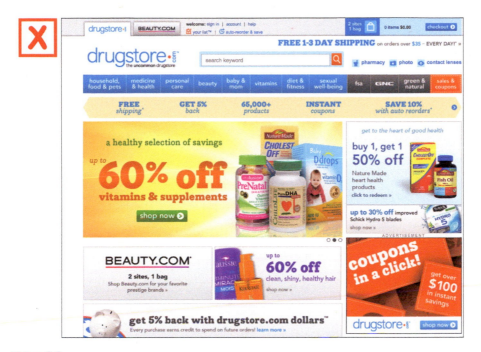

Figure 6.6.
Drugstore.com homepage displays many competing calls to action, potentially overwhelming older visitors.

6.2 Help users maintain focus

Present one task at a time *[Affonso de Lara et al., 2010; Campbell, 2015; Hawthorn, 2006; Jahn and Krems, 2013; Kurniawan and Zaphiris, 2005; NIH/NIA, 2009; Nunes et al., 2012; Phiriyapokanon, 2011; Silva et al., 2015; Strengers, 2012; Williams et al., 2013]*

- Allow users to focus their attention on one task at a time. Don't require them to multitask, i.e., monitor or switch back and forth between two or more tasks, subtasks, or locations.

- Aim for one page, one task.

Eliminate distractions *[Carmien and Garzo, 2014; Chisnell et al., 2006; Czaja and Lee, 2008; Hawthorn, 2006; Kascak and Sanford, 2015; Kurniawan and Zaphiris, 2005; Miño, 2013; NIH/NIA, 2009; Nunes et al., 2012; Pernice et al., 2013; Phiriyapokanon, 2011; Romano-Bergstrom et al., 2013; Strengers, 2012; Williams et al., 2013]*

- All content and screen elements should be relevant to users' goals. Avoid purely decorative graphics or multimedia content.

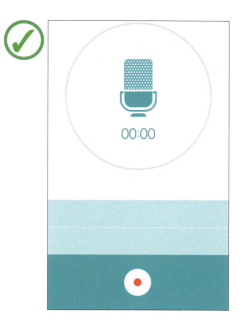

Figure 6.7.
The Android voice recorder app is focused on one task: recording sounds.

- Keep task paths clear of anything, such as animations, non–task-relevant images, and contextual advertising, that might distract users from reaching their goals (see Figure 6.7).

- Even advertisements, if they are necessary, should be relevant to users' goals.

Indicate current task prominently *[Silva et al., 2015]*

- Help users keep track of what they are doing by indicating the name and status of the current task prominently at all times.

6.3 Simplify navigation structure

Put most important information up front *[Chisnell et al., 2006; NIH/NIA, 2009; Nunes et al., 2012; Pernice et al., 2013]*

- Place the most important information and the most common tasks near the beginning of the website or app.

- Provide clear, short paths to commonly accessed content.

Make navigation consistent *[NIH/NIA, 2009; Patsoule and Koutsabasis, 2014; Pernice et al., 2013; Phiriyapokanon, 2011]*

- Make navigation consistent throughout the website or app.

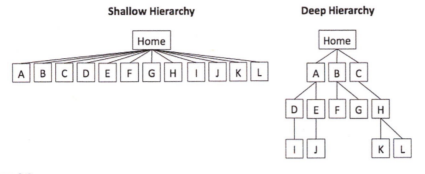

Figure 6.8.
Shallow versus deep page structure. Shallow is easier for older adults.

Make structure obvious *[Chisnell et al., 2006; Kurniawan and Zaphiris, 2005]*

- Make the structure of a website as obvious as possible.

Keep hierarchies shallow *[Carmien and Garzo, 2014; Chisnell et al., 2006; Czaja and Lee, 2008; Kurniawan and Zaphiris, 2005; Nunes et al., 2012; Reddy et al., 2014]*

- Choose broad and shallow navigational structures (see Figure 6.8), so users don't lose track of how deep they are in the hierarchy.

Make categories unique *[Pernice et al., 2013]*

- Make navigational categories unique and mutually exclusive.

- Make sure users can quickly see which category the product they are seeking is in, or which menu option the functionality they want is in. Don't make users guess which way to go. For example, an online food store should not have both "Seafood" and "Fish" product categories on the same page, and an airline website should not offer both "Use Award Miles" and "Book with Award Miles" functions.

6.4 Clearly indicate the progress and status of operations

Lead users step-by-step *[Hawthorn, 2006; Miño, 2013; NIH/NIA, 2009; Silva et al., 2015; Wirtz et al., 2009]*

- Use consistent and explicit step-by-step navigation. Divide complex sequences into substeps.

- Confirm steps with feedback.

- Show clearly how to go forward and back.

Show what step the user is on *[Carmien and Garzo, 2014; Hawthorn, 2006; Miño, 2013; NIH/NIA, 2009; Phiriyapokanon, 2011]*

- The starting point, ending point, and every step of a task should be marked, so users easily recognize and understand where they are.

- Show how many steps there are in multistep operations. Number each step.

- Clearly indicate users' current step, and show what has been done and what remains to be done.

Show progress *[Campbell, 2015; Phiriyapokanon, 2011]*

- During longer or more complex tasks, give clear feedback on progress and give reminders of goals. Consider providing wizards for complex tasks.

Provide immediate, clear feedback *[Arch et al., 2008; Chisnell et al., 2006; Kascak and Sanford, 2015; Kurniawan and Zaphiris, 2005; Patsoule and Koutsabasis, 2014; Pernice et al., 2013; Phiriyapokanon, 2011; Silva et al., 2015; Wirtz et al., 2009]*

- Prominently show the success/failure of every user action.

6.5 Make it easy for users to return to a known and "safe" starting place

Provide a link to Home *[Affonso de Lara et al., 2010; Carmien and Garzo, 2014; Chisnell et al., 2006; Correia de Barros, 2014; NIH/NIA, 2009; Silva et al., 2015; Stößel, 2012]*

- Provide an obvious link back to the Home or starting page on all pages or app screens (see Figures 6.9 and 6.10).

- Wherever a Back button is provided, ensure that it works as users expect by testing it on users.

Provide Next and Back *[Hawkins, 2011; NIH/NIA, 2009; Pernice et al., 2013]*

- In multistep situations, provide "Next" and "Back" buttons or links. Make sure they work as users expect.

Provide Undo *[Patsoule and Koutsabasis, 2014; Shneiderman et al., 2016]*

- Allow users to easily cancel or undo any action, if possible.

Figure 6.9.
Grand Circle Travel website has no clear link to homepage (the two company names in the banner both link to Home).

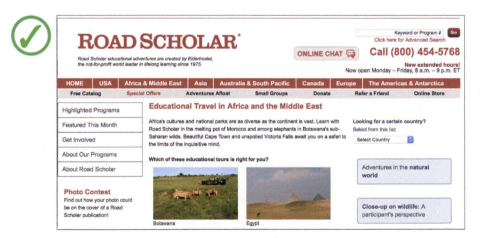

Figure 6.10.
Road Scholar's website has a clear link back to the homepage on every page.

6.6 Let users see where they are at a glance

Show current page *[Kurniawan and Zaphiris, 2005; Miño, 2013; Nunes et al., 2012; Pernice et al., 2013]*

- In websites, show page title and current location in page structure, e.g., navigation breadcrumb path on all pages.

Provide a site map *[Chisnell et al., 2006; Hawthorn, 2006; Kurniawan and Zaphiris, 2005; NIH/NIA, 2009]*

- On every web page, provide an obvious link to a site map that is easy to use.

- A site map should provide a quick overview of the whole site, rather than just repeating the main navigation links or just listing all the topics and pages.

Preserve page appearance *[Finn and Johnson, 2013]*

- Screens and pages should not change their overall appearance without user input, to avoid giving users the false impression that they have changed pages. Examples include autoplaying slideshows or images that change on each page visit or page refresh.

- If including autochanging images, make it easy to pause or stop them.

6.7 Minimize the need for users to manage multiple windows

Minimize number of windows *[Affonso de Lara et al., 2010; Kurniawan and Zaphiris, 2005; NIH/NIA, 2009; Pernice et al., 2013]*

- Display as few windows as possible. Avoid multiple or overlapping windows. Having only one window is an excellent goal if you can achieve it.

- In websites, avoid opening new windows or tabs; open new windows only for PDF and other file types, not for HTML pages.

- If multiple or overlapping windows can't be avoided, make sure the extra windows have prominent, standard *Close* [**X**] controls in the standard (top right) location.

Keep tasks together *[Campbell, 2015; Carmien and Garzo, 2014]*

- Keep information together that is to be used together. Avoid splitting tasks across multiple screens if that would require users to remember information between screens.

6.8 Avoid burdening users' memory

Don't strain working memory *[Kurniawan and Zaphiris, 2005; Miño, 2013; Silva et al., 2015]*

- Clearly indicate the name and status of the current task at all times, so users don't overtax their short-term working memory trying to keep track of task status.

Support recognition and avoid relying on recall *[Chisnell et al., 2006; Johnson, 2014; Kurniawan and Zaphiris, 2005; Silva et al., 2015]*

- Let users choose from buttons, menus, and lists, rather than requiring users to recall and type their choices.
- Provide strong cues to help users recognize their status and options.

Remind users *[Campbell, 2015]*

- Provide reminders and alerts as cues for habitual actions.

Make gestures memorable *[Stößel, 2012]*

- Design gestures to be familiar and easy to remember. Memorable is usually better than time efficient.

Bring task sequences to closure *[Kascak and Sanford, 2015; Shneiderman et al., 2016]*

- Design interaction sequences so that at the end, the task or transaction is complete, there is nothing more for users to do or remember, and the system is in a familiar "normal" state.

Avoid modes *[Johnson, 2007; Johnson, 2014; Kobayashi et al., 2011]*

- Avoid having actions, buttons, or keys that have modes, i.e., different effects or meanings at different times, so users won't have to mentally keep track of the mode.
- If modes are necessary, display the current mode clearly and continually.

6.9 Minimize impact of errors on users

Prevent errors *[Kascak and Sanford, 2015; Phiriyapokanon, 2011; Silva et al., 2015]*

- It is better to prevent an error than to let users make it and then help them recover from it.

- When possible, structure input fields so users cannot enter invalid values.

- Make frequently used functions quick and easy to execute. Request confirmation for functions that cannot easily be reversed.

Support easy error recovery *[Chisnell et al., 2006; Kurniawan and Zaphiris, 2005; Nunes et al., 2012; Pernice et al., 2013; Nielsen, 2013; Phiriyapokanon, 2011; Silva et al., 2015]*

- Make it simple and stress-free for users to correct errors.

- Error messages should be simple and easy for your intended users to understand.

- Avoid error messages that blame or frighten users.

- Describe the problem and how to recover from it. Fix the problem for the user, if possible.

- When there are errors in user-input fields, direct users' attention to those fields and explain how to fix the errors.

Allow users to report problems easily *[Affonso de Lara et al., 2010]*

- Provide a simple way for users to report bugs or problems, directly from the website or app.

6.10 Use terms consistently and avoid ambiguous terminology

Same word = same thing; different word = different thing *[Jarrett, 2003; Patsoule and Koutsabasis, 2014]*

- Ensure that each term has *one* and *only* one meaning within the software. Avoid different terms for the same concept (see Figure 6.11). Also avoid the opposite problem: using the *same* term for *different* concepts, i.e., a term with two or more meanings.

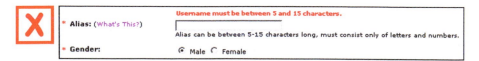

Figure 6.11.
Evite.com formerly used both "Username" and "Alias" for the same data field.

Same label = same action; different label = different action *[Kurniawan and Zaphiris, 2005]*

- Ensure that links or buttons that have the same effect have the *same* label or symbol. For example, if there are two links to a user's shopping cart, they should both be labeled "Shopping Cart."

- Conversely, if links or buttons have *different* effects, label them differently. For example, if one button displays the previous photo in a slide show and the other returns to the previous screen of the app, don't label them both "Back."

Link label = destination name *[Affonso de Lara et al., 2010; Chisnell et al., 2006]*

- Make sure link labels match the label on the destination (see Figures 6.12 and 6.13), so users see that they got to where they intended to go.

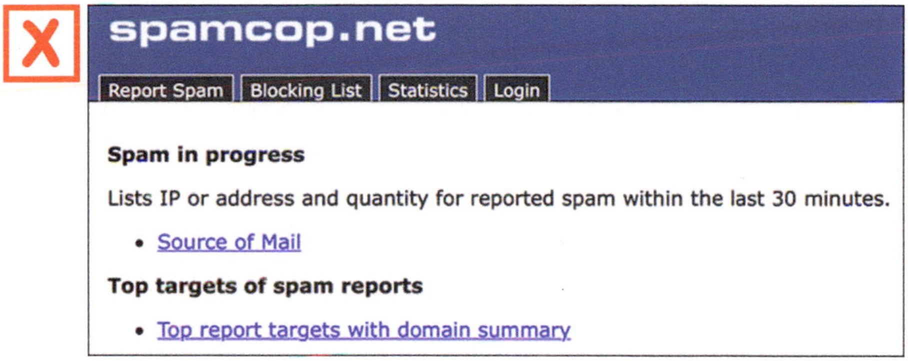

Figure 6.12.
At Spamcop.net, the Statistics navigation link goes to a page labeled "Spam in progress," so users cannot see if they are where they meant to be.

Figure 6.13.
At NAACP.org, the Advocacy & Issues navigation link goes to a page with the same label, showing users that they are where they meant to be.

6.11 Use strong words to label page elements

Use verbs *[Chisnell et al., 2006; NIH/NIA, 2009]*

- Use action words (verbs) for buttons and links.

Make labels semantically distinctive *[Chisnell et al., 2006; Pernice et al., 2013]*

- Use information-carrying words for all page elements, including links, headings, subheadings, summaries, and bulleted lists (see Figure 6.14). When possible, lead with the most descriptive term.

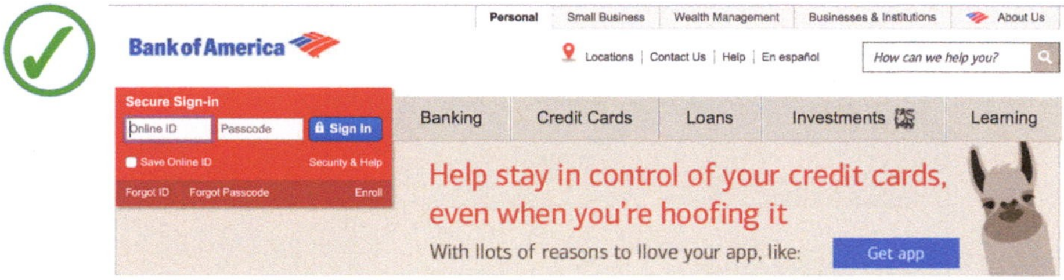

Figure 6.14.
Bank of America's homepage labels all links with words that clearly convey where they go.

6.12 Use writing style that is concise, plain, and direct

Be brief *[Chisnell et al., 2006; Hawkins, 2011; Kurniawan and Zaphiris, 2005; NIH/NIA, 2009; Nunes et al., 2012; Williams et al., 2013]*

- Keep instructions, labels, and messages as short as possible. Keep paragraphs and sentences short. Break body text (content) up into short paragraphs and bullet points.

Keep sentences simple *[Arch et al., 2008; Kascak and Sanford, 2015]*

- In content, instructions, and messages, use a simple sentence structure.
- Accommodate a wide range of literacy and language skills.

Get to the point quickly *[Chisnell et al., 2006; Dunn, 2006; NIH/NIA, 2009; Pernice et al., 2013]*

- Lead with the most important information, e.g., headline, summary, abstract, conclusions, or implications, as newspaper articles do.

- If content is long and detailed, provide a simple summary and let users drill down to see more details. This is called *information layering.*

Make language active, positive, and direct *[Chisnell et al., 2006; NIH/NIA, 2009]*

- Use active voice, e.g., "Plan your trip," not "Trip planning," and "Your search found no results," not "No results were found by your search."

- Use positive terms, e.g., "For your safety, use outside," not "For your safety, don't use inside."

- Talk directly to users. Address them as "you."

Be explicit *[NIH/NIA, 2009; Silva et al., 2015]*

- When providing instructions, be specific and detailed. Don't skip steps or assume users can fill in details. Don't make users guess what you mean (see also Chapter 7: Knowledge).

6.13 Don't rush users. Allow them plenty of time

Don't make messages time out *[Kurniawan and Zaphiris, 2005; Nunes et al., 2012; Silva et al., 2015]*

- When displaying a message, give users ample time to read and understand it. Don't take important messages away after a brief time-out; show them for many seconds—10 or more.

- Even better, provide an **OK** or **Close [X]** button to let users indicate when they are done reading the message.

Let users take their time *[Campbell, 2015; Miño, 2013; Nunes et al., 2012]*

- Allow plenty of time for users to enter data and complete tasks (see Figure 6.15). Test on older users to ensure that the time is sufficient.

- Better yet: don't require users to finish responding within a certain time interval; let them signal when they are done.

- If someone is logged into a public terminal to access private information, such as bank accounts or health-care data, session time-outs may be necessary if there is no input for several minutes, for security reasons. In that case, before ending the session, ask if the user is still there, preferably without losing any input they had started, and give them enough time to answer. Perhaps they dropped their reading glasses and needed to pick them up before continuing.

Figure 6.15.
Combination locks on doors sometimes time out (e.g., after 10 s), which can be frustrating for older adults, especially if the buttons are hard to see, are close together, or require bending down to press.

Make playback speed adjustable *[Affonso de Lara et al., 2010; Kascak and Sanford, 2015]*

- With video, audio, or animated content, provide a way for users to adjust the playback rate.

6.14 Keep layout, navigation, and interactive elements consistent across pages and screens

Consistent layout *[Carmien and Garzo, 2014; Chisnell et al., 2006; Hawthorn, 2006; NIH/NIA, 2009; Nunes et al., 2012; Pernice et al., 2013; Patsoule and Koutsabasis, 2014; Silva et al., 2015; Williams et al., 2013]*

- Use consistent screen layouts throughout an app or website.

- Error messages should always appear in the same place, so users are more likely to see them.

Consistent controls *[Chisnell et al., 2006; Czaja and Lee, 2008; Hawthorn, 2006; NIH/NIA, 2009; Patsoule and Koutsabasis, 2014; Pernice et al., 2013]*

- Make interaction elements functionally and visually consistent. Their placement, labeling, and color should be the same across pages or screens.

Consistent order and labeling *[Nunes et al., 2012]*

- Offer options in the same order on every screen or page, and label options the same way everywhere they occur.

Consistency across related apps *[Hawthorn, 2006]*

- Use the same or highly similar layout, labeling, and color palette in related apps or websites.

6.15 Design to support learning and retention

Show gestures *[Leitão and Silva, 2012; Stößel, 2012]*

- On touch-screen devices, provide training videos, animations, or illustrations to show users the correct control techniques and gestures (see Figure 6.16).

Repetition is good *[Hawthorn, 2006; Miño, 2013; Williams et al., 2013]*

- Repeat instructions; don't take them away after users have seen them once.

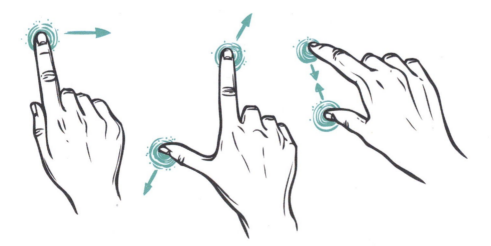

Figure 6.16.
On touch-screen devices, show how to make the required gestures.

- In instructions, encourage users to practice. If appropriate, design an element of fun into the operation, so users will want to do it repeatedly.

Tell users what to bring to task *[Affonso de Lara et al., 2010; Arch et al., 2008]*

- List at the outset what information the user will need to complete the task (see Figure 6.17).

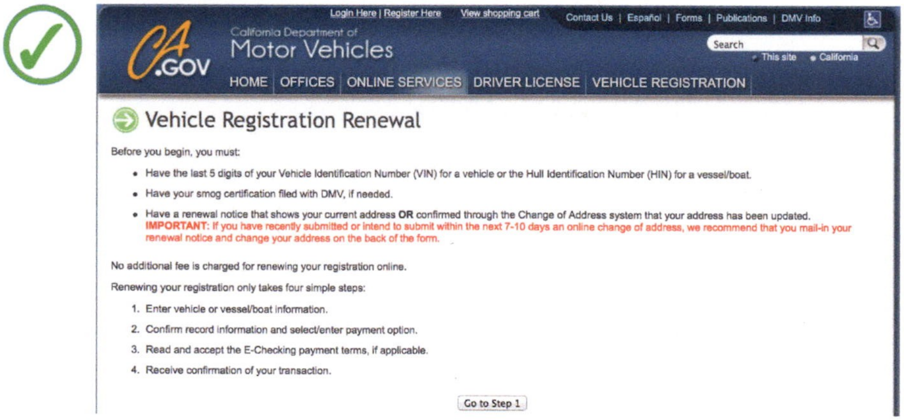

Figure 6.17.
The California Department of Motor Vehicles website lists everything users will need to renew their vehicle registration.

Let users reuse previous paths or choices *[Campbell, 2015]*

- Make it easy for users to repeat what they've done before or already know. Avoid forcing them to try new paths.

- Provide strong cues to help users recognize their status and options (repeated from Guideline 6.8).

6.16 Help users with input

Show what's valid *[Affonso de Lara et al., 2010]*

- Data entry fields should include labels that describe or show the format and range of acceptable inputs.

- Offer examples, such as "Product Serial Number (e.g., 123-45-6789)" or templates, such as "dd/mm/yyyy."

Preformat input fields *[Nielsen, 2013; Pernice et al., 2013]*

- If possible, prestructure input, so users cannot enter invalid values. For example, let users specify dates with a calendar control, let them choose times of day from a list, and break phone number fields into separate fields for country code, area code, and the rest (see Figure 6.18).

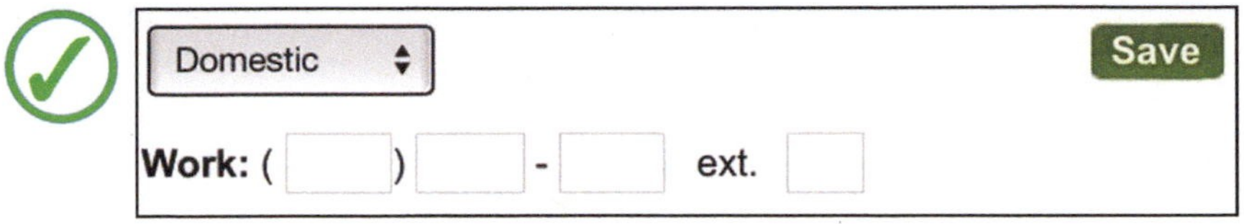

Figure 6.18.
Chase Bank's website preformats the phone number, so users cannot enter an invalid number.

Be tolerant *[Affonso de Lara et al., 2010]*

- Accept a wide range of possible input data formats, then reformat the data to your preferred format.

- Don't force users to enter multipart numbers—such as phone numbers and credit card numbers—with no spaces or punctuation (see Figure 6.19), because it is hard to see in a run-together 10-digit phone number or a 16-digit credit card number if you have made an error.

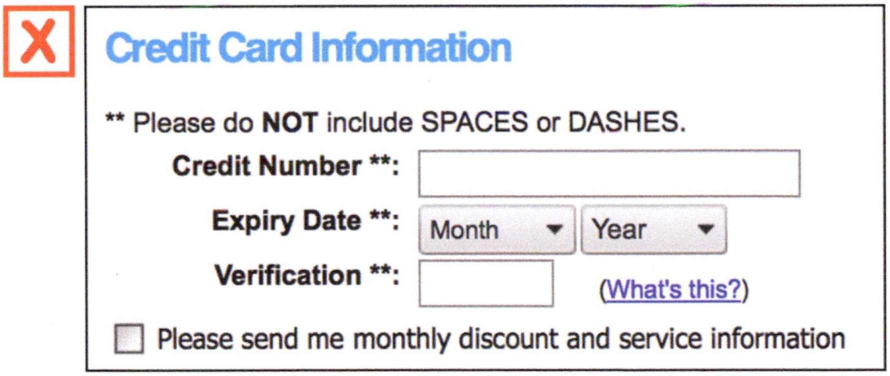

Figure 6.19.
Toronto Airport Express website does not allow spaces or dashes in credit card numbers.

Show what's required *[Arch et al., 2008; Patsoule and Koutsabasis, 2014; Pernice et al., 2013; Sanjay et al., 2006]*

- Clearly indicate which fields or steps are required. Mark them with a prominent symbol, distinctive color, separate placement from nonrequired fields, or a combination. Don't assume that a small asterisk will be visible and meaningful to everyone.

Provide reminders *[Miño, 2013]*

- Allow users to save memory cues for recalling information, e.g., passwords or PINs.

6.17 Provide on-screen help

Provide easy access to context-specific help *[Arch et al., 2008; Czaja and Lee, 2008; Patsoule and Koutsabasis, 2014; Phiriyapokanon, 2011; Silva et al., 2015]*

- Make context-specific on-screen help easily available at all times.
- If contextual help appears in pop-up windows, the pop-up windows should be small, movable, or translucent, so the original problem remains visible (see Figure 6.20).

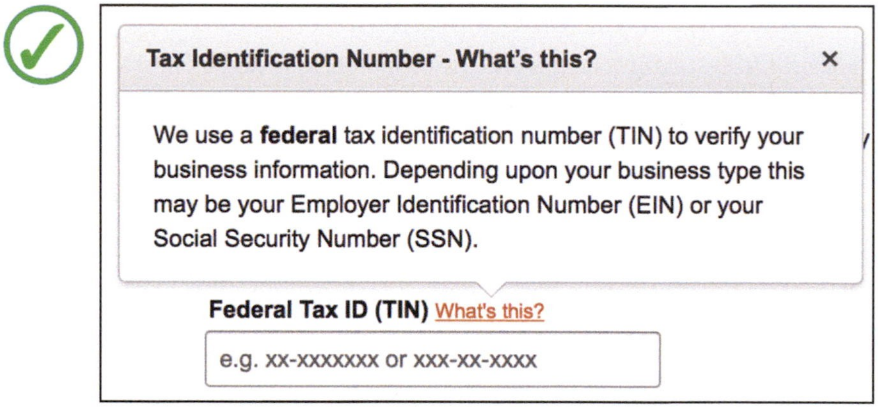

Tax Identification Number - What's this?   ✕

We use a **federal** tax identification number (TIN) to verify your business information. Depending upon your business type this may be your Employer Identification Number (EIN) or your Social Security Number (SSN).

Federal Tax ID (TIN) What's this?

e.g. xx-xxxxxxx or xxx-xx-xxxx

Figure 6.20.
On Amazon's form to apply for a Business Account, the Federal Tax ID data field provides contextual help.

Provide online help file or tutorial *[Affonso de Lara et al., 2010; Kurniawan and Zaphiris, 2005]*

- Provide an easy-to-access online help file or tutorial (see Figure 6.21).

Provide help desk chat *[Pernice et al., 2013]*

- Offer online help desk chat. Ensure that information previously provided by the user (name, problem) is provided to the chat representative.

6.18 Arrange information in order of its importance

Prioritize information *[Chisnell et al., 2006; Kascak and Sanford, 2015; Kurniawan and Zaphiris, 2005; NIH/NIA, 2009; Nunes et al., 2012; Patsoule and Koutsabasis, 2014; Pernice et al., 2013]*

- The most important content on any screen should be immediately visible without scrolling.

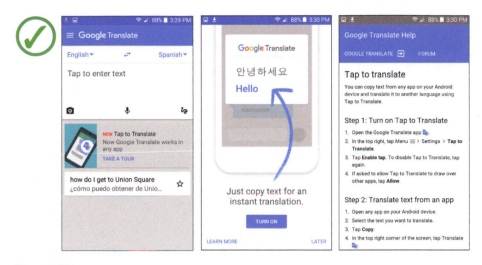

Figure 6.21.
Google Translate provides a simple built-in tutorial and easy access to more complete online Help documents.

- Prioritize each page's content; focus on users' top tasks and on answering their top questions (see box **Know Users' Goals**).
- Study your users to help you anticipate their top tasks and questions.

Know Users' Goals

To ensure that your design meets users' needs, you should study your intended users and their tasks. Why do people use your digital product or service? What do they want to accomplish? What information are they seeking?

For example, when people walk up to a bank automatic teller machine, they typically want to do one of a small number of tasks: get cash, deposit cash, transfer funds, check their balance. They probably *don't* want to open a new bank account; for that they would go into a bank office.

Use tables when appropriate *[Pernice et al., 2013]*

- Use tables to present data or to convey the properties or attributes of objects or concepts. Structuring information into headings, columns, and rows makes it easy for users to scan and understand it. Consider how many paragraphs of text would be required to convey the information in Table 6.1.

Table 6.1	Tables Present Information in a Way That Is Easy for Users to Scan and Understand	
Food	**Serving size**	**Calories**
Macaroni and cheese	4.9 oz.	200
Mashed potatoes	5.0 oz.	90
Herb stuffing	2.4 oz.	180
Cranberry chutney	1.0 oz.	50
Roasted turkey	3.0 oz.	100
Bone-in ham	3.0 oz.	120
Turkey gravy	2.4 oz.	45
Sweet potato soufflé	4.9 oz.	180
Broccoli rice casserole	4.0 oz.	80
Cinnamon apple slices	4.9 oz.	210
Pecan pie	1 slice	450
Cheesecake	1 slice	330

Summary of Cognition Guidelines

6.1 Design for simplicity	■ Minimize stimuli.
6.2 Help users maintain focus	■ Present one task at a time. ■ Eliminate distractions. ■ Indicate current task prominently.
6.3 Simplify navigation structure	■ Put most important information up front. ■ Make navigation consistent. ■ Make structure obvious. ■ Keep hierarchies shallow. ■ Make categories unique.
6.4 Clearly indicate the progress and status of operations	■ Lead users step by step. ■ Show what step the user is on. ■ Show progress. ■ Provide immediate, clear feedback.
6.5 Make it easy for users to return to a known and "safe" starting place	■ Provide a link to Home. ■ Provide Next and Back. ■ Provide Undo.
6.6 Let users see where they are at a glance	■ Show current page. ■ Provide a site map. ■ Preserve page appearance.
6.7 Minimize the need for users to manage multiple windows	■ Minimize number of windows. ■ Keep tasks together.
6.8 Avoid burdening users' memory	■ Don't strain working memory. ■ Support recognition and avoid relying on recall. ■ Remind users. ■ Make gestures memorable. ■ Bring task sequences to closure. ■ Avoid modes.
6.9 Minimize impact of errors on users	■ Prevent errors. ■ Allow easy error recovery. ■ Allow users to report problems easily.
6.10 Use terms consistently and avoid ambiguous terminology	■ Same word = same thing; different word = different thing. ■ Same label = same action; different label = different action. ■ Link label = destination name.

Continued

Summary of Cognition Guidelines—cont'd

6.11 Use strong words to label page elements	■ Use verbs. ■ Make labels semantically distinctive.
6.12 Use writing style that is concise, plain, and direct	■ Be brief. ■ Keep sentences simple. ■ Get to the point quickly. ■ Make language active, positive, and direct. ■ Be explicit.
6.13 Don't rush users; allow them plenty of time	■ Don't make messages time out. ■ Let users take their time. ■ Make playback speed adjustable.
6.14 Keep layout, navigation, and interactive elements consistent across pages and screens	■ Consistent layout. ■ Consistent controls. ■ Consistent order and labeling. ■ Consistency across related apps.
6.15 Design to support learning and retention	■ Show gestures. ■ Repetition is good. ■ Tell users what to bring to task. ■ Let users reuse previous paths or choices.
6.16 Help users with input	■ Show what's valid. ■ Preformat input fields. ■ Be tolerant. ■ Show what's required. ■ Provide reminders.
6.17 Provide on-screen help	■ Provide easy access to help. ■ Provide context-sensitive online help. ■ Provide help desk chat.
6.18 Arrange information consistent with its importance	■ Prioritize information. ■ Use tables when appropriate.

CHAPTER 7
Knowledge

If this book is still in print in, say, 20 years, and the publisher wants to update it, the chapters about age-related changes (Chapters 3–6 and 9) will probably not need much updating. Those chapters enumerate the ways in which people's abilities change with age, and present guidelines for designing digital technology so people who experience those changes can use it. Unless science finds a way to slow or halt aging, those perceptual, motor, and cognitive changes will continue to occur as people age, so designers of technology will still need to follow those guidelines.

This chapter is different. It is about the *knowledge* that today's older adults have—or don't have—that makes using today's digital information and communications technology difficult for them. Over the next 20 years, three big changes will render this chapter obsolete:

1. **A new generation will grow into older adults**. People now in their 70s and 80s will be in their 90s and 100s. Insurance companies predict that 20 years from now there will be some 120-year-olds. People now in their 50s and 60s will be in their 70s and 80s. People now in their 30s and 40s will be in their 50s and 60s and will, by this book's definition, be older adults.

2. **A greater percentage of older adults will have experience with digital technology**. The personal computer revolution started in the 1970s but didn't really get going until the 1980s, and the Internet took off in the mid-1990s. Most of today's people over 50—older adults by this book's definition—grew up with electromechanical devices, such as vacuum cleaners and toasters, or analog electronic devices, such as stereos, microwave ovens, and Walkman cassette players. They didn't experience computers and other digital technology until they were already well into adulthood. In contrast, the post-Baby Boom generation—Gen-X—has been using digital technology since their teenage years. They aren't as steeped in digital technology as the Millennials (born ~1982–2004), but they are more tech-savvy than Baby Boomers. In 20 years, Gen-Xers (born ~1965–1981) will be over 50 and therefore will qualify as older adults.

3. **Information and communications technology will change**. Technology does not stand still. It has advanced tremendously over the last 20 years. There is no indication that this advancement will stop or slow over the next 20 years. In fact, the indications are that major changes will occur. In 20 years, digital computing will probably be replaced by some combination of neural,

Designing User Interfaces for an Aging Population. http://dx.doi.org/10.1016/B978-0-12-804467-4.00007-4

biological, and quantum computing. Voice control and biometric control, now emerging, will replace keyboards, pointers, and touch screens, and direct thought control may start to emerge. Self-driving cars and trucks will be commonplace. With the rise of the Internet of Things, devices will communicate among themselves. Refrigerators will order milk, eggs, and vegetables when we run out. Robots, cuddly or utilitarian, will be everywhere. Digital implants will make people "bionic." What it means to be tech-savvy will have changed a lot. However, as we pointed out in Chapter 2, most of today's middle-aged people who live to see those changes won't adapt fully to them; they will be "stuck" in the comfort zone of today's technologies.

 I was cleaning out my garage and found an old floppy disk. I showed it to my granddaughter, and she said 'Cool! You 3D-printed the Save icon!' – John

Because of these three big changes, 20 years from now this chapter will need to be rewritten. Older adults will still face a knowledge gap, but they will be lacking *different* knowledge.

However, let's return to the present. For designers who are creating digital information and communications technology for the next 10 years or so, this chapter describes the gap between what *today's* older adults know and what they would *need* to know to be comfortable with *today's* technology. The chapter then provides guidelines for helping *today's* older adults use digital technology, despite that gap.

DIGITAL TECHNOLOGY KNOWLEDGE GAP IN OLDER ADULTS

As stated earlier, in addition to age-related declines that hamper their ability to use modern digital technology that wasn't designed for them, older adults also have less experience with digital technology [Jahn and Krems, 2013]. This lack of experience manifests itself in several ways.

Lack of familiarity with digital technology terms and acronyms

It is an unfortunate fact that using today's information and communications technology often requires becoming familiar with technical terms that came from engineering and software development. Consumers have to learn the meaning of jargon words such as app, gigabyte, router, download, upload, dialog, and Ethernet. They have to learn abbreviations and acronyms such as JPEG, HDMI, MP4, URL, and CAPTCHA (see Figures 7.1 and 7.2).

```
To enable your phone for voice and text:
1. Go to Settings
2. Go to Network Settings (this may be found under More Networks or More) and
is also sometimes called Mobile Networks
3. Make sure Network Mode is set to Automatic, CDMA, or LTE/CDMA depending on
which network you wish to use
4. In the Roaming Settings (also usually found within More Networks or "Data
Roaming"), make sure youve turned on International CDMA voice roaming
5. If your phone has Roaming guard settings, make sure it is turned off for
international voice roaming
```

Figure 7.1.
These emailed instructions from Credo Mobile customer support—specifically step 3—wrongly expect users to understand what type of cellular service is available where they are.

Figure 7.2.
The website of Pacific Gas & Electric uses the technical jargon term "Captcha," which few older adults will know. Also, the acronym should be in all caps: "CAPTCHA."

Today's adults who are above 50 years of age did not grow up using today's tech terms and acronyms and might not easily learn and remember their meanings [Leung et al., 2010; Burns et al., 2013]. This knowledge gap is exacerbated by the memory deficits discussed in Chapter 6.

Even worse, older adults have to learn new meanings for words they have used all their lives. For example, they might not know that the terms *drive* and *cloud* have acquired additional meanings in the digital age. They might think that *drive* is just what you do to a car, and *clouds* are only in the sky.

Older adults' lack of mastery of digital tech-speak is not surprising, but it is ironic, because older adults typically have greater vocabularies and verbal knowledge than younger adults [Pak, 2009; Youmans et al., 2013].

When I came to the U.S., I learned English. Now it seems like I have to learn another foreign language: tech-speak. – Carolina

Lack of familiarity with digital technology icons

Today's older adults have no trouble understanding symbols they grew up with, such as a skull and crossbones meaning "toxic," or a railroad crossing sign. However, many of today's older adults *do* have more difficulty than younger adults remembering the meaning of *new* symbolic labels of the digital age: icons. The currently common icons shown in Figure 7.3 are certainly not understood by everyone, regardless of age [Leung et al., 2010; Sayago et al., 2009].

Figure 7.3.
Common icons for Settings, Menu, and Share are unfamiliar to many of today's older adults.

I am an auto mechanic, so I know that is a gear. But I did not know what the gear meant, so I asked a young woman at the phone store. She told me it is the button to open the phone's settings. A gear means settings? OK, if you say so, but I don't get the connection. – Stefano

A lack of standard appearance and location of icons symbolizing common functions makes it difficult for users of all ages—but especially for older adults—to learn what the icons mean (see Figures 7.4 and 7.5).

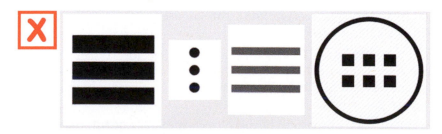

Figure 7.4.
Searching Google Images for "Android menu icons" yields at least four different icons.

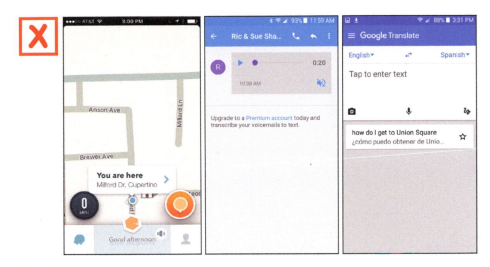

Figure 7.5.
In the way-finding app Waze (left), users may not realize that the blue speech balloon with feet at bottom left is the menu button. In Android's voicemail app (middle), the menu button is three vertical dots at top right. Google Translate (right) uses the three-line "hamburger" menu symbol at upper left.

Researchers have also observed that many older adults pay little attention to icons on a digital device screen; they pay more attention to the words, possibly because the words mean more to them than the icons do [Sayago et al., 2009].

Do not know control gestures

People who grew up using personal computers, game consoles, tablets, or mobile phones have learned the various common control gestures well enough that they can execute them automatically, without thinking. Not so with many of today's older adults, who encountered digital technology after attaining adulthood. Double clicking, two-finger scrolling, pinching and spreading, click-drag, and other complex gestures are new and unfamiliar to them, and so aren't necessarily automatic [Stößel, 2012].

When text on my iPad is too small to read, I tap three fingers twice to enlarge it. That took me a while to learn, and even now I don't always succeed on the first try. – John

Even older adults who often used computers during their working years some-times have trouble with today's newer touch screen user interfaces: they often try to scroll down a page by swiping their finger downward, probably because they are familiar with scrollbars on desktop systems, which *do* work that way (see Figure 7.6) [Stößel, 2012]. Once a gesture for achieving a certain result is learned to the point where it has become an automatic "muscle memory," it is

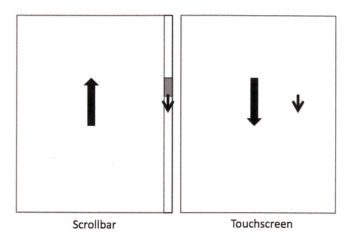

Scrollbar   Touchscreen

Figure 7.6.
With scrollbars, users swipe in the opposite direction that the page moves. With touch screens, users swipe in the same direction that the page moves.

difficult for people—especially older adults—to unlearn the gesture and learn a new one [Newell, 2011].

The lack of standardization of gestures across applications and devices makes it difficult for people to transfer gestures learned in one app or device to others. For example:

- Scrolling is accomplished with one-finger swipes on Apple iPhone and iPad touch screens, but with two-finger swipes on Apple Mac laptop touch pads.
- On desktop and laptop computers, a two-finger swipe zooms the map in Google Maps and MapQuest, but everywhere else on the screen, a two-finger swipe scrolls the content.
- On desktop and laptop computers, one-finger and two-finger swipes on the trackpad have different effects. On smartphones and tablet computers they have the same effect.

Such inconsistencies might not be the fault of the creators of these systems. In many cases the inconsistencies are dictated by fundamental differences in the platforms. Nonetheless, inconsistent gestures make it harder for users—especially older adults—to internalize the gestures as automatic "muscle memories."

Outdated understanding...

Chapter 6: Cognition explained the role of users' *mental models* in guiding their use of digital technology. That chapter concerned older adults' declining ability to develop, retain, and recall mental models. Here we are concerned with the specific *knowledge* embodied in users' mental models and how those models differ between generations of technology users.

Researchers who study human aging often separate people into technology generations [Docampo Rama et al., 2001; Lim, 2010; Sackmann and Winkler, 2013]. Technology generations are defined by the dominant technology during people's formative years: approximately ages 15–30. The main technology generations are:

- Mechanical (born before 1939)
- Electromechanical (born 1939–1948)
- Analog electronic (born 1949–1963)
- Digital computer (born 1964–1978)
- Internet (born 1979–1989)
- Internet + social networking + smartphone (born after 1989)

Older adults now in their 80s and 90s grew to maturity during the height of electromechanical technology. Those now in their 50s, 60s, and 70s grew up with analog electronic technology. Both types of technology operated differently from today's digital electronic devices, software applications, and websites. Each technology generation requires different background knowledge [Charness and Boot, 2009; Docampo Rama et al., 2001; Lim, 2010; Newell, 2011; Wilkinson, 2011; Wirtz et al., 2009].

Mental models that people learned and internalized to guide their use of mechanical (e.g., hand powered egg-beaters), electromechanical (e.g., electric mixers, toasters), and analog electronic devices (e.g., radios, tape recorders, and microwave ovens) do not work well for using websites, smartphones, and tablet computers [Docampo Rama et al., 2001; Leung et al., 2010; Lim, 2010; Sackmann and Winkler, 2013].

Most appliances from the electromechanical and analog electronic technology eras had user interfaces in which all functions were always directly accessible. Every button, knob, or dial had only one function. No navigating around in the user interface was required to get to what the user wanted—in fact there was no concept of navigation. In contrast, digital devices and the software that runs on them put multiple functions under each control. Users must navigate around in information spaces consisting of menus, pages, screens, and dialog boxes to get to the function or information they want [Lim, 2010; Lim et al., 2012]. As an example, compare automobile dashboards of the 1950s with those of today. Thus, understanding digital versus older technology requires quite different mental models. But as Chapter 6: Cognition explained, many older adults have difficulty forming new mental models.

In addition, many predigital consumer appliances are being reinvented as digital devices (e.g., clocks, cameras, coffee makers). User interface design expert Alan Cooper lamented that when this happens, the appliance often changes into something much more like a computer than it formerly was [Cooper, 2004]. Mental models that formerly worked well to operate the appliance no longer do.

I grew up fixing autos. I know them inside and out. I used to, anyway. These new autos – hybrids, electrics, and such – they have so many computers in them, most of my knowledge is useless. – Stefano

Thus, today's older adults operate with outdated knowledge and mental models [Carmien and Garzo, 2014; Dunn, 2006; Zajicek, 2001; Ziefle and Bay, 2005]. As a result, they are often confused or bewildered by today's information and communications technology [Broady et al., 2010].

However, over time, people—older adults included—*do* gain experience, and the population of older adults turns over. Consider the example of scrolling: studies conducted in the late 1990s and early 2000s found that older web users lacked the concept of browser windows that could scroll. Younger web users scrolled down, but older users rarely did. Recent studies show much less of an age difference in web users' tendency to scroll down. Apparently, most of *today's* older adults *do* know that pages may have to be scrolled to see all the information [Pernice et al., 2013].

Cognitive abilities and knowledge often interact. This makes it hard to determine whether difficulties that older adults encounter in using digital technology are caused by age-related cognitive declines or by outdated knowledge.

…But more domain knowledge

Aging is not just a downhill slide. Those fortunate enough to make it to old age have several advantages over younger adults: they have more life experience and wisdom—hence, better judgment and more common sense. They also have larger vocabularies [Newell, 2011]. Simply put: older adults may not know how computers work, but they tend to know more about how the world and society work.

Older adults have typically amassed a great deal of task domain knowledge related to their work, hobbies, and experiences. As we explained in Chapter 6: Cognition, this accumulated knowledge is sometimes called "crystallized intelligence" to contrast it with "fluid intelligence." Crystallized intelligence, unlike fluid intelligence, tends to increase throughout most of a person's lifetime, except in clear cases of dementia (see Figure 7.7).

As stated earlier, cognitive abilities and knowledge interact. One type of interaction is that older adults can often use their greater general and specialized task domain knowledge to compensate for their declining cognitive abilities and lack of knowledge about digital technology.

In addition to having greater general knowledge and knowledge of specific task domains, older adults tend to have more knowledge of their own strengths and

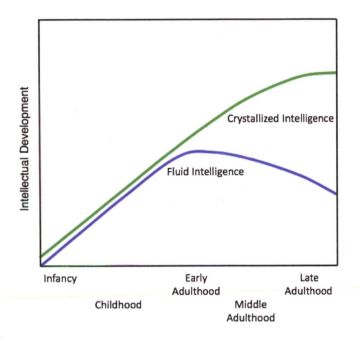

Figure 7.7.
Crystallized intelligence (knowledge) usually increases throughout a person's lifetime, while fluid intelligence typically begins to decline after early adulthood [Cattell, 1987].

weaknesses. When using digital technology, they use that knowledge to adopt different strategies from younger adults.

Nowhere are these strategy differences clearer than when older adults use the web. In general, they are more cautious than younger web users. They tend to work more slowly. They sometimes create step-by-step instructions—"cheat sheets"—for themselves. They write intermediate results down, so they remember them. They read more of what is on the screen before proceeding. They print things out. They avoid risky actions, i.e., actions for which they cannot foresee the result. They return to Home more often. And they abandon their efforts and call the company or organization much more frequently [Hansen, 2009; Pernice et al., 2013].

DESIGN GUIDELINES THAT HELP OLDER ADULTS (AND OTHERS!)

To ensure that adults of all ages can understand your app, website, or device, follow the design guidelines in this section. Note: some guidelines for supporting users who have plenty of knowledge but a lack of knowledge of digital technology are similar to guidelines for supporting people who have sensory and cognitive deficits. This means that some of these guidelines are also presented in other chapters. But as we learned in Chapter 6: Cognition, repetition is good.

7.1 Organize content to match users' knowledge and understanding

Group, order, and label content in ways that are meaningful to users
[Chisnell et al., 2006; Kurniawan and Zaphiris, 2005; NIH/NIA, 2009]

- Don't organize your content according to your organization's structure or by categories that only industry or technical experts know (see Figure 7.8).

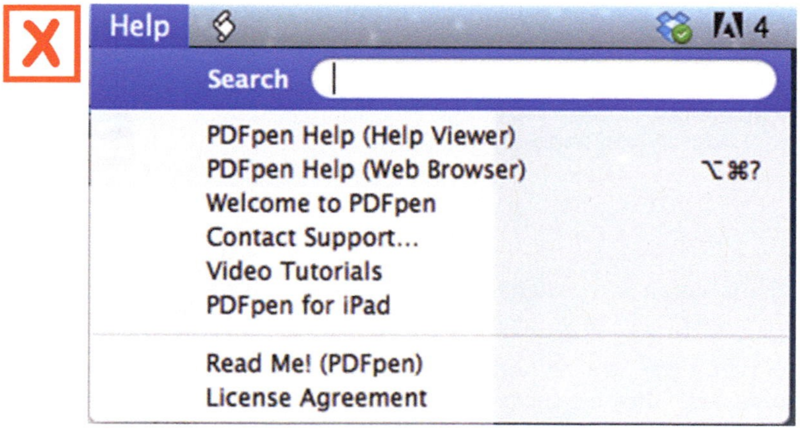

Figure 7.8.
The application PDFpen's Help menu requires users to choose between viewing Help information in the Help Viewer or the web browser. This choice will probably be meaningless to many users, especially older ones.

- Organize content into categories that are meaningful to users. Label content categories and sections clearly, from users' point of view. Order categories and sections in a way that makes sense to users (see Figure 7.9).

- To learn what content organization makes sense to users, conduct observational studies, interviews, or focus groups. Include older adults! See Chapter 10: Working With Older Adults for guidelines on how to work with older adults.

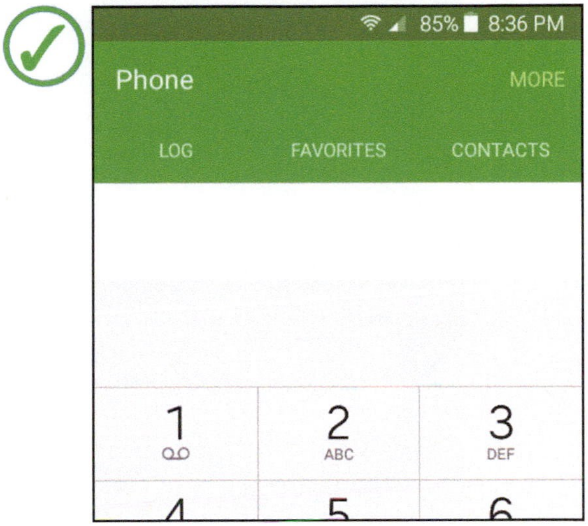

Figure 7.9.
Android's options for finding phone numbers (Log, Favorites, Contacts) make sense to most users, including older adults.

7.2 Use vocabulary familiar to your audience

Avoid technical jargon *[Arch et al., 2008; Carmien and Garzo, 2014; Chisnell et al., 2006; Correia de Barros et al., 2014; Dunn, 2006; Miño, 2013; NIH/NIA, 2009; Silva et al., 2015; Williams et al., 2013]*

- Use words familiar to your audience. Don't make them learn technical jargon or industry jargon (unless it's the users' familiar business jargon).

- Test the vocabulary on users of all ages to ensure that everyone understands it.

- If unfamiliar terms cannot be avoided, provide clear explanations or definitions of them (see Figures 7.10–7.12).

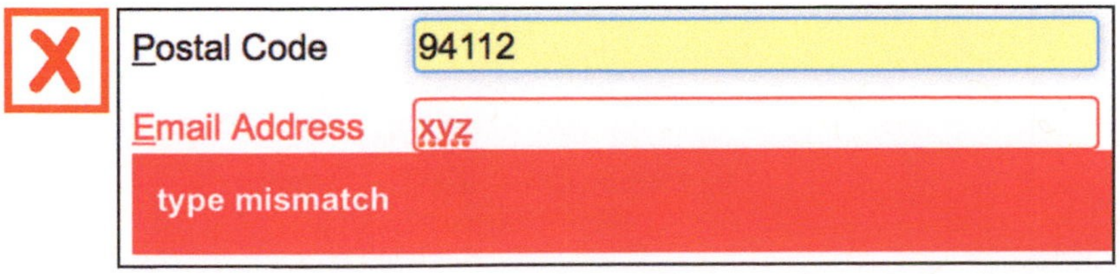

Figure 7.10.
YesFairElections.org's registration form uses technical jargon "type mismatch" to inform users that they entered an invalid email address. Users might interpret this as an instruction to type "mismatch." A clearer message would be: "You have not entered a valid email address" or "Invalid email address."

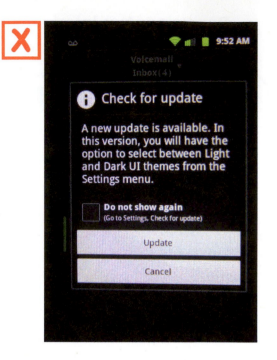

Figure 7.11.
Sprint smartphone software update uses the technical abbreviation "UI," an abbreviation for "user interface." Many users, not just older ones, won't be familiar with the term or its abbreviation.

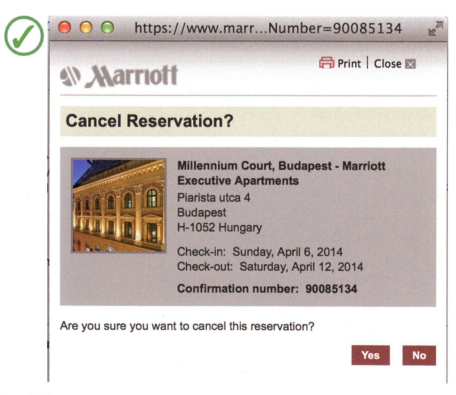

Figure 7.12.
Marriott's website uses very clear vocabulary when a customer prepares to cancel a reservation.

Spell words out *[Campbell, 2015; Chisnell et al., 2006; Dunn, 2006; Miño, 2013; NIH/NIA, 2009; Pernice et al., 2013]*

- Avoid abbreviations, acronyms, and technical or business shorthand, unless they are familiar to users.

7.3 Don't assume the user has a correct mental model of the device, app, or website

Design a simple, clear conceptual model *[Carmien and Garzo, 2014; Johnson and Henderson, 2011; Pak and McLaughlin, 2011; Silva et al., 2015]*

- Design a conceptual model that is so clear that it guides users to construct a suitable mental model.

- If users' existing mental models are known, leverage them in the design of the new conceptual model. Make use of such design metaphors as "electronic desktop," "e-book," or "address book."

Match users' mental model of navigation space *[Williams et al., 2013]*

- Conduct user research to discover users' mental models.

- Provide navigation that matches users' mental models.

7.4 Help users predict what buttons do and where links go

Make link labels descriptive *[Chisnell et al., 2006; NIH/NIA, 2009]*

- Label links clearly to allow users to predict where the links go (see Figure 7.13).

- Make sure labels and category names correspond to users' goals and knowledge. Not to your organization structure, categories that only industry insiders will know, or distinctions unique to your product.

7.5 Make instructions easy to understand

Be explicit *[Chisnell et al., 2006; Miño, 2013; NIH/NIA, 2009; Phiriyapokanon, 2011; Silva et al., 2015]*

- When providing instructions, be specific and detailed. Don't assume users have any technical background knowledge (see Figure 7.14). Don't skip steps or assume users can fill in details (see Figure 7.15). Don't make users guess what you mean (see Figure 7.16).

- If steps are to be executed in a certain sequence, number them.

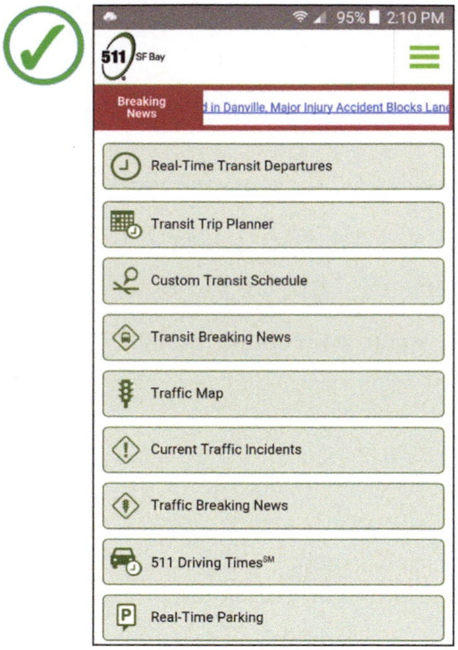

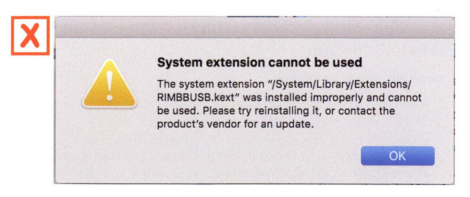

Figure 7.13.
The SF Bay Area 511 Transit Trip Planner mobile site labels its links clearly.

Figure 7.14.
Apple Mac OS Software Update displays a cryptic, complicated error message when an extension is installed incorrectly. Few older adults will know what the message means, who the extension's vendor is, or how they should proceed. Most will simply click OK and hope for the best.

Figure 7.15.
Vimeo displays a vague error message when it can't play a video. Few users, especially older adults, will know what "the current setup" is, or what to do next. Most will just stop trying to view the video.

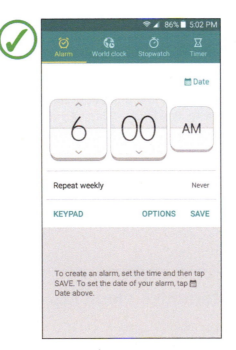

Figure 7.16.
The Android alarm clock app explains clearly what users can do and how to do it.

7.6 Minimize the negative impact on users of new versions

Avoid needless change *[Campbell, 2015; Finn and Johnson, 2013; Pernice et al., 2013; Phiriyapokanon, 2011]*

- Don't make changes just for change's sake or in response to design trends. Keep in mind that requiring users to learn a new interface has a cost: it may even cost you customers.

- Some researchers advise not changing the design radically, or often. Given market realities, this is not always feasible. Therefore, be mindful of the frequency and degree/scope of updates. Consider the impact on your existing users of having to learn the new version and the possibility that you will lose some of them.

Obviously, websites can't always stay the same forever. But it's worth trying to keep key steps as similar as possible for the most important tasks for as long as possible. To reduce the need for major future restructuring of websites, conduct extensive early usability research on workflow steps, information architecture (IA), and other foundational aspects. – Pernice et al., 2013

Change gradually *[Campbell, 2015]*

- If you plan many changes in a product or service, introduce them incrementally over time to avoid overwhelming your users with new things to learn.

Guide users from old to new *[Hawthorn, 2006]*

- In a new version, provide a way for users to revert to the old UI, built-in assistance for learning the new version, or both. For example, offer a quick "What's New" tutorial when a user first tries the new version.

7.7 Label interactive elements clearly

Label with text if possible *[Chisnell et al., 2006; Correio de Barros, 2014; Czaja and Lee, 2008; Phiriyapokanon, 2011; Williams et al., 2013]*

- Label interactive elements—links, buttons, and controls—with text where space allows (see Figures 7.17 and 7.18). In desktop applications, graphical labels (icons) can be augmented with textual tooltips.

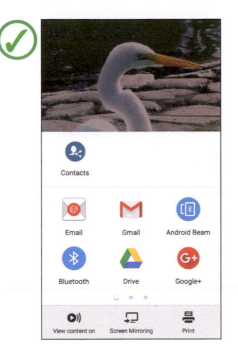

Figure 7.17.
Android's photo-sharing function labels its options with both text and graphics.

Figure 7.18.
The check image pop-up in Bank of the West's website labels options with both text and graphics.

Use easy-to-recognize icons *[Affonso de Lara et al., 2010; Carmien and Garzo, 2014; Chisnell et al., 2006; Czaja and Lee, 2008; Kascak and Sanford, 2015; Kurniawan and Zaphiris, 2005; Leung, 2009; Miño, 2013; NIH/NIA, 2009; Nunes et al., 2012; Or and Tao, 2012; Silva et al., 2015]*

- Use icons and graphical labels that are visually simple, familiar to your intended users, and relevant to users' tasks.

- Make sure icons are easily distinguishable from each other.

- Use industry-standard icons where possible; avoid icons that are unique to your product or service.

- Test on older users to ensure that the icons and labels work for them.

Summary of Knowledge Guidelines

7.1 Organize content to match users' knowledge and understanding	■ Group, order, and label content in ways that are meaningful to *users*.
7.2 Use vocabulary familiar to your audience	■ Avoid technical jargon. ■ Spell words out.
7.3 Don't assume the user has a correct mental model of the device, app, or website	■ Design a simple, clear conceptual model. ■ Match users' mental model of navigation space.
7.4 Help users predict what buttons do and where links go	■ Make link labels descriptive.
7.5 Make instructions easy to understand	■ Be explicit. ■ If steps are to be executed in a certain sequence, number them.
7.6 Minimize the negative impact on users of new versions	■ Avoid needless change. ■ Change gradually. ■ Guide users from old to new.
7.7 Label interactive elements clearly	■ Label with text if possible. ■ Use easy-to-recognize icons.

CHAPTER 8
Search

In Chapter 3: Vision, we explained that *visual* search—scanning a page for a specified item on a page or screen—usually slows down as people grow older. Older adults generally take longer to spot things than younger adults do.

This chapter concerns *another* type of search, in which users enter keywords or search terms and the software returns a list of results. What is searched can be a document, a collection of documents, a database, a product list, a website, or the entire Web. As with visual search, people also show age differences in keyword search.

AGE-RELATED DIFFERENCES IN KEYWORD SEARCH

The online search behavior of older adults differs from younger adults in several ways.

Slower entry of search queries

Researchers have found that older adults are slower than younger adults to enter search queries. This is due mainly to two differences:

- Older adults tend to enter longer search queries than younger adults do.
- They also make four times as many typographical errors while entering search terms [Pernice et al., 2013].

More repeated searches

After I search Baidu for something, I often forget which results I have looked at already and which ones I have not.
– Wong

Declining short-term memory (see Chapter 6: Cognition) impacts older adults' search behavior in two ways:

- Older adults tend to repeat searches for the same keywords more than younger adults do [Fairweather, 2008].
- Older adults show a greater tendency to look again at search results they've already checked [Nielsen, 2013].

Designing User Interfaces for an Aging Population. http://dx.doi.org/10.1016/B978-0-12-804467-4.00008-6

Repeated searches and repeated looking at search results may be due to people forgetting what they've done and seen, but it might also be a cognitive *strategy*. If you realize that your memory is unreliable, you might choose to store details such as contract addresses or prices in the *environment* rather than in your own brain. Then you simply requery the environment whenever you need the information again.

Less successful searches

Overall, older adults succeed when searching only a quarter of the time, while younger adults succeed in over half their searches [Pernice et al., 2013].

But greater knowledge can compensate

As mentioned in Chapter 7: Knowledge, age has some advantages. Because of their greater experience, older adults tend to know more about the topic in which they are working than a younger adult would. This increased domain knowledge ("crystallized intelligence") can allow older adults to compensate for declining memory and other deficits.

For example, it is only in *well*-defined search tasks—e.g., "What country hosted the 2016 Summer Olympics?"—that younger adults do better. With *poorly* defined tasks, where the goal is unclear and more perseverance is required, older adults often search *more* successfully than younger adults. An example is "What is the best inexpensive restaurant in Paris?" Not only are older adults more patient and diligent with that sort of search task, their superior domain knowledge gives them an advantage in selecting search terms and assessing search results [Gilbertson, 2014].

Handling my mother's health problems as well as my own has made me quite expert at finding medical information online. I can usually find exactly what I am looking for. – Monika

DESIGN GUIDELINES THAT HELP OLDER ADULTS (AND OTHERS!)

To make sure adults of all ages can successfully search your app or website, follow the design guidelines in this section.

8.1 Help users construct successful queries

Put the search box in upper right *[National Institute on Aging (NIH), 2009; Pernice et al., 2013]*

- If a website or app has a Search function, place the Search box or a button to display it in the standard, top right position on every page and screen, where people expect it to be. For bad versus good examples, compare Figures 8.1 and 8.2.

Figure 8.1.
The Washington Post's website displays no search box at top right—only a search icon at top left, where few users will spot it.

Figure 8.2.
The Oakland Tribune's website has a large and well-placed search box.

- Specialized search functions for specific types of information—e.g., stock quotes in a mobile banking app, or store locations on a shopping website—can appear in other positions as long as they are well labeled.

Show search terms in large font *[Pernice et al., 2013]*

- Use a large font size—at least 12 point—to display users' search query text and improve contrast between text color and background color (see Figures 8.1 and 8.2).

Make the search box long *[Fadeyev, 2009; Pernice et al., 2013]*

• Make sure the search box shows enough characters, so users can see most or all of what they enter (see Figure 8.2). Research has found that a width of 27 characters is enough to show users' entire query about 90% of the time, so that is the width we recommend.

Make the search box "smart" *[Kurniawan and Zaphiris, 2005; National Institute on Aging (NIH), 2009; Pernice et al., 2013]*

• Make your search box tolerant of what people type into it. It should be able to work with any reasonable keywords.

• A search box should suggest completions based on what a user has already typed. It should check for errors and offer to correct them (see Figure 8.3).

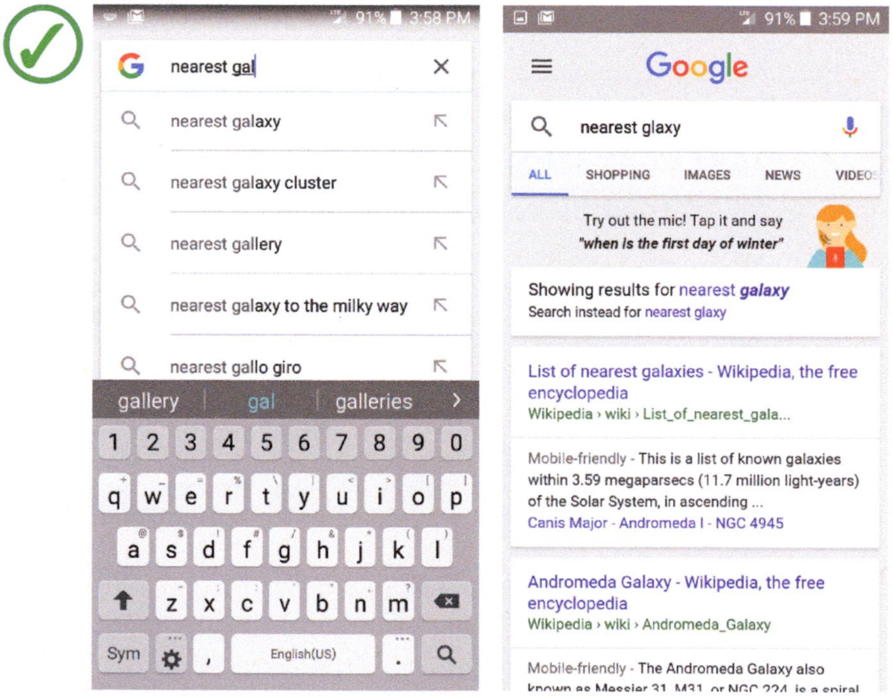

Figure 8.3.
Google's search function offers completions based on input so far and corrects spelling errors.

Anticipate likely searches *[Pernice et al., 2013]*

• Conduct tests with typical users—including older adults—to identify likely keywords and terms. Make sure that the search function returns relevant and appropriate results for those expected terms (see Figure 8.4).

Figure 8.4.
At AARP.org, a search for "membership fees" finds no information about AARP membership fees.

8.2 Design search results to be friendly to users

One quick note before the guidelines about search results: many websites and apps that include search functions don't have their own custom search engine. Instead, they use one offered by a search engine vendor. This limits the control the website or app developers have over how search results are displayed. However, developers do have *some* control over their website or app's search results.

First, they can choose which third-party search engine they use. The quality and usability of search results should be an important criterion for choosing a search engine.

Second, with any search engine, the quality of the results is influenced by the quality and internal consistency of the data it searches. For example, if a website's product database has many product items with incomplete or inconsistent metadata, *any* search engine will produce poor results, both in what items are found and in how the items are labeled.

Therefore, two important metaguidelines for making sure your search function is user-friendly and age-friendly are:

- Use a search engine that produces user-friendly results.
- Maintain a quality database.

OK, now here are guidelines for making your search results user-friendly.

Mark paid results *[Pernice et al., 2013]*

- Clearly distinguish paid results ("sponsored links") or listings from regular search results (see Figure 8.5).

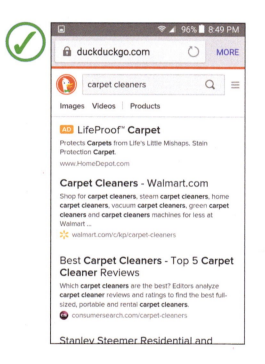

Figure 8.5.
Search engine DuckDuckGo's mobile results page shows what the user searched for and marks paid results with "AD" (for "Advertisement") to distinguish them from regular results.

Show search terms *[Pernice et al., 2013]*

- Display the user's query along with search results (see Figure 8.5).

Mark already visited results *[National Institute on Aging (NIH), 2009; Nielsen, 2013; Pernice et al., 2013]*

- Show users which results links they have already visited and which ones they have not (see Figure 8.6). Chapter 3: Vision explained that marking links as visited is helpful on some types of web pages and not on others. Search results pages are a type of page where it is helpful.

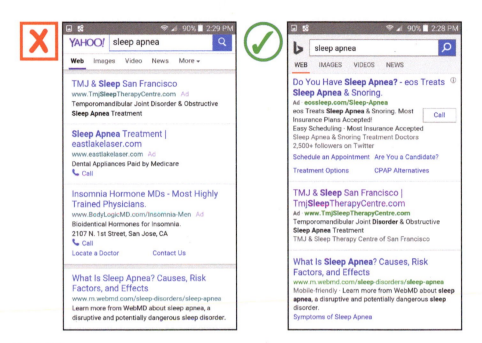

Figure 8.6.
Yahoo (left) does not display not-yet-visited and already-visited results links in different colors. Bing (right) does.

Summary of Search Guidelines

8.1 Help users construct successful queries	■ Put the search box in upper right. ■ Show search terms in large font. ■ Make the search box long. ■ Make the search box "smart." ■ Anticipate likely searches.
8.2 Design search results to be friendly to users	■ Mark paid results. ■ Show search terms. ■ Mark already visited results.

CHAPTER 9
Attitude

Older adults did not grow up with the latest technology. That is true of the current generation of older adults and today's digital technology, and it will also be true for tomorrow's older adults and tomorrow's latest technology—whatever that technology is.

In addition to the age-related declines and knowledge deficits described in the previous chapters, older adults differ from younger ones in their attitudes and feelings about new technology. These differences in attitude affect older adults' comfort with new technology, their willingness to adopt it, and their success in using it.

This chapter begins by describing attitudes about—and reactions to—digital technology that today's older adults often exhibit. It then provides guidelines to allow designers to make devices and online services easier to use for older adults, which will improve older adults' attitudes toward the technology. This, in turn, might make them more willing to try it and to use it.

OLDER ADULTS' ATTITUDES TOWARD TECHNOLOGY USAGE

More risk-averse

A common observation about older adults using digital technology is that they tend to be risk-averse. They are afraid of making mistakes, losing work, or embarrassing themselves. They are afraid of "breaking something" [Arch et al., 2008; Hill et al., 2015; Raymundo and da Silva Santana, 2014; Zajicek, 2001].

There may be an easier way to do this, but I know this way. So this is how I do it. – Hana

Aversion to risk can affect how older adults use digital technology in several ways:

- They might prefer to be certain of the outcome of an action *before* taking the action. Therefore, when trying an unfamiliar application or website, they tend to read everything on the screen before acting. They often scan the entire screen to find the *most promising* next step to their goal rather than clicking immediately on the first item that looks likely [Carmien and Garzo, 2014].

- They often prefer *familiar* paths, even when those paths are not the easiest or shortest.[1] Once they learn how to accomplish a goal, they might hesitate to try new ways or to explore alternate paths to that goal. Therefore, they may never discover a more efficient route and may even reject one if it is shown to them. This contrasts with younger adults, who are much more likely to explore and to try new paths in search of more efficient methods [Pernice et al., 2013].

- They often want to be sure they're right. Older adults take longer to complete tasks in part because they recheck their results more often than younger adults do. For example, they might run a mortgage calculator twice to make sure they entered the correct data. As Chapter 8: Search explained, older adults recheck search result items more often than younger adults do [Olmsted-Hawala et al., 2013].

- They tend to show more fear than younger adults do of the hazards of using digital technology: viruses, hackers, unauthorized access, and spam [Arch et al., 2008; Hill et al., 2015]. For example, one study found that older adults are less likely than younger adults to download files from the Internet [Dunn, 2006]. A second study found older adults to be more reluctant than younger people to put personal information online, both for e-commerce and for social networks, out of fear that someone could misuse the information [Grindrod et al., 2014; Waycott et al., 2013]. A third study found that today's adults above 80 years of age don't want to give up using checks, partly because they don't yet fully trust credit cards, online payments, and other newer ways to pay and transfer funds [Vines et al., 2012].

Often get frustrated, give up

Lower self-confidence concerning digital technology also prompts older adults to give up more easily [Leung et al., 2012]. For example, a study of web users found that older adults are twice as likely as younger adults to abandon tasks when they encounter difficulties [Pernice et al., 2013]. Among web users, abandoning a task often means picking up the telephone to call the organization or company (see box: **Quotes from Real Older Adults In a Usability Test of Tourist Websites**).

---

1 Older adults' preference for familiarity extends to food, music, and activities [Sapolsky, 1998]. Older adults are also more likely to be repeat buyers of products than younger adults are [Goddard and Nicolle, 2012].

Quotes From Real Older Adults in a Usability Test of Tourist Websites

A few years ago, we conducted a usability test of three tour company websites that are aimed at older travelers [Finn and Johnson, 2013]. The older adults who participated in our tests had many problems with the travel websites, including:

- difficulty returning to the Homepage;
- inability to tell whether or not an item was a link;
- not understanding terms used on the website;
- difficulty finding their way to their goals;
- being overwhelmed by highly cluttered pages;
- difficulty controlling pull-down and pull-right menus.

Participants were asked to try to book trips using different travel companies' websites. When we asked what they would have done without us present, some typical responses were:

I would have gotten on the phone very quickly... like within 3 or 4 minutes. Because for me... I'm not accustomed to using my computer this way and it's extremely frustrating. I didn't grow up with computers in my life. – Participant, age 75

I would screw this! I would say, if I can't get to what I want in reasonable tries, then I don't want to go with this company. – Participant, age 72

At this time, I would give it up. I would give this whole thing up. This, to me is like, crazy-making. Totally crazy-making. – Participant, age 68

If older adults are a significant part of your target audience, you will need to be able to handle phone calls. Hiring personnel to handle phone calls costs money, but turning away older customers may cost you more. Of course, it would be even better to make your website/app usable by all potential customers.

Tendency to assign blame (to self, app, or designers)

Another common observation is that when older adults have trouble with technology, they are more likely to assign blame than younger adults are. When they do, they often assign blame to themselves [Komninos et al., 2014; Nunes et al., 2012; Pernice et al., 2013; Reddy et al., 2014].

For example, one study found that when people have trouble using the Web, older adults blame themselves most of the time while younger adults blame themselves less than half of the time [Nielsen, 2013].

In another study, some older adults blamed themselves ("I don't really know what I'm doing"; "It's probably my fault"; "This always happens to me"), while other older adults blamed the *website* or its *designers* ("I hate it when websites do this"; "Well, that's stupid"; "That doesn't make any sense"). In contrast, when younger adults in that study encountered problems, most didn't assign blame at all [Dunn, 2006].

Some researchers, attempting to explain older adults' tendency to assign blame to themselves, suggest that they have lower self-confidence: they don't believe they can use modern digital technology [Leung et al., 2012].

> Technology is not my friend. – 60+ woman in supermarket checkout line, when the checkout clerk asked her if she had tried the store's online sweepstakes game.

Tendency to not consider oneself "old" and to avoid products designed for "elderly"

It should not be surprising that researchers find that most people above 50 years of age—even many above 75 years of age—don't consider themselves to be "old" [Durick et al., 2013]. This is due in part to large individual differences in the age at which the various perceptual, motor, and cognitive impairments begin to appear and the rate at which they progress. Some people are simply not very impaired until quite late in their lives, while others experience impairments earlier in life. Those who remain relatively unimpaired after 50, 60, or 70 are unlikely to consider themselves "old" when compared to their peers.

A second reason for our tendency not to think of ourselves as "elderly" is that it is easier to see changes and impairments in others than it is to see—or to acknowledge—such changes in ourselves. People are much more willing to label others as "old" than to apply that label to themselves [Durick et al., 2013].

> One thing I don't like about this place is that there are so many **old** people here. – Jeff's uncle, after moving at age 70 into a senior retirement community.

In addition, many modern societies—particularly in the industrialized western world—place a high value on youthfulness and much less value on age and experience. In such societies, the elderly are often (wrongly) assumed to be in poor health, incapable, unproductive, and dependent [Durick et al., 2013; Wilkinson, 2011]. It is no wonder that people in such societies don't want to be considered "elderly."

Because of the stigma about being considered "old," some older adults avoid technology designed especially for their age group. For example, using a simplified computer, smartphone, or web browser that was designed for seniors would mark the user as a "senior" who cannot handle "regular" products (see Figure 9.1) [Leung, 2009]. Similarly, using assistive technologies, such as screen magnifiers, hearing aids, or text-to-speech, can flag the user as "handicapped" and "elderly" [Roberts and Simon, 2009; Wilkinson and Ghandi, 2015]. To make matters worse, the designers of many assistive products and services focus more on function than on appearance, resulting in quasimedical designs that many older adults consider unappealing [Durick et al., 2013; Stößel, 2012].

Figure 9.1.
The Jitterbug smartphone and Wow computer, with simplified user interfaces "designed for seniors," may not appeal to some of the people it was designed for, because using it would label them as "old."

DESIGN GUIDELINES THAT HELP OLDER ADULTS (AND OTHERS!)

To make your app, website, or digital device appealing to adults of all ages, or at least to avoid having it be annoying or even repellant to substantial numbers of potential users, follow these design guidelines.

9.1 Be flexible in how users can enter, save, and view data

In Chapter 6: Cognition, Guideline 6.16 ("Help users with input") states that data entry fields should be labeled to show clearly what is expected. Data entry fields should either be structured, so users cannot enter invalid data, or they should allow variations in how users format the data. In Chapter 6, the purpose of this guideline is to facilitate learning, retention, and operational efficiency. This chapter has a similar guideline, but here its purposes are to enhance users' subjective experience and avoid annoying and frustrating them.

Provide "smart" data input *[Affonso de Lara et al., 2010; Nielsen, 2013; Pernice et al., 2013]*

- Design input fields and controls to facilitate the entry of valid data.

- If possible, use structured input fields—such as calendar date pickers and preformatted phone number fields—rather than generic text fields.

- If you must use unstructured text fields for data input, show the proper format in the label, but allow users to enter data in any reasonable format, then convert it to your format.

- If your software can determine what the user has done "wrong," don't scold them for it; just fix it and proceed (see Figures 9.2 and 9.3). You'll have happier users as a result.

> ✗ ✔ **Your message contains invalid characters.Please use only letters, numbers, and the special characters ! - : ' . , ? / $ % ( ) in your reply.**

Figure 9.2.
The "Contact Us" form on Kaiser Permanente's website provides no warning of its punctuation restrictions for messages, then scolds users for violating the restrictions.

Put users in control *[Arch et al., 2008; Chisnell et al., 2006; Kascak and Sanford, 2015; Kurniawan and Zaphiris, 2005; Miño, 2013; Silva et al., 2015]*

- Allow users to adjust aspects of the display, such as font size, color contrast, sleep timeout duration, audio volume, or text-to-speech speaking rate.

- Don't require users to complete long online forms in one session. Allow them to save the form and return to it later.

- If your system corrects user input as it is typed, make it easy for users to reject specific corrections or disable autocorrection.

9.2 Earn users' trust

Ask only what's necessary *[Arch et al., 2008; Czaja and Lee, 2007; Pernice et al., 2013]*

- Ask users only for information you really need. If you can complete the transaction without a piece of information, don't ask for it (See Figure 9.4).

- Explain why you need the information. Provide justification for personal questions.

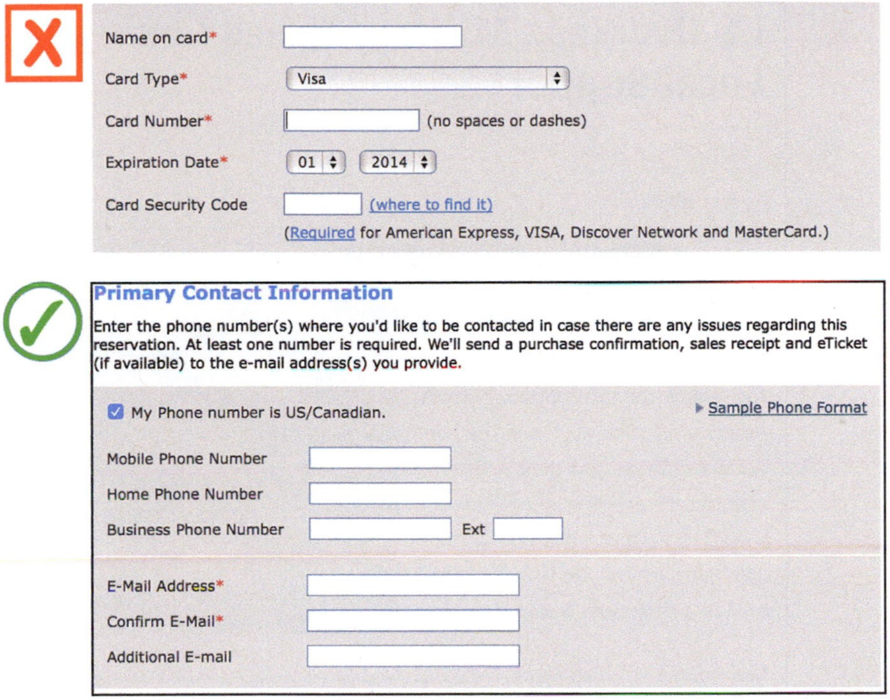

Figure 9.3.
Amtrak's ticket purchase form does not accept spaces or dashes in credit card numbers (above), but its contact form accepts phone numbers in almost any format (below).

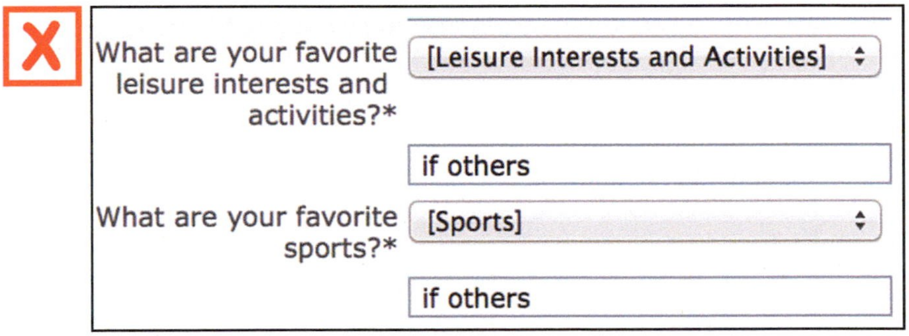

Figure 9.4.
Philippine Airlines frequent flyer registration form requires unnecessary information. To give you a frequent flyer account they don't need to know your favorite leisure interests and sports.

- Assure users that whatever data they give you will only be used by you and that you won't sell it to a third party.

- Assure users that you won't use their information to spam them.

Mark ads clearly *[Chisnell et al., 2006; Pernice et al., 2013]*

- Make it easy to distinguish advertising from regular content (see Figures 9.5 and 9.6).

US Overseas Military Bases Losing Local Support

July 15, 2016 4:46 pm

by Ben Richards

hisgo Fly to Japan with H.

The best prices to Japan on

Recent scandals involving US military
covered by the international media. I
American democracy" and the "defe
American bases and their occupants
lawlessness and crime, as evident by
voiced by various members of the int
countries around the world and num
held in a **desperate bid** to have these

Less than a week ago a new wave of p
Japan, after the arrest of yet another American soldier who was driving a
car while drunk on Okinawa.

Figure 9.5.
At the website of *Counter Current News*, links in articles display ads unrelated to the link.

How George Martin Changed Pop Music Production

By BEN SISARIO   MARCH 9, 2016

For the legions of musicians, producers and music executives who carefully
followed everything the Beatles did, one name on the band's records
mattered perhaps just as much as those of the Fab Four themselves: George
Martin.

As the producer for almost all of the band's classic recordings, Mr. Martin,
who died on Tuesday at 90, was an inseparable part of the Beatles
phenomenon. But he also had a vital role in shaping the art of music
production, and of defining a producer's role in pop music as equal parts
technical master and creative enabler.

Figure 9.6.
At the website of the *New York Times*, text links in stories go to related stories, as readers expect.

- In search results, ensure that users can easily tell which items are paid-for-placement items and which are not (see Figure 9.7).

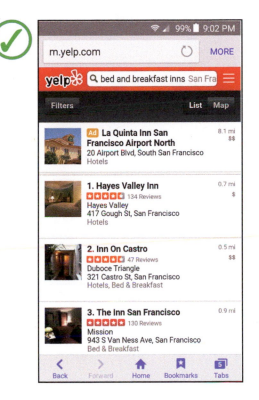

Figure 9.7.
Yelp marks paid search results with an "Ad" symbol and numbers nonpaid results. Making the Ad symbol easier to read—e.g., by making it larger or by using black-on-orange instead of white-on-orange—would help users even more.

- Test on typical users to make sure the ad indicators really work.

Don't make users log in *[Affonso de Lara et al., 2010; Kascak and Sanford, 2015; Pernice et al., 2013; Practicology, 2015]*

- Allow people to view content or to make purchases as guests, instead of requiring them to sign in or register for an account (see Figure 9.8).
- Clearly distinguish the links for signing in, creating a new account, and continuing as a guest.

I'm not here to enter into a relationship. I just want to buy something. – user study participant [Spool, 2009].

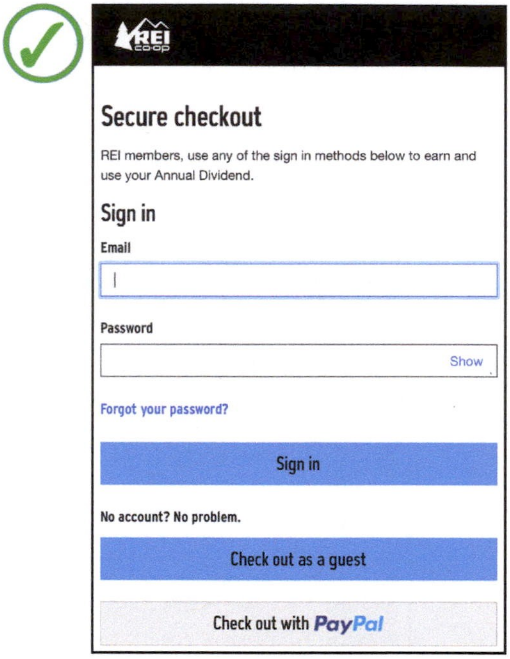

Figure 9.8.
REI.com allows customers to check out with their purchase, without first having to create an REI online account.

9.3 Make your design appeal to all your users, including older adults

Understand older adults' values *[Hanson et al., 2010]*

- Design for older adults' *values* as well as their accessibility and usability requirements. Interview older adults to learn what their values are and how they differ from those of younger adults.

Don't talk down to older adults *[Campbell, 2015; Kascak and Sanford, 2015; Pernice et al., 2013]*

- Don't patronize or stigmatize older adults. Older adults dislike being treated like dummies or like children. For example, it is fine for a device or app to have a "simplified" or "easy" mode, but don't call it "senior" mode.

- Older adults generally avoid products and services designed just for "seniors," because few people like to consider themselves old. Therefore, design so older adults can use the same products and services as younger adults.

Don't assume users are young adults *[Campbell, 2015; Kascak and Sanford, 2015; Pernice et al., 2013]*

- Avoid content, functionality, or questionnaires that assume a user is young or at a certain life stage. They may be students, working, or retired. Some may have a drivers' license; others may not. They may have young children, adult children, or no children. If you must ask the user's occupation, offer options such as "former occupation," "retired," or "not applicable." Assuming that users are still working will frustrate some people and annoy others.

Don't blame users *[Nunes et al., 2012]*

- Never imply that an error was the users' fault. For example, instead of scolding users with an error message like "Invalid date!", either transform their input into a correct date and ask them to confirm it or show them how to enter a date, "Please enter dates as mm/dd/yy."

Don't be scary *[Pernice et al., 2013]*

- Avoid displaying error messages that are frightening or threatening to users (see Figure 9.9).

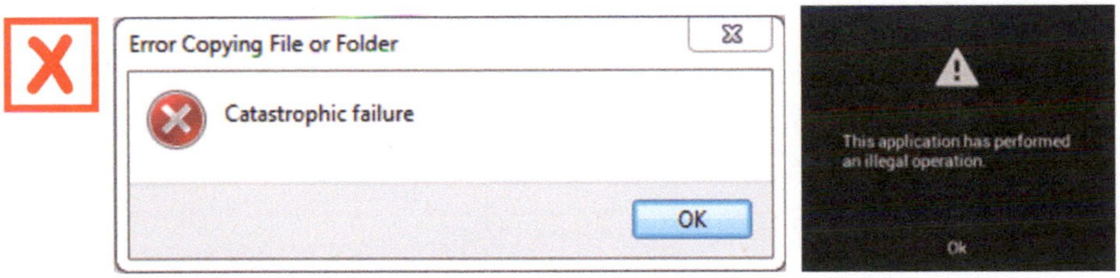

Figure 9.9.
Windows (left) and Android (right) sometimes display error messages that can scare users, especially those who are less familiar with computers.

Don't rush users *[Kurniawan and Zaphiris, 2005; Miño, 2013; Nunes et al., 2012; Silva et al., 2015]*

- Chapters 4: Motor Control and 6: Cognition explained how short response time-outs can cut users off before they finish responding due to slow movement or cognition. It is also annoying and frustrating to be cut off in the middle of responding. Therefore, avoid short time-outs that terminate an interaction before the user is finished.

- Give users plenty of time to read information and complete operations. Even better: let them indicate when they are done.

Don't skip steps *[National Institute on Aging (NIH), 2009; Silva et al., 2015]*

- When providing instructions, be specific and detailed. Don't skip steps or assume users can fill in details.

- Don't give instructions that nontechnical users won't be able to understand or execute. For example, "Connect a LAN cable to your computer and to the cable modem" requires users to know (1) what "LAN" means, (2) what a LAN cable looks like, (3) which socket the cable goes into, (4) what a cable modem is, and (5) where on the modem the cable connects.

9.4 Provide ready access to information users might want

Provide an easy way to contact you *[Chisnell et al., 2006; National Institute on Aging (NIH), 2009; Nunes et al., 2012; Pernice et al., 2013]*

- Make contact information easy to find. Customers, especially older adults, want to know that they can contact real people when necessary. Provide a customer support phone number, email address, "Chat with a representative" link, or Contact Us form.

- Put a Contact Us button or link prominently on your Homepage or screen.

- An alternative is to place contact information at the bottom of every page.

Provide a telephone alternative *[Finn and Johnson, 2013]*

- Make it easy for users to contact you or conduct transactions by phone rather than online.

Show summary *[Affonso de Lara et al., 2010]*

- Provide an easy way for users to see a summary of their actions. This gives them confirmation that they did what they intended to do, which inspires confidence. Providing a summary is especially important before a user commits to a transaction that is difficult or impossible to reverse. Examples include submitting a ballot in an election, purchasing a nonrefundable item, or transferring funds.

If you offer senior discounts, say so *[Pernice et al., 2013]*

- If you offer "senior discounts," they should be prominently shown, clearly described, and easy to obtain.

Summary of Attitude Guidelines

9.1 Be flexible in how users can enter, save, and view data	■ Provide "smart" data input. ■ Put users in control.
9.2 Earn users' trust	■ Ask only what's necessary. ■ Mark ads clearly. ■ Don't make users log in.
9.3 Make your design appeal to all your users, including older adults	■ Understand older adults' values. ■ Don't talk down to older adults. ■ Don't assume users are young adults. ■ Don't blame users. ■ Don't be scary. ■ Don't rush users. ■ Don't skip steps.
9.4 Provide ready access to information users might want	■ Provide an easy way to contact you. ■ Provide a telephone alternative. ■ Show summary. ■ If you offer senior discounts, say so.

CHAPTER 10

Working With Older Adults

Unlike most of the preceding chapters, this one does not present age-related changes in older adults. It does, however, describe ways in which working with older adults on usability studies or in participatory design may differ from working with younger adults. From recruiting participants to deciphering evaluation results, you might need to make some modifications.

Good user experience professionals understand that knowing their audience or users is an essential step in developing well-received products or services. But somehow, this is often overlooked when it comes to audiences and users that include older adults. The rationales for this range well beyond the usual "We don't have the time/budget for that." Other common excuses include [Finn, 2013]:

- *We don't know any older people.*
- *Older adults don't use technology.*
- *Not enough older adults use our products/services to make it worthwhile including them.*
- *General usability guidelines are good enough.*
- *People 50 and older are just like everyone else.*

In many ways, older people *are* just like younger people. For instance, everybody wants to feel respected, relevant, and included. But by this point in this book, you're aware of the many ways in which older people can differ from younger people and from *other* older people!

Because of their inherent diversity (see Chapter 2: Meet Some Older Adults), older adults present unique challenges to designers and developers.

Designers and developers new to working with the older population may be surprised to learn about successful projects that have involved older adults on participatory design teams or in usability studies (see the case studies in this book, as well as [Davidson and Jensen, 2013; Hakobyan et al., 2015; Massimi and Baecker, 2006]).

Usability and design researchers who have worked with older adults emphasize the importance of bringing them in at the earliest stage possible. They also emphasize the need to understand the issues and challenges older adults face, how willing they are to participate, and how valuable their contributions can be [Komninos et al., 2014; Lindsay et al., 2012].

Designing User Interfaces for an Aging Population. http://dx.doi.org/10.1016/B978-0-12-804467-4.00010-4

However, despite such inspirational examples as Barbara Beskind, who at the age of 90-something worked as a conceptual designer with IDEO, the design field has been more notable for the *lack* of involvement of older adults. Despite their own group's success with older adults and participatory design, Lindsay et al. [2012] report that:

- Most other groups are reluctant to work with older adults in the design process.
- Many groups just want to be able to say that they conducted participatory design or held focus groups, but are not willing to include older adults; and
- Many people have dismissive attitudes toward older adults and technology and don't believe that older adults can make valuable contributions.

It isn't enough to just read about the general technical abilities of older adults; you really do need to see it for yourself:

> When these [experienced user interface] designers finally met with and observed older people working with computers, they could fairly be described as stunned by the extent to which they would need to adapt their usual design practices to meet the older people's capabilities. Yet all the points that surprised the designers had been conveyed to them previously by people with extensive experience in design for older people – [Hawthorn, 2006].

As Gilbertson [2015] concluded from her survey of web developer companies: older people are "a hidden group."

OLDER ADULTS AS PARTICIPANTS IN DESIGN AND EVALUATION

Older adults may not have been a big part of design and evaluation so far, but we need to start including them. The previous chapters described some of the differences between older adults and younger adults and offered guidelines to help you design better user experiences for them.

When planning a participatory design project or a usability study that involves older adults, you should be aware of other considerations, as well.

Older adults may be unfamiliar with usability studies or participatory design

A number of years ago, one of us was conducting usability studies for Microsoft in the San Francisco Bay Area. The client jokingly explained their need to travel outside the Redmond, WA area (Microsoft headquarters): "Everyone in the state of Washington has already been in multiple Microsoft studies. We need fresh participants!"

But many older adults (outside the state of Washington) have not yet had the pleasure of participating in usability studies, focus groups, or participatory design teams. They may not be used to a computer or usability lab environment. It may be confusing or intimidating for them [Komninos et al., 2014].

Recruiting older adults as participants

Even recruiting older participants can offer some unique challenges. They might not be on your typical social media outlets and may not even be checking emails regularly.

Older adults' self-presentation to researchers

People who aren't familiar with usability studies are often unsure about what's being tested: the participant or the user interface. Older adults may not know how to relate to the researchers and developers, many of whom are much younger than they are, yet still somehow "official." Should participants be critical or polite? Casual or formal? Researchers report that older adults can be reluctant to make negative remarks about the subject at hand, even when they are clearly struggling with it [Neves et al., 2015].

These uncertainties can cause older participants to give short, uninformative responses or to respond in ways that seem intended to please the researcher [Franz et al., 2015]. On the other hand, older adults can provide useful comments on ideas put forward by other team members in a participatory design setting [Lindsay et al., 2012].

Older adults may be uncomfortable discussing their personal circumstances, and they are often reluctant to acknowledge what they consider their own frailties or shortcomings [Lindsay et al., 2012].

Usability researchers sometimes describe older adults as being afraid of breaking the computer or giving the wrong answer, making them less likely to explore the application, website, or device [Chisnell, 2011].

Older adults' behavior during a design or usability evaluation session

Older adults can be unfamiliar with current devices, technologies, and applications. It follows that many older adults may not be current on technical jargon (see Chapter 7: Knowledge). The strategies and mental models they bring to new experiences may be quite opaque to younger adults, including those conducting the study [Chisnell, 2011; Dickinson et al., 2007; Komninos et al., 2014; Neves et al., 2015].

Older adults have been described as having difficulties trying to envision new technologies (see Chapter 7: Knowledge). In participatory design situations, they sometimes have trouble separating their own personal experiences from the current situation. They may not be able to focus on how to solve the problem specified in a hypothetical scenario [Lindsay et al., 2012].

Researchers working with older adults on design and evaluation projects repeatedly mention that older adult participants require more time at every stage of the project or study. The researchers also often report having trouble keeping older participants focused, while at the same time encouraging older participants to voice their observations and opinions [Correia de Barros and Leitão, 2013; Dickinson et al., 2007; Hawthorn, 2006].

Data collection and evaluation with older adults

The classic technique of having participants think aloud while executing tasks can be problematic for some older adults who, due to diminished short-term memory capacity, might struggle to speak while simultaneously solving a problem, performing a task, or exploring something novel. If the study involves low-fidelity prototypes, some older adults may struggle with the extra mental work required to constantly "translate" between the tangibles they see in front of them (such as sticky notes) and what those tangibles represent (such as digital controls) [Hawthorn, 2006].

Using standard evaluation techniques with older adult participants can be difficult. Participants may have trouble understanding the psychometric scales often used in questionnaires and usability evaluation forms. For example, participants asked to rate items using a 5-point Likert scale couldn't quantify their answers; this seemed too abstract for them [Franz et al., 2015; Neves et al., 2015].

Self-reported data from older adults about their usage patterns, the difficulties they encountered, etc., is likely to be less accurate than data from younger adults. They often need a higher level of certainty before committing to a response to a researcher's question. Until then, their responses may not be very useful, due to incomplete or missing data [Komninos et al., 2014].

GUIDELINES FOR WORKING WITH OLDER ADULTS

Much of the literature on which this chapter is based is fairly recent. Despite the fact that technology and culture are rapidly changing, most of the guidelines offered should remain valid for many years.

10.1 Choose a study design or protocol suited to the population

Follow the examples and advice of others who have conducted user research with older adults *[Dickinson et al., 2007; Komninos et al., 2014]*

- An excellent table from Dickinson et al. [2007] is shown in Table 10.1 *Some considerations for planning research studies involving older participants.* This table presents Procedural issues (such as Written documentation or Cognitive testing), Suggested solutions (such as ways to ensure readability, language; ways to handle cognitive testing), and Reasons (e.g., participants' difficulty with small font, diversity in literacy and education levels, intimidating nature of cognitive testing for participants).

Table 10.1	Some Considerations for Planning Research Studies Involving Older Participants.	
Procedural issue	**Suggested solutions**	**Reasons**
Written materials shown to participants	Ensure readability. Font size should be at least 14 pt. Language should be straightforward, "every day" English, with particular effort taken to avoid jargon and terminology.	Older participants may find small font size harder to read.
Experimental instructions	Ensure that participants understand instructions before you begin. Be prepared to repeat them (if necessary using different words) throughout the experiment.	Inexperience with experimental conditions can mean uncertainty about appropriate behaviors. Additionally, memory issues may make it necessary to repeat instructions.
Companions	Be prepared for participants to ask to bring—or to simply bring—companions. Have a strategy for accommodating companions, so they don't affect the study.	Attendance at a research venue can be an intimidating experience. Companions, while helping to reduce participant anxiety, can also interfere with experimental conditions if not situated properly.
Cognitive testing	Explain clearly at the start the instructions and level of performance expected. If necessary, when failure occurs, make it clear that this is to be expected. Use "age-specific" scales with caution.	Oder adults can worry about the effects of aging on their memory and cognition. Diversity and effective strategies cause age-specific scales to produce a ceiling effect.
Think-aloud procedures	Be aware of potential problems with both "concurrent" and "retrospective" think-aloud techniques.	Concurrent think-aloud can stress inexperienced computer users and often fails to produce useful data. Conversely, retrospective think-aloud often yields excellent data, but may complicate the study.
User diaries	Be aware that inexperience and other factors affect the data received; check regularly that desired data is being collected; follow up rapidly with one-on-one discussions.	Difficulties with memory, processing, and physical problems with writing can reduce the usefulness of diaries. One-on-one discussions are normally the best way to elicit information from inexperienced computer users.
Balanced measures	Combine subjective and objective measures.	Beginners can have difficulty describing problems in an interface. Additionally, explanations by participants often differ from those by observers. Richer information from multiple approaches makes it more likely that useful data will be gathered.

Continued

Table 10.1	Some Considerations for Planning Research Studies Involving Older Participants. —cont'd	
Procedural issue	**Suggested solutions**	**Reasons**
Timing	Be as flexible as possible. In more formal experiments, where flexibility may be more difficult, budget generously for time.	Older participants commonly take longer to complete tasks and to achieve autonomy than researchers anticipate.
Recruitment	Choose appropriate recruitment strategies. Be cautious about having people outside the research team screen participants.	Strategies vary according to the research. It is often wasteful and inefficient to depend on others to vet participants.
Instructions for visit to research venue	Make directions to the venue clear and explicit; provide a range of information and contact numbers. Include what to bring (e.g., reading glasses, hearing aid) and check by telephone that the information has been received and understood.	Older participants may have to travel some way to the experimental venue. Variations in literacy mean that directions should be as clear as possible. Telephoning to check beforehand helps to reassure participants and encourages attendance.
Reaching research venue	Minimize the amount of walking that participants need to do to reach the research space. Avoid stairs.	Some older participants may find it difficult to walk further than a few meters. Many find stairs a significant barrier.
Retaining participants	Adopt an appropriate strategy to retain participants. The offer of free computer classes is often very effective.	Offering something in return for participation increases participant retention and can create a more positive relationship.
Longer-term study maintenance	To maintain participation in a longer-term study, it is important to be flexible about session times and any rescheduling.	Participants or their family members may be ill, or busy, and occasional rescheduling is preferable to losing participants in a study.

Reproduced by permission [Adapted from Dickinson et al. (2007)]

- Another great resource appears in Komninos et al. [2014], Table 10.2 *Factors that influence the use of design methods with older adults.* This table lists physiological, psychological, cognitive, and social factor categories, and the issues that arise with each.

Decide between individual or group designs *[Dickinson et al., 2007; Komninos et al., 2014; Lindsay et al., 2012; Silva and Nunes, 2010; Tullis, 2004]*

- Sometimes only single individuals are appropriate. Individual sessions are the best choice if you want to study select characteristics, or you don't want a participant to be influenced by other participants' opinions, or you're using someone's personal space as your testing site.

Table 10.2	**Factors That Influence the Use of Design Methods With Older Adults.**
Factor category	**Issues**
Physiological	Age factors that make self-reporting inaccurate Limited endurance Medical conditions that hinder motor skills, hearing, or verbal expression
Psychological	Tendency of blaming themselves instead of designers for issues Fragility of confidence while using technology Anxiety toward computer use Perception that computers are not much use to them Difficulty in focusing on the design process if they feel that it is going toward a direction that is not valuable to them
Cognitive	Lack of understanding of technical language and metaphors Lack of underlying understanding of computer concepts Difficulty in envisioning new technology Disapproval of deep explorations in subjects that are forced on them by the designer Tendency to digress into unrelated subjects during discussions
Societal	Participatory design meetings are seen as social events Positive predisposition toward prototypes and tendency to praise rather than offend researchers by offering objective views

Reproduced by permission Komninos et al. [2014]

- Otherwise, consider groups. Examples are focus groups and participatory design teams. There are many advantages to conducting group studies. Participants may be more willing to sign up if they feel there will be safety in numbers, or the prospect of a "social" gathering is more appealing to them. Peer-to-peer tutoring and retention of learning is seen more often in groups. For multisession projects, long-term attendance is better with groups. Participants can arrive at novel ideas from the input of other members. You do need to watch out for "group think" and to make sure each participant has a chance to form and voice their own opinions, rather than being overwhelmed by a perceived majority or dominant personalities.

- Consider a twosome. As mentioned in Table 10.1, older adults sometimes bring along a spouse, friend, or family member. If the study design allows for this (and if the privacy permissions are in order), consider allowing the "extra" person to sit in and participate. You might get two sessions instead of one! Or you can relabel the session as one of "codiscovery." However, be careful about the "extra" person being more technically adept (or at least, seeing themselves that way) or talking over your main participant. Just decide ahead of time how you will handle this situation, if it comes up.

Make sure the study situations are relevant to your participants *[Lindsay et al., 2012; Newell et al., 2007; Silva & Nunes, 2010]*

- Make it real...: Older participants may have trouble imagining "real-life" situations that don't actually reflect their own real lives. Use scenarios, circumstances, or events that ring true for your participants. Role-play situations and video prompts have both worked well for this purpose. Role-plays consist of you creating scenarios or scripts and assigning roles to multiples participants (or to the facilitator and one participant).

- ...or make it someone else's reality. When participants' reality isn't going to work, such as when you need to get their opinions about a future technology or situation and they have no idea how to respond, encourage pretending.

- Ask participants how they think someone in that situation would react or respond.

- Create short videos (with actors fulfilling the roles) to serve as prompts for discussion.

- Present various points of view in your scripts or videos.

- Include humor, which has been especially successful.

- These techniques serve to open up the participants' minds and free them to respond from someone else's viewpoint.

Choose between concurrent and retrospective think-aloud protocols *[Chisnell, 2011; Dickinson et al., 2007; Olmsted-Hawala and Bergstrom, 2012; Wilkinson, 2011]*

- Concurrent or retrospective? A concurrent thinking aloud (CTA) protocol is when you ask the participant to think out loud while they're working through tasks, evaluating interfaces, etc. This gives the researcher real-time insight into the participant's thought processes and allows them to stop the participant and ask for further clarification. However, CTA can cause problems for anyone who struggles with multitasking, such as keeping up a running commentary on their technical actions. For such people, the retrospective think-aloud (RTA) protocol might be better.

- With RTA, however, you may find that participants cannot recall their previous thought processes or actions in great detail or with great accuracy. Instead, they may make up after-the-fact justifications for their actions. You also run the risk of not capturing their fleeting emotions and thoughts with the RTA protocol.

- Studies have shown no difference in accuracy, efficiency, or satisfaction for older adults using either a CTA or an RTA protocol.

Avoid using user diaries *[Dickinson et al., 2007; Komninos et al., 2014]*

- Self-reporting may not be your best option when working with older adult participants (refer to Table 10.1).

- Keeping a user diary may force participants to divide their time and attention between the task at hand and the diary itself.

- Participants struggling with motor control, memory, or fatigue may make only minimal entries or may completely neglect to make entries.

- Electronic diaries force participants to deal with yet another layer of complexity.

- An (arduous) option is for you to collect the data as the process moves along by talking to each participant, either in person or by phone.

Make it easy for older adults to participate *[Hawthorn, 2006; Lindsay et al., 2012]*

- Involve them early. Bring older adult participants into the design process as early as possible.

- Provide familiar office supplies and low-fidelity mock-ups. In addition to the standard supplies for design sessions (post-its, tape, markers, white boards, etc.), consider "seeding" the discussions with mock-ups, blank dummy devices, or even simple, iconic cutout shapes.

- Develop an advance plan. Prepare a list of the topics you want to cover, with estimates of how long you'll spend on each topic. For ongoing sessions: review what was covered in the previous session, and specify for participants the goals of the current session. Keep the group on topic, but make sure everyone understands the issue. Direct them toward productive discussion and, hopefully, resolution.

Avoid between-subjects experimental design *[Dickinson et al., 2007]*

- If you are conducting a scientific study investigating effects of variables on behavior, the diversity of older adults makes it difficult to control all the potential sources of variance.

10.2 Identify potential design or usability study participants

Know your population *[Hawthorn, 2006; Silva and Nunes, 2010; Tullis, 2004]*

- Become an informal observer or volunteer as an assistant in environments frequented by older adults, such as computer classes.

- Talk to community contacts: doctors, caregivers, and service providers who already know members of your intended study population.
- Start with some likely places: community/senior centers, libraries, adult/continuing education programs, health clinics, senior day centers, community/local newspapers, fitness centers, and places offering computer classes for novices (e.g., YMCA).

Approach group living settings with caution *[Franz et al., 2015]*

- Access to older adults who live in group senior homes or care settings can be difficult, due to privacy rules and regulations or due to a lack of spare time or training among staff.

10.3 Recruit and schedule participants

Having a personal connection helps *[Chisnell, 2011; Ostergren and Karras, 2007; Tullis, 2004; Wilkinson, 2011]*

- Avoid "cold calling." Whether by phone or Internet, this usually doesn't work with older adults. Unscrupulous scammers often target older adults, who might be very cautious.
- Mention how you obtained the person's contact information and the name of your personal connection when contacting potential participants.
- Older adults can also be susceptible to pressure or persuasion, whether from you or from their family members, friends, or caregivers. If an older adult does agree to participate, be sure that it's for their own personal, well-informed reasons.

Select the most suitable contact method to use with your participants *[Chisnell, 2011; Lindsay et al., 2012]*

- Phone calls may be difficult for people with hearing impairments, and electronic communications may be difficult for those with limited access to, or experience with, technology.
- Older people may be less receptive to strangers phoning them, but calling someone can help establish an ongoing connection; older adults are often "glad to hear from a real person."
- And talking to them by phone gives you a chance to assess them.
- Recruiting by email or social media can take longer with older adults, who may not check their email or social media outlets very often.

Recruit early, recruit extras *[Dickinson et al., 2007; Lindsay et al., 2012]*

- Begin your recruiting of older participants earlier than you might with younger ones (e.g., 8 weeks in advance).

- Plan on recruiting 20% more individuals than you actually need, to allow for last-minute cancellations due to health, transportation, or caregiving issues. This becomes increasingly important as the age of your participant group increases. For example, if you're working with people in their 80s, you should probably recruit a comfortable number of extra participants.

- For focus groups, one recommended size is four to five participants.

Decide the desired diversity level in advance *[Dickinson et al., 2007; Komninos et al., 2014; Lindsay et al., 2012; Neves et al., 2015; Newell et al., 2007]*

- Keep in mind the range of diversity among individuals. Differences exist in the "normal" factors: age, location, education level, professional experience, literacy, fluency, income level, technology experience and aptitude, etc.

- Remember the "extra" diversity among people aged 50+. There are often more numerous, and broader, differences in technology familiarity, health conditions, physical abilities, risk aversion, living situation, and social attitudes (privacy, security, appropriateness).

Plan to modify your screening tool *[Chisnell, 2011; Tullis, 2004]*

Now We Know Better

We should have done this ourselves: as we found when compiling the returned surveys we used in developing our personas for this book, many older people don't offer the level of detail you might hope for.

When we initially asked people what they did online or what they used their devices for, they tended to just say "email" and "phone calls." When we offered a list of examples, we got better responses (although some people just circled the entire list).

We also discovered that frequency of use (e.g., every day, every week) and length of use was unhelpful in determining someone's level of proficiency; some people simply answered that they had been "using computers since 1980." That didn't correlate with their actual expertise; neither did their self-reported level of expertise. You may need a more explicit screening tool.

- "Test" your surveys, screeners, or assessment forms in advance. You might find that you've misjudged what your target participants do online or how they interact with technology. You might assume they just read news, play games, and look for health information, only to learn that they actually spend all their time on social media or binge-watching TV. In other words, while their habits might not match your own, they might not match your assumptions, either.

- To help you get started with a screening tool, Figures 10.1 and 10.2 offer a couple of well-considered assessment matrices from Chisnell [2011].

How often do you do these activities on the web? Please pick the closest answer.

[Recruiter or researcher: Mark an X in the appropriate box. For example, when you ask "Send and receive email" and the participant selects "once per week" mark that box with an X. In the Totals column, multiply the number of Xs in that row by the number of points that appears in the left hand column.]

Points	Send and receive email	Read news items on websites	Totals
Never (0)			(number of Xs * 0)
Once per month (1)			(number of Xs * 1)
Once per week (2)			(number of Xs * 2)
Daily (3)			(number of Xs * 3)
Several times a day (4)			(number of Xs * 4)
			(total Xs * point value in each row)

_____ Novice – 0 to 2 points
_____ Competent – 3 to 5 points
_____ Expert – 6 to 8 points

Figure 10.1.
Screening tool for frequency of general web activities. (From Chisnell [2011], reproduced by permission).

Schedule your participants based on their needs, not yours *[Chisnell, 2011; Dickinson et al., 2007; Ostergren and Karras, 2007; Tullis, 2004]*

- Be flexible. The more flexibility, the better. Many older adults lead active lives and are not just sitting around waiting to be invited to participate in a study. However, they are more likely than younger adults to be constrained by health, caregiving, and transportation issues.

How often do you do *these* activities on the web? Please pick the closest answer.

[Recruiter or researcher: Mark an X in the appropriate box. For example, when you ask "Send and receive email" and the participant selects "once per week" mark that box with an X. In the Totals column, multiply the number of Xs in that row by the number of points that appears in the left hand column.]

Points	Research health information such as conditions, treatments, or drugs at websites	Take part in online auctions	Play games alone or with others on websites	Pay bills through a website	Totals
Never (0)					(number of Xs * 0)
Once or twice a year (1)					(number of Xs * 1)
Three or four times a year (2)					(number of Xs * 2)
Every month (3)					(number of Xs * 3)
Every week (4)					(number of Xs * 4)
					(total Xs * point value in each row)

_____ Novice – 0 to 4 points
_____ Competent – 6 to 8 points
_____ Expert – 9 or more points

Figure 10.2.
Screening tool for frequency of specific web activities. (From Chisnell [2011], reproduced by permission).

- Short sessions are better than long sessions. To avoid participant fatigue, consider scheduling two short sessions per week, instead of one long session. Shorter sessions also offer more chances for repetition of material, and thus, more successful learning. However, multiple sessions per week can introduce more scheduling problems. Consider increasing the number of sessions in your study, but making each session shorter.

- Be mindful of transportation issues. Older participants tend to dislike being out during peak travel times. This may also be true of any friends or family members responsible for driving them. Public transportation fares often increase during rush hour. Consider holding the study at a very central location that is accessible via public transportation.

- Be prepared for early birds, who often travel in pairs. Older participants tend to be at their best in the mornings, although some are okay with afternoons (or even prefer them). Avoid scheduling evening sessions. Also, be aware that they tend to arrive earlier than the scheduled start time (like, an hour earlier). And they often have someone with them, for transportation or just for moral support. Make sure you have someone there to welcome any early arrivals. You will also want to have a nice place for them to wait, and something to occupy their companions during the session.

- Build in pilot sessions. As with any study, it's a good idea to schedule one or more pilot sessions in advance of the main body of the study. This gives you a chance to revise your procedure, in case it doesn't play out as planned.

Do yourself a favor: use reminders *[Chisnell, 2011; Dickinson et al., 2007]*

- Be multimodal in your reminders. Remind your participants by phone, and by post and/or email (as appropriate).

- Be specific in your reminders. At least for email and post, include the following information: day and date; starting and ending times; contact and alternate contact details, address, map; parking and public transportation details.

- Prevent unpleasant surprises. If there are multiple entrances to the building, specify which one they should use. Ask them to bring their reading glasses, hearing aids, and any mobility aids for the activities they'll be doing. The incidence of diabetes is several times higher among older adults than younger adults [CDC, 2015], so be sure to let your participants know if they should eat beforehand, or if you will be providing food. Remind them what type of session they'll be in (one-to-one or group). Mention whether you'll be recording the session and whether extra observers will be present.

Take extra steps to increase participant attendance *[Dickinson et al., 2007; Komninos et al., 2014; Lindsay et al., 2012; Silva and Nunes, 2010]*

In addition to being flexible in your scheduling, you can increase your attendance rate in the following ways:

- Put it in writing. Make a formal payment agreement in advance. This "can have a contract effect with better attendance."

- Assign homework. This is especially advisable for multisession designs. Having homework assignments keeps participants engaged, and can increase their learning and retention between sessions.

- Make it a social event. If you are conducting a group study, you may find that this increases the likelihood of registered participants actually showing up. Reasons may include shared rides, the promise of free food, or a sense of obligation to a group. And don't discount the possibility that group events can be regarded as more fun and less threatening than individual sessions.

10.4 Plan the activity with extra attention to older-adult-centric details

Be patient, be nice *[Chisnell, 2011; Correia de Barros and Leitão, 2013; Dickinson et al., 2007; Komninos et al., 2014; Lindsay et al., 2012; Ostergren and Karras, 2007; Pernice et al., 2013; Silva and Nunes, 2010]*

- Allow for extra time at every step of the study. Many older adults take longer to do things. One suggestion is to allow up to 25% more time than you would plan for younger adults. Another is to add in an extra 10–20 minutes at the beginning and ending of each session.

- Keep participants on task. Some older adults tend to be chatty. They may be nervous, start reminiscing, or just get off track. You need to keep them on topic (especially challenging in a group setting), but you also want to be polite and respectful. Reassure them that you are interested in their (on-task) contributions. You may need to wait longer before prompting participants, but don't let them become frustrated.

- Start and stop on time. As mentioned earlier, many older adults lead quite busy lives. They may also have other people depending on them, or be relying on other people, and so they are very aware of those people's schedules. Be respectful of participants' time.

- Have fewer tasks, shorter sessions, and built-in breaks. Don't cram as many individual tasks into a session as possible. Keep each task focused, and keep it short.

- Although there isn't any "magic" time limit, older adults in general will be better off with shorter sessions. Design sessions that are shorter than typical sessions with younger people.

- If this isn't possible, remember that some older adults may tire more quickly, and lose their focus more easily, than many younger people. If you must have a long session, schedule breaks, preferably between activities. Make sure participants know they are free to take additional breaks (as necessary—not for socializing and snacks!).

- Keep in mind that maintaining your participants' well-being is more important than your data.

Be on the alert for any access issues *[Chisnell, 2011; Dickinson et al., 2007; Lindsay et al., 2012; Ostergren and Kraas, 2007; Silva and Nunes, 2010]*

If you are conducting sessions anywhere other than the participant's residence, there are particular things you need to pay attention to. Although you should do this for participants of any age, it is even more important for older adults.

- Choose an accessible location. Ideally, use a place already familiar to your participants. Be prepared to help with transportation arrangements. Make sure the site is wheelchair accessible. Use locations that don't require participants to use stairs, or to walk long distances (including long hallways). Having restrooms nearby is very desirable.

- Arrange workspace to suit each participant. Adjust the height, distance, angle, etc., of the desk, chair, digital device, and input device. Make sure there is a stand to support devices such as tablets, so participants don't have to hold them all the time. Set the font size large enough for your participants to be able to read easily (unless you're testing whether or not they can figure out how to do that themselves).

- Eliminate distractions. Use a quiet location, with minimal distraction from people walking through during your session, and without background noise such as phones ringing, public announcements, etc.

- Provide optimal lighting. Make sure the space you're using is well lit, preferably with natural light. On the other hand, avoid glaringly bright light (beware of reflective surfaces and be considerate of participants with light sensitivity). Having several light sources, as well as ways to control them (dimmer switches, window coverings), can help.

- Make participants as comfortable as possible. Always make sure your participants are comfortable and at ease. Don't leave them waiting outside; don't leave them alone.

- Control the temperature; be especially careful that the room isn't too cold.

Take control of the logistics and security *[Franz et al., 2015; Komninos et al., 2014; Tullis, 2004]*

- Be prepared for red tape. As mentioned earlier, it can be difficult to connect with people residing in group living situations. When you request access to the residence's Wi-Fi, passwords, and devices, house managers tend to get alarmed. Researchers' access to and control of devices and networks can present a significant bureaucratic problem.

- Be prepared to provide extra support. If your study involves participants operating anything on their own, such as when they can take a device home with them, they will need extra support. This could be as straightforward as preparing a simple user manual or providing a name and contact for help. Or, you might need to enlist and train participants' friends, family members, or staff, so they can provide more instantaneous and real-time support.

- Provide familiar setups. Okay, this may not always be feasible. But within reason, provide a testing environment that closely matches the one that participants already know. Unless you're testing people's ability to adapt to new systems, avoid the extra "noise" that would be introduced by having them use unfamiliar computers, mice, keyboards, etc.

- Don't leave participants alone. Their ability to understand you, and the results of their feedback, will be better if the moderator or facilitator is in the same room with them, where participants can see the moderator's face and hear their natural, unmodulated voice (see Chapter 5: Hearing and Speech).

Take the pressure off data collection *[Dickinson et al., 2007; Franz et al., 2015; Neves et al., 2015; Silva and Nunes, 2010]*

Most of the guidelines in this section center around making the data collection process better suited to older adults, and relieving the pressure your participants might feel.

- Use collection methods that fit your participants. Aim the data collection at the participants' literacy, ability, and technology levels.

- If you ask questions directly, instead of expecting participants to fill out a hardcopy or online form themselves, it may be easier on them, and yield responses that are more informative. Guided interviews work well for this.

- Consider relying more on your observations than on user-supplied data. Use user-friendly evaluation forms, such as those used by Silva and Nunes [2010] (see Figure 10.3).

Figure 10.3.
A scale used for evaluating participant mood and fatigue. (Based on Silva and Nunes [2010]).

- Make sure your participants don't become stressed. Instead of having them think out loud while performing the task, they might do better talking about their thought processes after performing the task (concurrent vs. retrospective think-aloud protocols are discussed under Guideline 10.1).

- Consider using the indirect method. Ask participants how someone they know would respond to a question, rather than asking them for their own response; or ask them how they would explain something to someone else.

- Make selection easy for them. Ask them if they prefer A over B; for example, if they prefer swiping over tapping.

- Consider doing a "community" evaluation. This might relieve some of the performance stress that individual participants might feel. This is not just for focus groups; you can ask for feedback from the participants' friends, family members, or caregivers.

One of the ice breakers I found with older adults was to get them to choose which alternative of a design feature was better and to get them to say why. I also used reframing to present their difficulties as positives – 'You are finding this bit hard – excellent – you have found something we will need to change, thanks for that.' – [Dan Hawthorn, personal communication, 2016]

10.5 Be especially mindful when conducting an activity with older adult participants

Be polite, considerate, and respectful [Chisnell, 2011; Correia de Barros and Leitão, 2013; Silva and Nunes, 2010]

- Ask each participant how they would like to be addressed, e.g., by their first name, as "Mrs./Mr.," or with some other title.

- Use more expressions of politeness—please, thank you—and be a bit more formal than usual.

- Avoid being patronizing or using ElderSpeak.[1]

- Keep in mind that their beliefs about anything (not just technology) may be quite different from your own, or from the beliefs of younger participants, but deserve equal respect.

- Don't ask participants anything personal.

---

1 "ElderSpeak": Speaking quite carefully, slowly, and loudly, using simple words and exaggerated facial expressions and using terms of endearment such as you might use with a child ("Sweetie," "Dearie," "Baby," "Honey").

- Let people know that you might prompt them for more (or less) detail, or that you might redirect their attention.

- When prompting or redirecting, be gentle!

- Keep participants on task, while encouraging communication.

- Reassure them with reminders that there is no wrong or right answer.

- Express your gratitude for their participation.

Be as clear as possible *[Chisnell, 2011; Lindsay et al., 2012; Silva and Nunes, 2010]*

- Speak while facing your older adults, in a reasonable volume and at a reasonable pace.

- Make eye contact to help with communication.

- Make sure that any written materials are easy to read (normal font of at least 12 points, regular weight, dark on a plain pale background, with a line spacing of 1.5 or 2).

- Keep questions and instructions short and simple.

- Make sure that participants understand any terms you use, even those that you assume are well known.

Set expectations *[Correia de Barros and Leitão, 2013; Komninos et al., 2014; Lindsay et al., 2012; Pernice et al., 2013; Silva and Nunes, 2010]*

- Emphasize (as often as necessary) that you're testing the software, device, or application, not *them*; that they're not going to be judged on their performance; and that there's no such thing as a "wrong" answer.

- For multisession studies, tell participants at the beginning of each session what the current status of the study is, the goals for the current session, and what to expect for the next session (and any homework you've assigned).

- Remind your participants of the duration of the current session, details (such as breaks, restrooms), whether it's being recorded, and what they'll be doing (e.g., operating something, thinking out loud, codesigning).

Warm up first *[Chisnell, 2011; Komninos et al., 2014; Pernice et al., 2013]*

- Plan to spend more time with older adults in your introductory remarks.

- If it won't bias your results, consider giving them a demonstration or allowing them to perform a brief "warm-up" or practice task. Seeing what's involved can help put them at ease.

10.6 Have an ethical "exit strategy" for your older adult participants

Wrap it up *[Finn and Johnson, 2013; Silva and Nunes, 2010]*

- As with any study, conduct a debriefing. If you haven't already explained the background and goals of the study, as well as the specific research questions, do so at the end of your participant's session.

- In addition to thanking your participants for their time, mention some specific way in which each individual has contributed to the session: something they pointed out that you hadn't realized, an insight that could help in future sessions, or a new way of interpreting something.

- Make sure they have your contact information, and encourage them to follow up with any questions or concerns.

Teach your participants something new *[Chisnell, 2011; Finn and Johnson, 2013; Pernice et al., 2013]*

- At the end of the session, offer to show your participants how to do something. This could be related to the session, their own (home) system, or the smartphone or cell phone they've got. It could be something they struggled with during the session, or something they've always wondered, or just something you think they might enjoy or find helpful.

- If they ask you to teach them something during the session, promise to do so at the end, after you have collected your data.

Return everything to its place *[Finn and Johnson, 2013]*

- If conducted in their own space, be sure to put everything back the way it was.

Do no harm *[Waycott et al., 2015]*

- Even if you are not reporting to a medical ethics review board, you should still act with the greatest integrity. When working with any vulnerable populations who might not be able to look out for themselves, you must be particularly careful not to take advantage of them.

- Some older adults might be socially isolated, might not understand the boundary between their care plan and your study/design, or might not grasp the conditions of the study or design activity. You do not want to leave them worse off than they were before you came along.

- Manage participants' expectations. If you're providing them with some software or a device for the duration of the study, what happens at the end of it? Assuming they liked it: do they get to keep it, or is there some easy, low-cost or no-cost method for them to obtain it? If you've been spending a lot of time with your participants over a prolonged period, they might assume that your relationship is more than just a professional one. Are you going to maintain contact with them? Will there be some way for participants to be in touch with one another afterward? These issues should definitely be addressed.

What Happens When the Research Ends?

When older adults participate in research on how they use—and learn—digital technology, one issue that arises is: what happens after the research is complete? Here is an example:

Waycott et al. [2015] conducted a study to examine an iPad app intended to reduce loneliness and foster friendship among older adults, called Enmesh. The participants were all socially isolated seniors who had been recommended by their care providers. One ethical concern that arose was that, at the end of the study, participants had to return the iPads and the prototype Enmesh app. To ease the transition for participants, the researchers arranged for participants to receive iPads to keep. In addition, the researchers helped participants keep in touch with each other via email, phone, and social events.

Summary of Guidelines for Working With Older Adults

10.1 Choose a study design or protocol suited to the population.	■ Make use of the advice offered by other age-related researchers. ■ Decide between individual or group designs. ■ Make sure the study situations are relevant to your participants. ■ Choose between concurrent and retrospective think-aloud protocols. ■ Avoid using user diaries. ■ Make it easy for participants to participate. ■ Avoid between-subjects experimental design.
10.2 Identify potential design or study participants.	■ Know your population. ■ Approach group living settings with caution.
10.3 Recruit and schedule participants.	■ Having a personal connection helps. ■ Select your contact method. ■ Recruit early, recruit extras. ■ Decide the desired diversity level in advance. ■ Plan to modify your screening tool. ■ Schedule your participants with their needs in mind, not yours. ■ Do yourself a favor: use reminders. ■ Take extra steps to increase participant attendance.
10.4 Plan the activity with extra attention to older-adult-centric details.	■ Be patient, be nice. ■ Be on the alert for any access issues. ■ Take control of the logistics and security. ■ Take the pressure off data collection.
10.5 Be especially mindful when conducting an activity with older adult participants.	■ Be polite, considerate, and respectful. ■ Be as clear as possible. ■ Be patient. ■ Set expectations. ■ Warm up first.
10.6 Have an ethical "exit strategy" for your participants.	■ Wrap it up. ■ Teach your participants something new. ■ Return everything to its place. ■ Do no harm.

CHAPTER 11

Case Studies

OVERVIEW

This chapter highlights five case studies. The first three are examples of participatory design and applied research. Some of the usability guidelines presented in the present volume are based, in part, on these case studies.

The last two case studies are a bit different. One relates a case in which human interface engineers designing an automobile "infotainment" system discovered that most of their customers were older adults, and had to refocus their design and evaluation efforts. This case study also includes the timetable, demographics, and procedural overview for each step of the process. The final case study reports on a project to address designers' lack of understanding and empathy by simulating the effects of age-related conditions on the user experience.

eCAALYX TV User Interface. First up is eCAALYX, contributed by Francisco Nunes and Paula Alexandra Silva, who worked on the project while they were affiliated with the Fraunhofer Portugal Research Center for Assistive Information and Communication Solutions (Fraunhofer AICOS). eCAALYX, which ran from 2009 to 2012, arose from the Ambient Assisted Living program (AAL). The case study describes the design and implementation of a TV-based user interface to a health-care monitoring system. The goal of eCAALYX was to help older adults who are living with chronic conditions continue living independently. The in-home systems connected to hospital-based clinicians. Team members worked with both clinicians and patients to develop a better understanding of the different perspectives and needs of stakeholders. Patients were involved in iterative stages of prototyping. Participants with low technical literacy evaluated the user interface. The case study presented here explains how the team used participant feedback to choose an icon that would mean "watch video," and to remove a poorly understood display option.

Smart Companion to GoLivePhone. Ana Correia de Barros and Ana Vasconcelos coauthored the second case study, Smart Companion. As with the eCAALYX project, some of whose team members also worked on Smart Companion, the Smart Companion authors conducted their research while based at Fraunhofer AICOS. Like eCAALYX, this study illustrates extensive involvement of older adults from the earliest stages of the project. The project centered on a simplified smartphone, with an optimized task flow to support the users' mental models and goals. From the underlying metaphor to the selection and presentation of applications, everything was designed to minimize distraction and complexity. Over time, the general look-and-feel of the user interface evolved. So did users' experience: at the outset of the project, the target audience was generally less familiar with smartphones than by the project's end. Since 2013, AICOS has licensed the Smart Companion technology to Gociety, which began marketing it as the GoLivePhone.

ASSISTANT, a Support Tool for Elders Using Public Transportation. In ASSISTANT, the third case study in this chapter, contributing authors Stefan Carmien and Samuli Heinonen describe another Ambient Assisted Living effort that was developed to help older people use public transportation. ASSISTANT combined web-based trip planning with a stripped-down smartphone, called the Personal Navigation Device (PND). The PND assisted users through selecting a destination, planning the route, getting on the right bus, getting off the bus at the right stop, and getting from the bus stop to the door of the destination. Throughout the project, the team's commitment to including representative people was reflected in focus groups, heuristic evaluations, and field testing with participants. The research phases of the project ran from 2012 to 2015. Commercialization is underway at the time of writing.

Subaru Auto Infotainment System. The fourth study, Subaru Auto Infotainment System, presents an overview of the entire user interface design process for the infotainment system used in the 2017 Impreza. The author, Sean Hazaray, is with Subaru Research and Development. He describes the human–machine interface team's surprise at learning that most of their customers are older adults, and how that changed their whole design approach. As is often the case, the design team members tended to be young adults and were not familiar with older adult populations. After including older adults in their studies, the design team learned that age alone was not a determining factor in whether or not an interface would be usable. More important was the users' familiarity with other, existing interfaces (e.g., smartphones, Google Maps). People preferred user interfaces they were already comfortable with, rather than the innovative ones automakers often aim for.

The Virtual Third-Age Simulator for Web Accessibility. Finally, we learn about the Virtual Third-Age Simulator, developed by Teri Gilbertson for her 2014 PhD thesis at Loughborough University. Gilbertson's initial research had determined that many developers and project managers (1) were unaware of age-related accessibility guidelines and (2) did not regard aging as an accessibility issue. For her dissertation, she drew on her experience with virtual learning environments (VLEs) to create a "novel, engaging, and awareness-raising tool" for developers. Other simulators of vision impairment have been developed, but Gilbertson's is distinct in that it allows you to simulate multiple conditions at the same time, uses an eye tracker for real-time effects, and uses live websites. The Virtual Third-Age Simulator also differs in that it provides actual lessons to educate designers and increase their empathy for older adults. The resulting Virtual Third-Age Simulator provides developers with education on several age-related changes and conditions, and allows them to experience simulations of those changes and conditions. Participants who used the simulator said they learned a great deal, had increased empathy for what older adults experience in using technology, and found the experience enjoyable.

These case studies illustrate some of the ways in which other researchers and designers have approached the issue of age-friendly digital interfaces. To varying degrees, these projects all deal with usability considerations and design guidelines. The main purpose of including them here is to inspire you.

eCAALYX TV USER INTERFACE

Francisco Nunes, Vienna University of Technology

Paula Alexandra da Silva, Department of Design Innovation, Maynooth University, Ireland

Background

Developed from 2009 to 2012, eCAALYX (Enhanced Complete Ambient Assisted Living Experiment) was intended to help older adults continue to live independently. It was funded by the European Commission under the Ambient Assisted Living Joint Program, part of their push to develop remote monitoring tools for older people with chronic conditions.[1]

Fraunhofer AICOS (Fraunhofer Portugal Research Center for Assistive Information and Communication Solutions) was one of 11 consortium partners working on eCAALYX. The Fraunhofer AICOS team included human computer interaction researchers, software engineers, and visual designers. We were responsible for designing and implementing a TV-based user interface for older adults, whose chronic health conditions could be monitored remotely by health-care professionals.

The technological setup in the home of the patients consisted of a TV-based user interface, a router, and wireless sensors (e.g., weight scale, blood pressure monitor). In the hospital, clinicians used a web interface to visualize and interact with the older adults at home. The two components were connected through a central server. The work reported in this document refers to the TV-based user interface for older adults to use in their homes. The prototyping and the development of the design were tailored to cardiovascular disease and diabetes.

The work of the design team responsible for the development of the TV-based user interfaces unfolded in three phases.

---

1 After 2014, the Ambient Assisted Living Joint Program was renamed Active and Assistive Living (AAL). It was renewed for a second phase of funding under the Horizon 2020 umbrella (www.aaleurope.eu/).

User Research Phase

During the User Research Phase, we conducted a thorough review of the literature on telecare technologies, chronic care, and the perspectives of patients living with chronic conditions. To better understand the issues of people living with chronic conditions, we also interviewed project clinicians. Based on the data collected, we defined users' requirements and goals and developed personas of the main user types.

Prototyping, Evaluation, and Redesign Phase

The Prototyping, Evaluation, and Redesign Phase consisted of iterative development of low-fidelity paper prototypes for six main tasks:
1. Watch Health Status
2. Contact Doctor
3. Browse Agenda
4. Watch Health Videos
5. Questionnaires
6. Emergency Call

In total, 15 participants were involved in this phase. Their ages ranged from 54 to 92 years (average 79), and there was an average of eight participants in each test. Participants were from a diversity of backgrounds and levels of education. Four of them were living with chronic conditions: two with hypertension and two with diabetes. All of them used a TV daily, but only two had ever used a computer. When testing the main functionalities of the system, the researchers used the Wizard of Oz technique.

We also had participants perform card-sorting tasks, both to improve the navigation structure and to identify the optimal icons and labels.

Example 1. Card sorting to choose appropriate icons

As an example, participants were asked to prioritize their choices for an icon that would represent the "Watch Health Videos" function (Figure 11.1). Participants' choices were equally distributed between the projector and the VHS cassette. The other icons—a clackett, a film reel, and a film strip—were never selected. The team chose to use the projector icon, because cassettes are becoming less and less common, and future users might not be able to correctly interpret a cassette icon.

Figure 11.1.
Choices of icons to be used on "Watch Health Videos" menu item.

Formal usability evaluation

A formal usability evaluation phase was conducted to assess the user interface before the project went on to trials and validation. The evaluation included all the main functionalities of the system, as well as the use of sensors.

For this phase, we had new participants who had not been exposed to any previous versions of the user interface. Ten participants from diverse backgrounds took part, aged 61–78 years (average 69.5). Seven participants lived with hypertension and three with diabetes. All participants used a TV on a daily basis. Six participants had never used a computer before; three of them used a computer regularly; and one reported having used a computer in the past.

One aspect of the user interface which we tested extensively was the participants' ability to successfully access and use a hidden control panel on the TV screen.

Example 2. Testing ability to access hidden video control panel on full screen TV

Technical setup: A 42-inch screen TV, connected to an STB running a modified version of XBMC[2] and a regular remote control, was set up in a living lab apartment. The TV screen was placed 3 m away from the test participant's chair. We covered the non-eCAALYX buttons on the remote control with paper, thus eliminating any usability issues stemming from the design of the remote control (as shown in Figure 11.2). Participants were asked to verbalize their thoughts during the task.

Figure 11.2.
Remote control, with paper covering the unrelated buttons.

---

2 XBMC is an open-source media player software that can be highly customizable. In the meanwhile XBMC has been renamed to Kodi.

Participants were invited to watch a health video. Initially, the video content and the control panel were both visible (Figure 11.3). However, a few seconds after starting the video, the control panel would disappear by sliding to the bottom with an animation.

Figure 11.3.
Health video on large-screen TV, with the control panel displayed at bottom.

At this point, the participants were asked to pause the video. They needed to use the remote control to make the TV screen control panel reappear, and then press the control panel's Pause button before the panel disappeared once more.

There were seven possible buttons to choose from on the modified remote control: Home, Up, Right, Down, Left, Back, and Info. Participants tried multiple remote control buttons before hitting the Up key, which made the video control panel visible again. Only 4 of the 10 participants were able to press the Pause button, and then only with great difficulty.

We had been hoping to use the disappearing control panel to maximize the display size of the video for the older adults. Because of the great usability challenge this posed for them, however, we decided to keep the video control panel visible at all times (except when in full screen mode).

Our team and the participants worked together throughout the course of the project. One result of the collaboration was the reordering of the options on the menus. Figure 11.4 shows the evolution of the menus.

Other usability issues included:
- Health plots:
  - what to display on the health data plots
  - how to navigate between different time frames (moments of the day, this week, last 4 weeks)
  - displaying blood pressure values (differences between Portugal that uses a scale of 10 and Germany that uses a scale of 100)

Figure 11.4.
eCAALYX menu items: paper prototype, intermediate, and final versions.

- What to show in the appointment calendar
- What to show in the medication reminders

Current status of eCAALYX

After the final revisions, the user interface was validated as a follow-up within the project CAALYX-MV (www.caalyx-mv.eu/project). Since then, the team has been exploring eCAALYX's commercial viability as a care solution, under the new branding name Care-Box (www.youtube.com/watch?v=pFGJloXIyW0). Further details about the eCAALYX project can be found at www.aal-europe.eu/projects/ecaalyx/ and www.ecaalyx.org/ecaalyx.org/index.html.

SMART COMPANION TO GOLIVEPHONE

Ana Correia de Barros and Ana Vasconcelos,

The Fraunhofer Portugal Research Center for Assistive Information and Communication Solutions (Fraunhofer AICOS)

Overview

Smartphones already account for 65% of mobile devices in the world [GSMA, 2015], and this market share is growing. For older adults—the fastest-growing demographic group—access to these increasingly powerful tools can mean independence, dignity, and an increase in well-being and quality of life.

Smart Companion, developed by Fraunhofer AICOS (The Fraunhofer Portugal Research Center for Assistive Information and Communication Solutions), was specifically designed to address older users' goals and needs. It replaces the default Android Launcher with a customizable Android application. Once installed, it supports users in their daily activities and connects them to relatives or caregivers. It is like a Swiss Army knife, from which users can choose the functionalities they need.

Begun in 2010, Smart Companion has enabled older adults, especially those who are novice technology users, to perform common mobile phone tasks and to have a companion supporting their daily activities. It also allows users and their relatives, caregivers, or physicians to be remotely connected at all times. This improves users' sense of self-confidence and security, and keeps caregivers informed.

Smart Companion researchers have relied on the principles of participatory design and cocreation with older adults, who are designing their own future technology. The team strives to achieve exceptional levels of accessibility and usability, aiming for empowerment rather than patronization. Seniors have been involved in the process from the earliest stages of requirements gathering, participating in activities such as focus groups, observations, questionnaires, and interviews.

A typical development cycle begins with a user research phase, followed by the creation of low-fidelity prototypes (Figure 11.5). Data collected during initial stages of the design process is of great importance to inform the consequent design. Researchers then produce prototypes, which are iteratively improved and evaluated with senior participants (Figure 11.6).

Figure 11.5.
An assortment of paper prototypes.

The COLABORAR user network

The need for close cooperation with older adults led to the creation of "COLABORAR," a user network. Signed protocols with health-care, day-care, or home-care institutions secured the conditions for researchers' ongoing contact with older adults. Benefiting from this user network, Smart Companion has been evaluated in more than 250 usability sessions, conducted either off-site or at Franhofer AICOS's facilities.

Our usability sessions focus on content, navigation, interaction, and graphic design. They assure efficiency, learnability, and memorability of the component applications, reduce error in action/task performance, and promote user satisfaction.

Figure 11.6.
Senior testing paper prototypes.

Deciding what applications and features were to be included in the solution was a result of bringing together the creativity of older adults with insights from the researchers at Fraunhofer AICOS. Through this process, we arrived at the concept of a tool that would assist its users in a broad and ever-expanding set of activities and environments. From core functionality to more meaningful and specific applications, every detail has been created, discussed, designed, and evaluated with the feedback of real users. Over the past 5 years, the differences between consecutive versions of the Smart Companion screen to the next have been quite substantial.

Developing the basic metaphor

When the project began in 2010, smartphones were less prevalent than they are now. Seniors tended to have difficulties when first interacting with touch screen devices. The Smart Companion team felt that the first time seniors activated a smartphone screen by unlocking it, their chances for success could be improved by using a metaphor they would immediately understand.

In our usability studies, we first tried using zipper and lock metaphors. Those evolved to threading a needle or scoring a goal. Later, the design was simplified to the current version: using a key on a lock. The metaphor-based screen developed to accommodate seniors' feedback and to introduce new relevant information and functionality. Figure 11.7 shows the different versions of the Unlocker screen.

Evolution of the contacts application

Basic applications such as the Contacts and Messages were designed to allow seniors to easily focus on the task they are performing. The Contacts List included arrows to navigate the list, since scrolling in a touch screen was still a novel and difficult gesture for most seniors. A zoomed-in version of the selected contact was shown on the top part of the screen. It was also a button for getting access to the Contact's details.

Figure 11.7.
Different versions of the Unlocker screen, from initial to current.

As our target audience became more comfortable with touch screen interactions, we replaced the up-and-down arrows with scroll lists (Figure 11.8).

Figure 11.8.
Contact List screens, initial and scrollbar versions.

We provided users with the minimal options needed, so they could follow step-by-step guidelines through a use case completion. In Contacts, for example, they were given the choice of View Contacts or Add Contact (Figure 11.9).

Figure 11.9.
First and second iterations of Contacts screen, showing option View Contacts and Add Contact.

Over time, our seniors indicated that it was too complicated to reach the Contacts List. A better solution was to merge the View Contacts and Add Contact screens (middle image, Figure 11.10).

Figure 11.10.
Contacts List with scrollbar, version showing merged View and Add options, and final version with color.

Transformation of the Smart Companion look-and-feel

Another aspect that changed over time was the look and feel of some elements, particularly buttons. Color was introduced in the last iteration of Smart Companion, as shown in Figure 11.11. This refreshed the overall design and made it more appealing to users.

Figure 11.11.
Several iterations of the main Launcher screen.

The main screen of the application—the Launcher—has also changed to reflect user feedback and experience. One example was the replacement of navigational arrows with a scroll gesture. In a second iteration of the Launcher, tabs were introduced. However, as our seniors never fully understood them, we removed the tabs. Launcher buttons were enlarged, and icon colors were associated with application groups (e.g., red for help or emergency, blue for communication, etc.). The most recent iteration featured a less-intrusive status bar (Figure 11.11).

Current status

When AICOS presented Smart Companion during the AAL Forum 2012 (Active and Assisted Living Forum) in Eindhoven, it caught the attention of Gociety (www.gociety.eu). Gociety is a Dutch company interested in business opportunities related to the "Best Ager" (55+) market.

In 2013, AICOS and Gociety worked together to create a solid solution based on Smart Companion. The current solution—commercialized as GoLivePhone—has been thoroughly tested with end users and satisfies the requirements of both end users and secondary users (caregivers). GoLivePhone includes a rebranded and improved Smart Companion, as well as GoLiveAssist, a companion website. Among other things, GoLiveAssist allows caregivers to manage older adults' smartphone settings, contacts, photos, and alerts.

Further information about Smart Companion can be found at smartcompanion.projects.fraunhofer.pt.

ASSISTANT, A SUPPORT TOOL FOR ELDERS USING PUBLIC TRANSPORTATION

Stefan Carmien, Tecnalia, San Sebastian, Spain

Samuli Heinonen, VTT, Espoo, Finland

ASSISTANT (www.aal-assistant.eu) helps European elders maintain their independence by supporting their use of public transportation. ASSISTANT builds its technology on platforms already familiar to older people: the PC and the mobile phone. It guides users to their destination by combining web-based trip planning with a Personal Navigation Device (PND). The PND is a stripped-down smartphone, which can simply make phone calls and run the ASSISTANT app.

ASSISTANT provides the traveller with relevant information, at the right time, and in the appropriate format. It identifies which vehicle to board, signals the vehicle's arrival, and informs the user when to exit the vehicle. The design has been guided by a Design for Failure approach, which means accommodating both human error and failure of system components. Our design motto was "Things always go wrong; why not build a system around this?"

The main target group for the project is mobile older people, particularly those travelling to unfamiliar places or just beginning to use public transportation. By mobile older people, we mean those who may need a little help to use transport: for instance, finding the bus stop, knowing when to get off the bus, or reaching their destination after getting off the bus.

ASSISTANT was funded by the Active and Assisted Living (AAL) Programme of the information and communication technology for active and health ageing. The consortium consisted of researchers from Finland, UK, France, Austria, and Spain. We had experts in public transit, end user advocacy, middleware and systems programming, mobile and distributed system development, embedded systems, and human computer interface design.

The project ran from June 2012 to June 2015. Initial end user and stakeholder requirement gathering was performed in San Sebastian (Spain), Paris, Vienna, and Helsinki. Pilot (formative evaluation) and Prototype (summative evaluation) were performed in 2014 and 2015 in the same cities. ASSISTANT followed an open user-centric and cocreative design. Short, iterative cycles of the user interfaces assured the end results would earn user approval.

Differences between ASSISTANT and other public transit systems

ASSISTANT provides safety for the traveller by monitoring, identifying, and resolving conditions, such as batteries dying, phone getting lost, or sleeping past the intended exit. With one touch, it also allows users to reprogram the smartphone route (to return to either their home or the route starting point) or to summon help. If the phone itself is inoperable, the ASSISTANT system can send an SMS message to an escalating sequence of caregivers (e.g., daughter, doctor, emergency services).

ASSISTANT also offers last kilometre guidance. Pedestrian GPS urban navigation guidance systems are notorious for unreliability. The ASSISTANT design team created a threefold robust guidance system, including (1) a smartphone-sized map from the stop to the final destination, (2) an "as the crow flies" compass showing the general direction of the destination, and (3) monitoring of the user's position (to warn them if they have gone the wrong way for more than a minute, with a compass pointing the right way).

Two versions of the ASSISTANT server help bridge the digital divide that can exist within smaller transportation agencies. The first uses data from large agencies' API (application program interface); the other uses open source systems for smaller transit systems.

ASSISTANT provides an easily configurable route editor, smartphone application, and route selection behavior via a user preferences selection page. If a user finds the options daunting, they can choose a theme from a set of typical user types.

ASSISTANT uses the real-time location data of both the user and the vehicle. If neither one is available, the system informs the user, switches to schedule-based guidance, and requests user confirmation at each stage.

Devices are easily connected in ASSISTANT. The design guideline is to ensure that both devices are easy to use, and both the interface and data transfer will be seamless and transparent.

A phased and iterative approach

The preliminary concept of operation consisted of a set of practical tasks to perform during the project's scenarios. A user questionnaire and a recorded user observation complemented the preliminary tests to gain insights and develop the project's architecture and tools further to the pilot level.

The pilot level evaluation was formative, testing the system's basic functionality and interface, and gathering information for application improvement and debugging. Besides utility, the focus of this evaluation phase was on ergonomic aspects. Results of this phase's user tests were used to verify and validate the design specifications, and to further develop the ASSISTANT system to the prototype level.

During the Prototype phase, the system design and architecture were further refined, and the final ASSISTANT integrated system was developed. The second field trial was summative, evaluating the whole system with respect to the original design requirements and user needs. This evaluation was held in an uncontrolled environment: participants took the ASSISTANT application home and tested it in real conditions.

To harmonize the testing, users received identical training at their local trial sites before taking ASSISTANT home. During training, they were given a brief scripted introduction to the system and smartphone. Then the participants spent the next week on their day-to-day activities, using the ASSISTANT system for their use of public transportation. At the end of the week, a feedback session was held to collect the results of the trial.

Participants used trial evaluators as the contact for route problems. Additionally, a member of the development team supported each trial evaluator. The development team pretested the system several weeks before the summative trials, resulting in capturing and debugging problems with the integration of the new system modules.

Every PND interaction between the phone and system was captured in a log file, and participants completed post-trial questionnaires. These provided valuable insights for the pre-commercialization phase, which was to begin right after the project's end.

The initial focus groups were shown three different mock-ups for both the PND and the route editor. Their responses were collated to build the pilot interfaces. The process of gathering research-based design guidelines for small device interfaces for elders resulted in a metapaper [Carmien and Garzo, 2014]. The guidelines were used as the basis of a heuristic evaluation of the PND pilot interface. Similarly, the Route Editor's browser–based interface was evaluated and refined using WCAG and results of research on websites for elders. Table 11.1 is a sample of the set of updates made to the system before the prototype trials.

Table 11.1	Usability Issues Observed and Resolved in the Personal Navigation Device and Web-Based Route Editor
Observation	**Solution**
Personal Navigation Device	
Compass was not always accurate.	Need to recalibrate after phone reboot.
Real-time information was accurate, but presentation to users in GUI was not clear enough. Real-time information works perfectly with trams and some bus lines.	Tweaks needed for real-time information representation in GUI. Information format in GUI specified.
Default walking speed is not appropriate in urban environment.	Need to use lower speed for default walking speed while creating routes.
System does not work with metros.	Navigation module improved.
Error trapping: Missed bus stop etc., tested with no errors	No need for further development.
GUI: 1. HELP screen layout needs improvement. 2. Currently loaded routes have unneeded EXIT button. Unclear that old route can be opened to see details. 3. Too many buttons in Settings screen	GUI: 1. HELP screen revised, adding CALL and SMS buttons. 2. Currently loaded routes layout redesigned. 3. Unnecessary buttons removed from Settings screen.
Some tram stops were so close to each other that app does not always recognize the correct one.	Need to add text on the screen that tells the current stop ID while awaiting the vehicle at the stop.
Map/Compass button is not placed well in Navigation screen.	Call button replaced by Map/Compass button. Call button moved to the HELP screen.

Continued

Table 11.1	Usability Issues Observed and Resolved in the Personal Navigation Device and Web-Based Route Editor—cont'd	
Observation		**Solution**
Web-Based Route Editor		
Translation errors observed.		Translation errors fixed.
Estimated time to reach first bus stop was too short.		It was improved, based on research paper.
Tested option of sending SMS contact accessing from different ways. It did not work in Spain.		It was because in Spain we were using special characters (accents). Developers fixed it.
The message for getting off the bus was confusing: "You should get off at the next stop" was not clear.		Changed message to "This is your second-to-last stop."

The web-based component

Figures 11.12 and 11.13 show the web-based component of ASSISTANT. The Route Editor Preference Tab shown in Figure 11.12 allows customization of the PND and the route editor interface and functions. The same tab also provides templates, or "themes," with complex, preset options for general types of end users.

Figure 11.12.
ASSISTANT Route Editor Preferences tab.

From the Route Creation page shown in Figure 11.13, the user can enter their start and finish points, as well as the date and time (either arrival or departure) for the route being generated. To the right of that panel, a high-level map of the offered route is displayed.

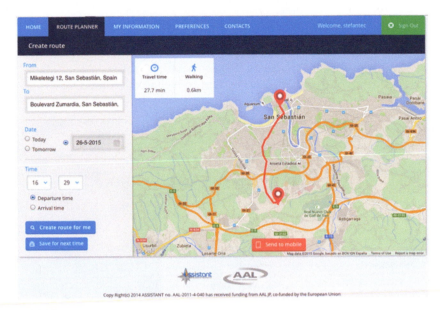

Figure 11.13.
The Route Planner page on the web-based route editor.

The Personal Navigation Device screen

Several screens of the PND are shown in Figure 11.14. From left to right:

- Error screen on PND while user is en route: This informs the user that they are possibly lost and offers the option of creating a new route or requesting help via SMS or phone call.
- Help Requested screen: When the user brings this up, it presents a series of options for the user.
- Typical SMS message sent to a contact's cell phone. In this case, the system is informing a caregiver that it has detected that the end user may have a problem. The system also tells the caregiver where the end user was when the potential problem was detected.
- Compass Guidance: This appears during the first and last kilometer of the trip.

Figure 11.14.
Sample Personal Navigation Device screens.

Figure 11.15 shows ASSISTANT in use. From left to right:

- Guidance for underground metro use, giving instructions based on the metro schedule.
- Photos of the PND in use in San Sebastian, Spain.
- Field trials of the ASSISTANT system in Helsinki, Finland.

Figure 11.15.
ASSISTANT in action.

Critical to the success of ASSISTANT is the coordination of the various complex parts of the interlacing systems. Following this is the careful design of the route editor and smartphone applications. Designing small-screen graphical interfaces for seniors is a nontrivial task. Other challenges include selecting the minimal information needed, personalizing the information to accommodate a wide range of needs, and retaining enough similarity in use to make the applications usable by those who may be on the "wrong" side of the digital divide.

SUBARU AUTO INFOTAINMENT SYSTEM

Sean Hazaray, Subaru Research & Development

Really, just how bad is last place?

In 2013, JD Power released their annual Navigation Satisfaction results focused on comparing in-vehicle infotainment systems across 26 brands, with Subaru claiming the infamous "last place." Several other media outlets had similarly low opinions; *TheStreet* spent most of its review of Subaru's Forester ranting about the infotainment system, which it called "a fatal flaw" [Wahlman, 2015]. Customers were filing record numbers of complaints about the infotainments with the Subaru dealerships.

In Consumer Reports' 2015 Annual Auto Reliability Survey, infotainment systems "continued to be among the top issues reported by new car owners" [Hard, 2015]. Clearly, (intuitive) infotainment systems matter to car owners. This all added up to a none-too-subtle indication that we needed to do something about our in-car tech and infotainment.

What does "intuitive" mean for Subaru buyers?

But what exactly makes a car infotainment system "intuitive"? For us, the answer lay with the customers, or more specifically, our Subaru customers. What do we know about Subaru customers?

Examining data obtained through about 20,000 customer surveys, we learned that Subaru buyers were older than we had expected. The median age was above 50, and a significant percentage indicated that they were retired. To us, this finding seemed strange, if not flat-out wrong.

After all, isn't Subaru's marketing directed at rock-climbers, kayakers, and other adventurers? In other words, the powerful and sexy Millennial generation? Missing the target demographic wasn't only our problem, but also it was common throughout the industry. This may seem very nearsighted, but can be explained by the following:

- Both the Subaru team members and the suppliers' team members were relatively young (average age was late 20s–early 30s) and very tech-savvy. It was difficult for us to relate to people who weren't as dependent on technology as we were.
- With Subaru's heavy bias toward outdoor and adventurer commercials, we tended to have a "feel" for who was buying the cars: younger people. (But, as the marketing data proved, we were quite mistaken.)
- The latest automotive features are technically very complex. Even our "older" team members were still engineers, and they had developed intimate working knowledge of the features. They simply couldn't understand why consumers couldn't learn, or weren't willing to learn, the features.

We took this data and did something unheard of in the auto industry: we designed our infotainment system for older consumers, rather than for consumers in their early-to-mid-20s.

Groundbreaking methodology (at least, for the auto industry)

Our design process was unique, and not just because it focused on older consumers. One of our most significant decisions was to go for a design that was familiar, rather than "cutting edge" or "unique."

Intuitive = Familiar: "Intuitive" is difficult to define, and the definition differs for everyone. However, one way to approximate "intuitive" is to focus on designs already familiar to the user. Thus, by using design motifs and animations that were similar to existing (and popular) devices, the system would be more "intuitive." For these reasons, we pushed a "smartphone-like" design, taking advantage of the ubiquitous nature of smartphones in today's society.

But intuitive design was only one piece of the puzzle. Another critical piece was understanding why easy-to-use products were, in fact, easy to use.

Ease-to-Use > Prioritized Features: Everyone wants an intuitive design, but are they willing to remove the clutter? This can be challenging because of the demographics. If we were to focus on 100% of our customers, then adding every different use case might be justified. However, we were simply focusing on the **majority** of consumers, specifically those who were older and those who were not tech-savvy. Stripping the infotainment system to its core functionality made the user interface quite simple to navigate. This may not satisfy the "power" users or the Millennials, but our usability research showed that not all Millennials are power users—a common misconception.

Consistency. Consistency. Consistency: The most important ingredient in an intuitive design is consistency. If the interface is similar to the iPhone interface, the user can learn and understand the system much more quickly. This is especially important for in-vehicle technology, due to potentially dangerous operating conditions, such as driving at high speeds or in poor weather.

"Agile" Development with a "Waterfall" Timeline: Automotive designs typically use a "waterfall" timeline with clear deadlines for handing off specifications to suppliers. Here, however, we opted for an "agile" development strategy with a focus on iterative testing. We tested each phase of the design with consumers and modified the specification to improve the results for the next round of testing.

An iterative process with constant testing

Making design decisions was challenging, partly because of our inherent bias. In fact, our biased opinions were the biggest obstacle in design. To combat this, we built a number of different prototypes at different stages and completed major usability testing with potential consumers (Figure 11.16).

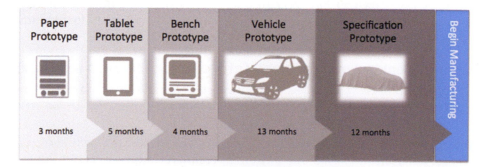

Figure 11.16.
A rough timetable of the progression of prototypes used during development.

Paper prototype: For the beginning of our design process, we humbly started with paper testing or quick mock-ups using paper cutouts. This helped keep the cost very low, while allowing us to brainstorm creative solutions to UI flow issues. With this low-fidelity prototype, we tested across a majority of internal Subaru staff at our main US research facility (about 20 people), and homed in on a design direction.

Although this testing was cheap and easy, a growing concern was the prevalent bias, as internal Subaru staff members were not representative of the Subaru consumer population. Figure 11.17 describes a rough breakdown of the demographics used for the internal testing.

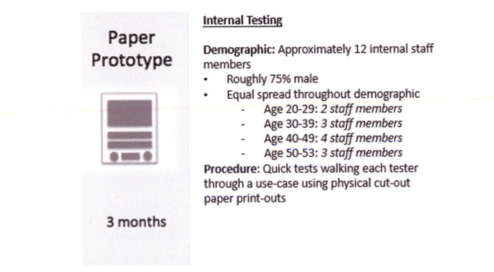

Paper Prototype

3 months

Internal Testing

Demographic: Approximately 12 internal staff members
- Roughly 75% male
- Equal spread throughout demographic
  - Age 20-29: *2 staff members*
  - Age 30-39: *3 staff members*
  - Age 40-49: *4 staff members*
  - Age 50-53: *3 staff members*

Procedure: Quick tests walking each tester through a use-case using physical cut-out paper print-outs

Figure 11.17.
Paper Prototyping was low cost and quick, but had major limitations.

Tablet prototype: Once we had a clear image of the prototype, we developed a simulated version in a tablet app. The fidelity wasn't high, with many images missing and with a number of bugs. However, this helped better visualize some of the more complicated use cases, and we continued to test, primarily using internal staff. Figure 11.18 describes a rough approximation of the procedure of evaluations using tablets.

Bench prototype: Using an automotive-grade processor and display screen, we developed a "bench" prototype that simulated the interior of a vehicle. This made it much clearer to participants that the interface would be inside a car, rather than just on a tablet.

Figure 11.19 describes the background for the first consumer evaluation using the bench unit. In this evaluation, the prototype was compared to a similar, but noticeably different, prototype. Prior to evaluating each prototype, the testers were shown four benchmark vehicles and performed various tests. Although

Internal Testing

Demographic: Approximately 12 internal
staff members
- Roughly 75% male
- Equal spread throughout demographic
  - Age 20-29: *2 staff members*
  - Age 30-39: *3 staff members*
  - Age 40-49: *4 staff members*
  - Age 50-53: *3 staff members*

Procedure: Quick tests walking each tester
through a low-fidelity mock-up similar to
PowerPoint on a tablet

Figure 11.18.
Testing with a tablet helped improved the flow, but was limited in scope with a lack of gestures or complicated use
cases.

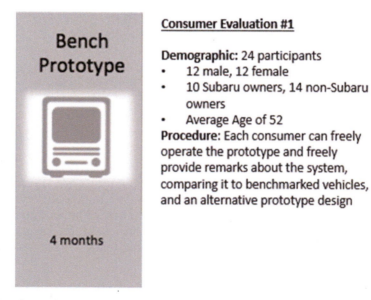

Consumer Evaluation #1

Demographic: 24 participants
- 12 male, 12 female
- 10 Subaru owners, 14 non-Subaru
  owners
- Average Age of 52

Procedure: Each consumer can freely
operate the prototype and freely
provide remarks about the system,
comparing it to benchmarked vehicles,
and an alternative prototype design

Figure 11.19.
Major red flags were identified using a bench prototype.

the evaluation was very short (approximately 10 min per prototype), it helped
determine both the main framework for the UX and the general direction of the
graphic design. Figure 11.20 shows a rendering of a bench unit used at an early
stage of development.

Figure 11.20.
An example rendition of a bench unit at an early stage.

Vehicle prototype: Once the design was further refined, a vehicle prototype was developed to simulate use cases and graphics. This provided the most realistic version of the system. Additionally, consumer behaviors and preferences changed when they saw the concept in a vehicle instead of on a computer screen. For example, safety became much more important, and gestures in the vehicle became much tougher for users to perform. Pictures of the prototype vehicle that was used are shown in Figure 11.21. Although the prototype vehicle did not possess full technical functionality, it could simulate the functionality of all features (such as FM radio and navigation). This provided the clinic's consumers with the illusion of a production vehicle.

Figure 11.21.
The exterior and interior of a prototype vehicle nicknamed "Vader."

Figure 11.22 provides insight into the procedures for the second and third consumer evaluations. The evaluations were completed and designed by two different companies, using different methodologies, to minimize potential bias from the Subaru team. The demographics were matched to Subaru's past data of recent owners.

In the second consumer evaluation, users were free to operate the vehicle prototype for each given use case. Although this was very informative, testers quickly discovered many bugs in the prototype system. The numerous bugs

Vehicle Prototype

13 months

Consumer Evaluation #2

Demographic: 24 participants
- 12 male, 12 female
- 12 Subaru owners, 12 non-Subaru owners
- Balanced by gender, age, income, and education

Procedure: Each consumer is asked to operate through a set of 10 use-cases. The consumer will perform the same tasks through a competitor benchmark vehicle either before or after.

Consumer Evaluation #3

Demographic: 24 participants
- 12 male, 12 female
- 50% over 50 years old
- 100% recent car buyers (within last 2 years)
- Balanced income

Procedure: The vehicle and 3 competitor vehicles are masked and anonymized. Each consumer is walked through a set of 4 main use-cases by an administrator. The consumer will rate how they feel each vehicle's use-case. After the conclusion, the 3 consumers will enter a focus group discussion, and explain their reasoning on why they liked or disliked certain aspects of each vehicle.

Figure 11.22.
The vehicle prototype provided the most realistic experience; consumer's comments were noticeably different in the vehicle environment.

in the prototype significantly impacted the testers' feelings and experiences—especially when compared to a competitor's vehicle, which had the final and stable software.

In the third consumer evaluation, we aimed to prevent the biases of prototype bugs. We masked the prototype vehicle and the three benchmark vehicles to keep the user from identifying the prototype. In this clinic, each tester saw—but could not touch—each use case demonstrated by an administrator in the car. The tester would then rate each use case based on a reference to three masked vehicles. After the evaluation, testers conveyed their reasoning in a small group discussion (three testers and one moderator). Although this helped prevent the bias of the bugs, it wasn't ideal, as the testers did not actually operate the prototype. Due to the ergonomics of the vehicles, it became more of hindrance to the users.

Specification prototype: Next we developed the "specification prototype," which was nearly identical to the final production unit. A design should be pretty locked by this point, as any further changes to the software or hardware would be incredibly expensive. The specification prototype mostly served to validate our design decisions.

Figure 11.23 describes the final consumer testing, which was nearly identical to the third consumer evaluation, but with new competitor vehicles. Although this provided the most realistic prototype, there were many lessons learned from the limitations of the setup. This prototype had many wires running through the system, and the car itself did not look like a fully functional vehicle. The infotainment system was using the same hardware as the production unit, but many users could not get past its "prototype feel."

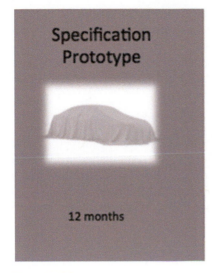

Specification
Prototype

12 months

Consumer Evaluation #4

Demographic: 36 participants
- 18 male, 18 female
- 50% over 50 years old
- 100% recent car buyers (within last 2 years)
- Balanced income
- **Procedure:** The vehicle and 3 competitor vehicles are masked and anonymized. Each consumer is walked through a set of 4 main use-cases by an administrator. The consumer will rate how they feel each vehicle's use-case. After the conclusion, the 3 consumers will enter a focus group discussion, and explain their reasoning on why they liked or disliked certain aspects of each vehicle.

Figure 11.23.
Final consumer testing.

Lessons learned from testing

Automakers continue to design their vehicles for the younger Millennial buyer, despite the fact that typical car buyers are older. The Subaru infotainment system was designed through consumer clinics and usability testing, a unique proposition for the automotive industry. From our consumer testing, some notable insights helped shaped our infotainment system.

Older consumers are not radically different from younger consumers: There is a preconception that consumers aged 40+ struggle with technology more than younger consumers (aged 20–30) do. Although this was evident in the testing, it was not a very reliable predictor of usability.

A more reliable predictor was familiarity with technology. Users who were more familiar with today's popular gadgets, from iPhones to tablets to smart TVs, were much more likely than other users to successfully complete use cases.

Older consumers might complain more, become more frustrated, or be more likely to give up. Their age alone, however, did not make them much less effective at navigating through the system.

Knobs and buttons are critical in the right environment: During the "bench prototype" phase, we tested designs both with and without knobs and hard buttons. The trend in consumer electronics is to reduce and remove knobs and buttons. Consumers didn't mind the lack of knobs and buttons in the earlier paper and tablet prototypes. However, in later prototypes with a full vehicle, consumers demanded these features. This shows the importance of realistic prototypes as early as possible in the development cycle.

Familiar UX framework is paramount to intuitiveness: To design an easy-to-use and intuitive device, it helps to use a model that's already familiar to your target audience. In the case of Subaru's infotainment interface, we leveraged the target audience's existing familiarity with iPhones and Windows PCs. Although this may sound very obvious and reasonable, this is a difficult direction for automakers, who are more inclined to innovate and lead.

> The display feels easy to understand and clear – reminds me of my smartphone – Consumer at clinic

Consumers preferred a smartphone-like design: We established a UX flow similar to the iPhone's, using icons similar to the iPhone's. Consumers had a strong preference for such familiar designs. Figure 11.24 shows an example of consumers preferring iPhone-like icons to those that were more in keeping with the overall theme of the system.

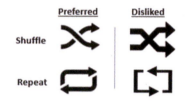

Figure 11.24.
Consumers preferred iconology similar to iPhones and Macs (left) rather than iconology that embodies the general design direction of the system.

Color coding proved to be vital to consumers: We allowed each engineer to design and create their own home screen icons, and let the consumers vote for their favorites. Overwhelmingly, the consumers chose designs that used color to differentiate categories, displayed schematically in Figure 11.25. The major trade-off is that the color coding makes the design resemble children's toys such as "Fisher-Price" and may not be the most appropriate for a luxury vehicle.

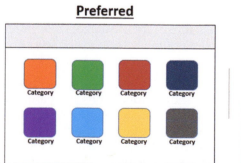

Figure 11.25.
Colored and uncolored schematic displays of categories.

The colors are great – very intuitive – Consumer at clinic

The icons look cheesy – a bit Fisher Price – Consumer at clinic

US consumers trusted a map interface that resembled Google Maps and Garmin's classic UI: Consumers had an overwhelmingly positive response to styling cues from Google Maps and Garmin. Trust has already been established between users and these successful mapping companies. Even if the core navigation algorithm is completely different, consumers preferred a styling similar to Google Maps, with the green boxes and gray/beige mapping color scheme.

This was particularly clear when conducting A/B testing, where Google Map's styling was significantly preferred 75% of the time over Apple Maps (21%) and the TomTom.

From our internal evaluation, we believe this is because Google Maps and Garmin have a significant market share in the US, where their products can be considered the de facto experience for navigation. However, we feel the results could not be replicated in China, where Google Maps has a very small market share. Figure 11.26 shows the final software in the vehicle.

Figure 11.26.
The navigation UI was styled to consumers' preference for a Google-like experience.

Basing design decisions on consumer testing

One of the most important aspects of this development strategy was buying into the value of consumer testing. By doing so, we acknowledged our own opinions were inherently biased and resolved to find the UX issues experienced by our actual users.

Reducing biased opinions: With a hunger for constructive criticism, we learned that the best way for unbiased opinions was to use two different third-party companies to conduct usability testing. During the bench prototype and vehicle prototype, we organized three major consumer testing studies. Additionally, we had about 10 "expert consultants" evaluate the system, including magazine journalists, academic professors, UX consultants, and automotive gurus. If a number of consumers and experts had the same issues or discussed the same complaints, we understood that these UX problems needed to be solved.

Low-cost internal studies are great initially, but are "somewhat biased": The internal studies certainly predicted a number of these problems, but an important finding was that our internal staff members were not a perfect reflection of actual Subaru owners. Specifically, our internal and local staff knew a lot more about cars than most Subaru owners. This may sound obvious, but too often, it is overlooked by automakers.

Recommendations and key findings

Based on our user testing, we are very confident in our design. We really believe we achieved some fantastic results, mainly due to our insistence of testing at each step of the process. Although we can't share the results of our product (because it hasn't been released as of time of writing), here are the top lessons we learned:

"The customer is always right": If need be, conduct surveys and testing to truly understand who your customer is. Don't dismiss the behaviors and attitudes of the participants in your usability tests. They're real.

Think "use cases" rather than "features": Once you understand your customer, don't focus on "features." Instead, determine which features are necessary to help your customer complete important use cases.

"Easy-to-use" is a trade-off: An "easy-to-use" device could be considered boring or even childish. However, simplicity can also be a real positive, which is arguably more important for a device driving 70+ MPH on the highway.

Know your consumer and build interfaces based on FAMILIAR design: The final design (Figure 11.27) has clear inspirations from Apple iPhone, Google

Figure 11.27.
The design is featured in the 2017 Impreza (left), which uses a layout of buttons designed to be familiar to the consumers (right).

Map, Garmin's Navigation systems, and Windows XP. Because those devices have strong resonance with Subaru consumers, our consumers can enter the car *already* knowing how to use the system. However, if we were to build a device for a different consumer population, it would be important to learn what devices a majority of those consumers used to strategize the design.

Consumers expectations are constantly changing: Consumer evaluations should be viewed as a "snapshot" of today's consumer, rather than a rule. For example, during our initial testing, many consumers could not understand gestures, such as swiping through a list by using a dragging motion with one finger. However, many consumers in the later tests had a better understanding of gestures. In fact, even some of the older consumers *expected* gestures.

We suspect that this change of expectations was due to the increasing penetration of smartphones in the US marketplace. The target population is always changing because the environment is always changing: newer gadgets, the latest apps, and more futuristic movies.

At the time of the study, smartphone market share was split evenly between Apple and Android users. However, Android's surge in increasing market share in recent times is a variable that can impact consumer's expectations for future development.

Final remarks

At the time of this write-up, the system launching in the 2017 Impreza has not yet entered the market and faced consumers, so we are unsure of the response from actual consumers. Based on consumer clinics, we certainly have an idea of their first impressions, but a 10-minute evaluation at a consumer clinic is likely to produce a different reaction than owning the product for an extended duration of time. Regardless, we are optimistic that our testing will prove beneficiary, and we're looking forward to any negative feedback. Yes, negative (!), because armed with this information, we will make sure to build a better next generation that addresses those concerns.

VIRTUAL THIRD-AGE SIMULATOR FOR WEB ACCESSIBILITY

Teresa D. Gilbertson, PhD, Loughborough University, UK

Introduction

The Web Content Accessibility Guidelines (WCAG 2.0) [W3C-WCAG2.0, 2008] provide best practice advice for making accessible websites, and are freely available from the World Wide Web Consortium (W3C). However, these guidelines are often centred on making sure that websites can be used by people using ATs (Assistive Technologies), such as screen readers. Often, they are also quite complex and confusing.

The W3C has also given advice specific to how the WCAG guidelines apply to older people in the Web Accessibility Initiative: Ageing Education and Harmonisation Project (WAI-AGE) [W3C-WAI-AGE, 2010]. Unfortunately, due to the structure of the original guidelines, much of the advice most suited to older people is not prioritized. As a result, the advice given is somewhat inaccessible for novice web designers and for those not familiar with the needs of people with age-related capability change.

The Virtual Third-Age Simulator for Web Accessibility was part of a PhD [Gilbertson, 2014] and built on earlier[3] research [Gilbertson, 2015] that showed:

1. designers (indeed most people in the web industry) have a poor understanding of age-related change and
2. that affects how a person experiences an interface/website.

Neither age nor experience was associated with a web professional or designer seeing age-related change as an accessibility issue. The goal of the third-age virtual simulator was to see if the use of simulation could improve professionals' attitudes toward, and understanding of, how aging affects the user.

Overview of simulator

The simulator contained six lessons dealing with age-related sensory changes and some common age-related conditions, plus a seventh, summary lesson:

1. Vision focusing changes associated with aging (presbyopia/far-sightedness)
2. Color and contrast vision changes associated with aging
3. Age-related diseases affected vision (for example: diabetic retinopathy; age-related macular degeneration)
4. Age-related hearing changes (for example: high frequency hearing loss; tinnitus (ringing in the ears))
5. Age-related motion changes (such as bradykinesia/slowness of movement; tremor)
6. Age-related changes to cognition (such as less ability to ignore distractions; increased cognitive load)
7. A summary, bringing all the lessons together and showing how having multiple conditions can amplify the effect of each of the conditions experienced

Each lesson introduced the condition, presented an activity involving a simulation of the condition, provided an explanation of why web professionals should be aware of the condition presented, and gave guidance on how web professionals could help ameliorate the effects of such conditions using good design practices. Parts of a sample lesson are shown in Figures 11.28–11.31.

---

3 Gilbertson's dissertation was completed in 2014, but the paper describing her earlier research was not published until 2015.

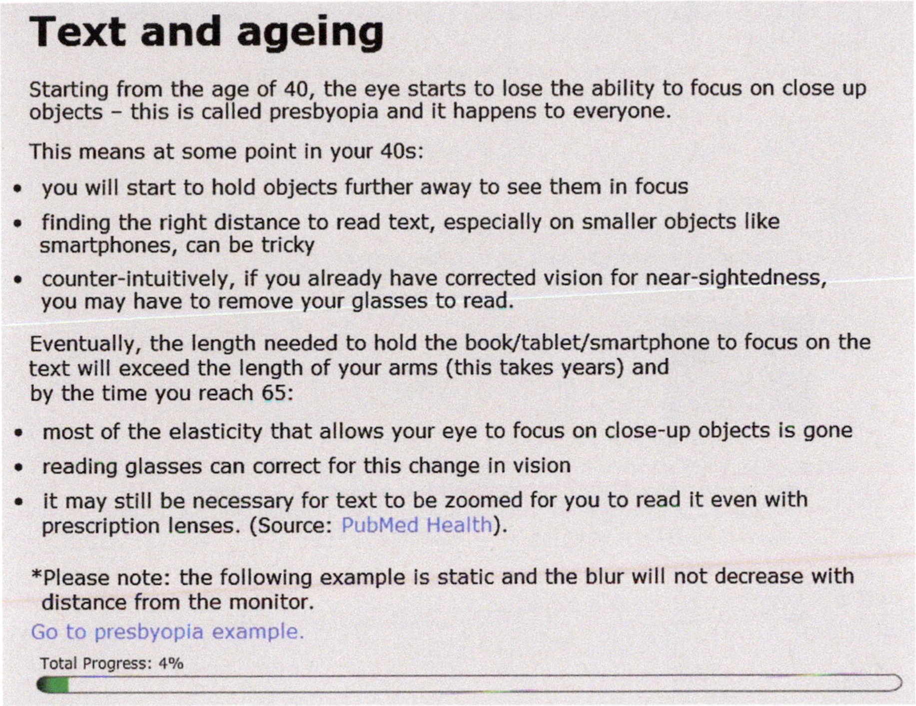

Text and ageing

Starting from the age of 40, the eye starts to lose the ability to focus on close up objects – this is called presbyopia and it happens to everyone.

This means at some point in your 40s:

- you will start to hold objects further away to see them in focus
- finding the right distance to read text, especially on smaller objects like smartphones, can be tricky
- counter-intuitively, if you already have corrected vision for near-sightedness, you may have to remove your glasses to read.

Eventually, the length needed to hold the book/tablet/smartphone to focus on the text will exceed the length of your arms (this takes years) and by the time you reach 65:

- most of the elasticity that allows your eye to focus on close-up objects is gone
- reading glasses can correct for this change in vision
- it may still be necessary for text to be zoomed for you to read it even with prescription lenses. (Source: PubMed Health).

*Please note: the following example is static and the blur will not decrease with distance from the monitor.

Go to presbyopia example.

Total Progress: 4%

Figure 11.28.
Introduction to "Text and Ageing" lesson.

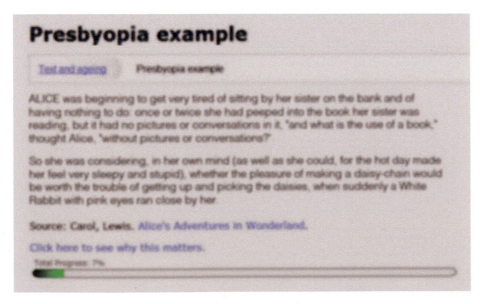

Figure 11.29.
Presbyopia (farsightedness) example from "Text and Ageing" lesson. Note: blurring is intentional.

Why does this matter?

Text and ageing 〉 Presbyopia example 〉 Why does this matter?

Why is this the problem for designers and developers if people can just buy glasses? There are a number of reasons.

Presbyopia develops slowly and can take up to a decade for you to go from having no presbyopia to you needing glasses to help you read. Reasons for not getting glasses when you first notice presbyopia may include:

- If you already wear glasses you may not want to buy bifocals until absolutely necessary
- cost of bifocals
- worry that the glasses will make you **look** weak and old
- worry that the glasses will make you **feel** weak and old.

Click the image below to play video about reading glasses:

Read the transcript here

So, in the video above we see a very strong character given pause due to his own sense of weakness caused by the simple fact that he needs to wear reading glasses. While this is a fun example, the idea that needing reading glasses can cause people to feel uncomfortable is an all too real experience.

Go to next page: How can I help?

Total Progress: 11%

Figure 11.30.
"Why does this matter?" screen from "Text and Ageing" lesson.

How can I help?

Text and ageing 〉 Presbyopia example 〉 Why does this matter? 〉 How can I help?

You can help reduce the effects of presbyopia by:

- Making sure that text can be zoomed.
- Being aware that many older people don't know how to zoom using their browser
- keeping the font size to the default of the browser or no lower than 85% of the default setting (Source:WebAim).

Arial 12 point text and Times New Roman 12 point text with presbyopia

There was nothing so very remarkable in that, nor did Alice think it so very much out of the way to hear the Rabbit say to itself, "Oh dear! Oh dear! I shall be too late!" But when the Rabbit actually took a watch out of its waistcoat-pocket and looked at it and then hurried on, Alice started to her feet, for it flashed across her mind that she had never before seen a rabbit with either a waistcoat-pocket, or a watch to take out of it, and, burning with curiosity, she ran across the field after it and was just in time to see it pop down a large rabbit-hole, under the hedge. In another moment, down went Alice after it!	There was nothing so very remarkable in that, nor did Alice think it so very much out of the way to hear the Rabbit say to itself, "Oh dear! Oh dear! I shall be too late!" that when the Rabbit actually took a watch out of its waistcoat-pocket and looked at it and then hurried on, Alice started to her feet, for it flashed across her mind that she had never before seen a rabbit with either a waistcoat-pocket, or a watch to take out of it, and, burning with curiosity, she ran across the field after it and was just in time to see it pop down a large rabbit-hole, under the hedge. In another moment, down went Alice after it!

In the above example, although both fonts are the same size, the even shape of the sans-serif font is more readable.

Other ways to improve readability of your content is to:

- avoid writing words in all capitals.
- avoid overuse of italics and underlines.
- use san serif fonts ex. Verdana, Arial
- leave text with a ragged right margin due to limitations of computer-based text justification.

Figure 11.31.
"How can I help?" screen from "Text and Ageing" lesson.

The simulator also included a web browser (Figure 11.32), which allowed the user to go online and apply a number of conditions to any web page of their choosing. All of the conditions in the lessons could be simulated in the browser. The user also could increase or decrease the severity of the condition simulated.

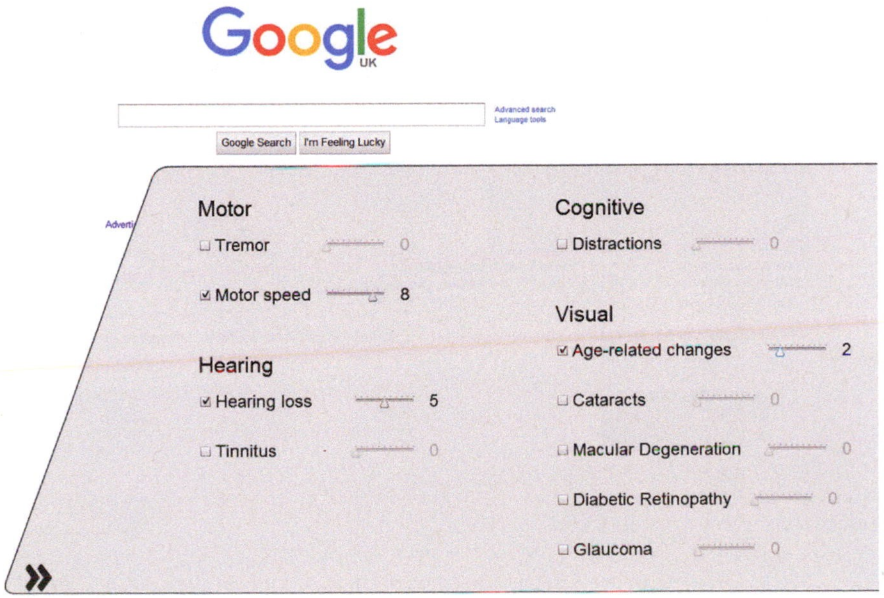

Figure 11.32.
Interface for using the simulator in a web browser.

Online instructions for calibrating the eye tracker are shown in Figure 11.33. The eye locator graphic, which tracked calibration, is shown in Figure 11.34. The eye tracker was used to move any visual disturbances in line with the users' vision.

That is, the simulated impairment affected whichever part of the screen the user was looking at, at any given moment (Figure 11.35). The use of the eye tracker made the visual simulations appear as realistic as possible. This marked a step up in fidelity of previous simulators, which did not have the ability to move with the user's gaze (the simulation was only shown on a fixed image of the screen).

The evaluation of the impact of the Virtual Third-Age Simulator was aimed at both people working in the web industry (including project managers and content authors, as well as designers and developers) and students who were taking web design/development courses at the Bachelor or Master's level. The project was carried out by the PhD candidate at Loughborough University and at

How to Calibrate

Please sit facing forward about 60cm from the screen.
Get the pair of eyes graphic in the middle of the green circle. Keep your head as still as possible during calibration.
Press the "Calibrate" button when you are ready to start.

Look at the white target circle and follow it with your eyes only
When the current point is calibrated, the circle will move to the next point
There are 9-12 points in total.

When completed check the calibrabration. If you recieve a score less than 'Good' or 'Perfect' please calibrate again.

Figure 11.33.
Instructions for calibrating the eye tracker.

How to Calibrate

Please sit facing forward about 60cm from the screen.
Get the pair of eyes graphic in the middle of the green circle. Keep your head as still as possibl
Press the "Calibrate" button when you are ready to start.

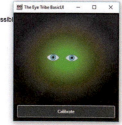

Look at the white target circle and follow it with your eyes only
When the current point is calibrated, the circle will move to the next point
There are 9-12 points in total.

When completed check the calibrabration. If you recieve a score less than 'Good' or 'Perfect' please calibrate again.

Figure 11.34.
Eye locator graphic for tracking calibration.

Figure 11.35.
How Google's homepage might look to a person with AMD (age-related macular degeneration).

businesses in the East Midlands during early 2014. The candidate had considerable previous experience working on large-scale web and virtual learning environment (VLE) projects. The evaluation had two phases, a usability/validation phase and an evaluation phase.

For the usability phase, three doctors and one high school–level media teacher tested the simulator. Each of the testers was informed that the test would take 40 minutes to an hour to complete, including discussion time. The system was launched for them, and the developer was present. The testers were observed interacting with the device and encouraged to mention any interaction or fidelity concerns as they arose in an informal think-aloud protocol.

Notes were taken during each test after each simulation presented, and evaluators were asked whether the simulated impairment conformed to their medical knowledge. Any problems noted by the developer in terms of bugs or interaction difficulties were also noted. The comments from the testers also helped to determine the minimum acceptable calibration output of four out of five stars on the calibration screen ("good" or "perfect"). Any other comments added by the testers were noted and informed the next iteration of the software. The simulator interface was updated after each usability test, so the testing/validation conformed to a spiral-type, iterative development model.

These testers were consulted on whether what they read and experienced matched their medical knowledge of the conditions discussed. The teacher was asked whether the information met the intended learning objectives in a way that younger people would find engaging. A secondary benefit to having the doctors for validation was that they had a good level of IT literacy (current medical training involves VLE use), a commitment to lifelong learning, and experience with peer teaching. The same sessions also served to validate the UI of the content and to identify any major interaction barriers.

After conducting the tests, the following usability improvements were made:

- Addition of a progress bar
- Inclusion of breadcrumbs to make current page more obvious
- Improvement to eye tracker instructions

The main barrier encountered by testers was in the amount of information presented. It was noted that all of the doctors skimmed the information presented, which was initially quite text heavy. As a result, the text content was reduced by about half, and bullet points replaced prose. The text and media information presented was used to introduce the conditions simulated and then to explore why it was important to understand how people experience these conditions. Suggestions followed on how to make simple changes to increase accessibility.

In this way an introduction and debrief for each of the simulations was included within the structure of the software. The introduction to the simulation was important in allowing the user to make an informed choice about whether they wished to proceed with the simulation. The debrief was similarly important in keeping participants mindful of the aim of the simulator: to provide information and examples of techniques that ameliorate the effects of age-related capability changes, rather than fostering pity.

Evaluation phase

The evaluation phase tested whether the software had any impact on attitudes toward accessibility and aging, as well as on participants' intention to use age-aware design practices in future projects. Questionnaires about user attitude toward aging and accessibility were given pre- and post-simulator use.

The findings showed that the simulator did have an effect on changing the attitude to aging and accessibility. The attitude changed from one of believing that technology and accessibility would only be a problem for the current older generation, to one of understanding that changes related to aging will have an ongoing effect on the use of technology.

Several participants mentioned that they enjoyed the simulator. In general, they found it "useful" and "enlightening." The simulator also helped in raising awareness of age-specific guidelines and good design practices for elder-friendly user interfaces.

Excellent and terrifying if you are over 40. – A study participant

In terms of the impact of the simulations, people responded that there were "some good illustrative examples." Another called the simulation an "eye opener" about what older people could potentially face. Two mentioned that it would make them think about their own designs more in terms of accessibility for older people. The visual simulations using eye tracking were mentioned frequently.

A positive experience — you do not fully realise how various impairments can affect others until you experience them yourself. – A study participant

Others specifically mentioned that they felt "empathy" for older people. The simulations were seen as having "a lot more impact than just reading something," and as helping the participants "understand how hard simple things can be."

The lessons were also well received, with one person saying that, while they had known about general accessibility guidelines, those guidelines do not talk specifically about aging. Another echoed the sentiment, saying it taught "the specifics."

[I now have a] much better appreciation for the struggle of others. Lots I hadn't realised. – A study participant

CHAPTER 12

Summary and Conclusions

In the first chapter, we presented the case for designing for older adults. Both the numbers and percentages of older adults are increasing, especially in developed countries. Older adults' technology usage differs from younger adults' technology usage, and older adults face more challenges in using current digital technology. Some age-related characteristics can contribute to those challenges. Older adults want to maintain their independence and can be at risk of social isolation, health concerns, and limited technology access, so it is very important that we help them become, or remain, digitally engaged. And since digital technology is becoming more necessary to function in today's world, we need to design applications, websites, and appliances that are usable by people of all ages and abilities.

Chapter 1 also mentioned earlier sets of general and age-related design guidelines compiled by other authors, and explained that accessibility guidelines are necessary, but not sufficient, for age-friendly usability. We stated our strategy for the book: presenting age-related characteristics should give you, our readers, a solid understanding of the issues older adult technology users' experience; and deriving usability guidelines from hundreds of relevant publications should give you confidence in those guidelines.

In Chapter 2: Meet Some Older Adults, we discussed what to call older adults and why we chose 50 years of age as a cutoff. We showed how usage of the Internet and various digital devices varies across age. We introduced the concepts of birth generations and technology generations, to help you understand the experience, skills, and knowledge of your intended users. We also introduced the first of many reminders in the book that older adults are a very diverse age group. Chapter 2 ends with images and brief descriptions of six fictional older adults. Although fictional, these individuals are representative of digitally engaged older adults from several developed countries. They are our personas, used throughout the book's chapters to illustrate older adults' experiences with digital technology.

In Chapters 3–10, we described common age-related changes and other ways in which older and younger people differ. Chapters 3–5 focused on sensory changes: Vision, Motor Control, Hearing, and Speech. Chapters 6–9 presented less tangible changes and differences: Cognition, Knowledge, Search, and Attitude. In Chapter 10, we described how to include older adults in your research and design projects. For each category of age differences, we provided guidelines to help older people use digital technology productively and enjoyably.

Designing User Interfaces for an Aging Population. http://dx.doi.org/10.1016/B978-0-12-804467-4.00012-8

Chapter 11, Case Studies, presented five different projects. Most of the projects showed how researchers used older adults in participatory design and in usability evaluation, to iteratively develop age-friendly user interfaces for a variety of devices and applications. The infotainment case study also provided a very clear outline of that project's different phases. The last case study detailed the author's research and development of a third-age simulator, designed to educate designers and managers about the effects of aging on people's user experience.

In this final chapter, we "zoom out" to see a larger picture: how age-related differences interact, handicapping older adults in multiple ways.

We finish with a few parting words on how to use the guidelines in this book to make your products and services usable and useful for older adults.

COMBINATIONS OF AGE DIFFERENCES

As we age, most of us experience changes in *many* of the abilities and attitudes described in Chapters 3–9. We don't just have poorer vision; we have that plus hearing loss, declining motor control, waning strength and stamina, and poorer cognition. Our knowledge and understanding of new technology, and our attitudes toward it, also change.

As we explained in Chapter 4: Motor Control, declining vision and motor abilities can interact to hamper older peoples' hand–eye coordination, which can make a wide variety of computer-related tasks difficult. For example, opening a pull-down menu and selecting one of the options require reading, visual search (if the user has not memorized the menu), and motor control. Similarly, scrolling through a document requires both vision and manual dexterity.

Similarly, we explained in Chapter 6: Cognition that age-related deficits in short-term memory, long-term memory, attention, reasoning, and other aspects of cognition can combine to create multifaceted difficulties for older adults trying to use digital technology. For example, if older people take longer to choose between competing options, it may be because of slower processing speed, declining short-term memory, or a combination of the two.

Interactions between age-related deficits can be even more complex. When we scan a display for a likely route to a goal, our vision, short-term memory, ability to ignore distractions, and long-term memory, all contribute to our task completion time and success. Researchers find that older adults need about 50% more time than younger adults need to complete web tasks, and have lower success rates [Pernice et al., 2013].

Another example of how age-related changes can interact: digital reminders, alerts issued by calendars or alarm clock apps in computers or smartphones. Such reminders are often of little use to older adults, for two reasons:
1. Many older adults have hearing loss, and so don't hear alarms, especially high-pitched ones.
2. Some older adults either don't carry their computers or mobile devices with them, or they power them off when not using them [Grindrod et al., 2014].

Either way, alerts and reminders are useless. Therefore, many older adults don't bother to set reminders or alarms on their computers and smartphones.

 I cannot read the appointments on my phone's calendar because the text is too tiny, and I cannot hear it when it peeps to remind me of an appointment. So I do not use it. I keep a calendar on the kitchen wall and look at it every day, and it works just fine. – Monika

Additional ways age-related differences can interact to compound the difficulties that older adults experience in using digital technology include:

- **Vision + hearing**. Many older adults have both hearing and vision deficits, so they have difficulty understanding videos—even captioned videos.
- **Vision + knowledge**. When people have trouble reading words on a screen due to blurred vision, poor lighting, or glare, they can often guess some of the words based on the overall context. However, if the text is full of technical jargon, people unfamiliar with that jargon—including many older adults—won't understand it and won't be able to guess the words.
- **Hearing + cognition**. Some computers, tablets, and smartphones provide text-to-speech capabilities to allow users to have information read to them. If the reading speed is too *fast*, users with hearing impairments may not be able to follow what is being said. On the other hand, if the reading speed is too *slow*, users with diminished short-term memory capacity will have trouble processing the information [Nunes, 2010].
- **Vision, motor, hearing, cognition + attitude**. Imagine a person using a computer or smartphone to buy something, but struggling because the design fails to accommodate their declining eyesight, motor skills, hearing, or cognition. What happens next depends on the person's level of confidence with digital technology and their attitudes toward it. If they are confident, have a positive attitude toward new technology, and are willing to take risks, they will probably continue trying. However, if they lack confidence, have a negative attitude, or are risk-averse, they will probably give up and either go to a brick-and-mortar store or decide they don't really need what they were trying to buy. Older adults tend to be in the latter group.

Poor Design + Poor Vision + Shaky Hands = Unhappy Customers

One of us was in line at a doctor's office. The patient ahead of us, who was in her mid-70s, was paying for her doctor visit. The young receptionist asked the woman to swipe her credit card in the card reader. The older woman eventually managed to swipe her card through the reader, despite her hand tremors. Next, the screen displayed the amount to be charged and an OK button. The woman said she couldn't read it because she didn't have her glasses. The receptionist, getting annoyed, told her the amount, reached around, and hit OK to display a signature box. The woman wasn't sure what to do. The receptionist said impatiently, "You have to sign." "Sign where?" the woman asked. "There on the screen," said the receptionist. "I can't see it," said the woman. The receptionist just loudly repeated, "You have to sign." The poor woman finally used her shaky finger to make a scribble on the screen. The receptionist reached around again and hit the OK button to finish the transaction. We suspect that neither the receptionist nor the patient would rate the experience favorably.

PARTING WORDS

A few final points before we send you on your way to designing better—meaning more age-friendly—digital products and services.

Design and test with older adults

Definitely test your product or service on actual users before releasing it. Don't succumb to the temptation—or budgetary pressure—to "test in the marketplace." That is far too risky and often leads to few or no customers, out-of-control customer service costs, or a poor reputation.

If your intended audience includes older adults, include some as participants in your usability tests. Test the *whole* user experience, including (if applicable) registration, logging in and out, installation and deinstallation, workflows, common tasks, data backup, incomplete transactions, troubleshooting, and customer support. Even test aspects of your product that you did not create, such as components provided by the OS or development platform, or back-end services upon which your product relies [Campbell, 2015].

Review and discuss what you have learned

If you have read this far, good for you! Loan the book to your work colleagues and urge them to read it. Then discuss it with them. Assess your team's product or service compliance with the guidelines presented in this book. Brainstorm ideas on how your team can make its product or service friendlier, or at least less hostile, to older adults.

What's that, you say? You doubt your team's management will buy into the idea of spending time and resources to make its products or services more age-friendly?

If you skipped Chapter 1 because you felt you didn't need an introduction and wanted to get right to the guidelines, fine, but now would be a good time to go back and read it. Chapter 1 provides facts and figures that should help convince your managers that designing to include older adults will pay off in several ways:

- Higher market acceptance and market share
- Better company reputation and higher customer loyalty
- Lower training and customer support costs

OK, enough said. Go forth and design for all ages!

Appendix: Design Guidelines

VISION

3.1 Maximize legibility of essential text	■ Use large fonts. ■ Use plain fonts. ■ Use mixed case. ■ Make text enlargeable. ■ Make information easy to scan. ■ Use plain backgrounds. ■ Use static text. ■ Leave plenty of space.
3.2 Simplify: Remove unnecessary visual elements	■ Present few calls to action. ■ Keep graphics relevant. ■ Don't distract. ■ Minimize clutter.
3.3 Visual language: Create an effective graphical language and use it consistently	■ Maintain visual consistency. ■ Make controls prominent. ■ Indicate strongly, not subtly. ■ Change links on hover. ■ Mark visited links or not? ■ Label redundantly.
3.4 Use color judiciously	■ Use color sparingly. ■ Mix colors carefully. ■ Use distinguishable link colors. ■ Combine color with other indicators. ■ High contrast. ■ Adjustable contrast.
3.5 Position important content where users will start looking	■ Lay elements out consistently. ■ Place important information front and center. ■ Make error messages obvious.
3.6 Group related content visually	■ Group related items.
3.7 Take care when relying on scrolling	■ Minimize vertical scrolling. ■ Don't require horizontal scrolling.
3.8 Provide text alternatives for nontext content	■ Supplement images and videos with text.

MOTOR CONTROL

4.1 Make sure users can hit targets	Desktop/Laptop Computers	Touch-Screen Devices
	■ Big click targets. ■ Maximize clickable area. ■ Put space between click targets. ■ Big tap targets. ■ Maximize tap target.	■ Big swipe targets. ■ Put space between tap targets? Maybe. ■ Place important tap targets near users' hand. ■ Place swipe targets bottom or right.
4.2 Keep input gestures simple	■ Avoid double click. ■ Avoid drag. ■ Leave menus open. ■ Multilevel menus: avoid or design carefully.	■ Avoid multi-finger gestures.
4.3 Make it obvious when a target has been selected	■ Make feedback obvious. ■ Provide feedback immediately.	
4.4 Minimize the need to use the keyboard	■ Gesture input preferred. ■ Structure user input.	
4.5 For touch-screen devices, provide within-app training on gestures, if possible	■ Provide in-app demos.	
4.6 Allow users plenty of time to complete operations	■ Avoid time-out.	
4.7 Avoid causing physical strain	■ Keep user's body position neutral. ■ Minimize repetition. ■ Minimize movement.	

HEARING AND SPEECH

5.1 Ensure that audio output is audible	■ Avoid high-frequency sounds. ■ Ensure that sounds are loud enough. ■ Make auditory signals long.
5.2 Minimize background noise	■ Avoid distracting sounds.
5.3 Convey important information in multiple ways	■ Supplement images with text. ■ Make alerts multimodal. ■ Provide text-to-speech.
5.4 Allow users to adjust device output	■ Make volume adjustable. ■ Let users replay audio. ■ Make play speed adjustable. ■ Let users select alert sounds. ■ Provide alternative voices.

5.5 Make speech output as normal as possible	■ Not too fast. ■ Avoid robot speech.
5.6 Provide an alternative data entry method for people who cannot use the main one	■ Allow speech input. ■ But don't require speech input.

COGNITION

6.1 Design for simplicity	■ Minimize stimuli.
6.2 Help users maintain focus	■ Present one task at a time. ■ Eliminate distractions. ■ Indicate current task prominently.
6.3 Simplify navigation structure	■ Put most important information up front. ■ Make navigation consistent. ■ Make structure obvious. ■ Keep hierarchies shallow. ■ Make categories unique.
6.4 Clearly indicate the progress and status of operations	■ Lead users step by step. ■ Show what step the user is on. ■ Show progress. ■ Provide immediate, clear feedback.
6.5 Make it easy for users to return to a known and "safe" starting place	■ Provide a link to Home. ■ Provide Next and Back. ■ Provide Undo.
6.6 Let users see where they are at a glance	■ Show current page. ■ Provide a site map. ■ Preserve page appearance.
6.7 Minimize the need for users to manage multiple windows	■ Minimize number of windows. ■ Keep tasks together.
6.8 Avoid burdening users' memory	■ Don't strain working memory. ■ Support recognition and avoid relying on recall. ■ Remind users. ■ Make gestures memorable. ■ Bring task sequences to closure. ■ Avoid modes.
6.9 Minimize impact of errors on users	■ Prevent errors. ■ Allow easy error recovery. ■ Allow users to report problems easily.
6.10 Use terms consistently and avoid ambiguous terminology	■ Same word = same thing; different word = different thing. ■ Same label = same action; different label = different action. ■ Link label = destination name.

Continued

COGNITION—CONT'D

6.11 Use strong words to label page elements	■ Use verbs. ■ Make labels semantically distinctive.
6.12 Use writing style that is concise, plain, and direct	■ Be brief. ■ Keep sentences simple. ■ Get to the point quickly. ■ Make language active, positive, and direct. ■ Be explicit.
6.13 Don't rush users; allow them plenty of time	■ Don't make messages time out. ■ Let users take their time. ■ Make playback speed adjustable.
6.14 Keep layout, navigation, and interactive elements consistent across pages and screens	■ Consistent layout. ■ Consistent controls. ■ Consistent order and labeling. ■ Consistency across related apps.
6.15 Design to support learning and retention	■ Show gestures. ■ Repetition is good. ■ Tell users what to bring to task. ■ Let users reuse previous paths or choices.
6.16 Help users with input	■ Show what's valid. ■ Preformat input fields. ■ Be tolerant. ■ Show what's required. ■ Provide reminders.
6.17 Provide on-screen help	■ Provide easy access to help. ■ Provide context-sensitive online help. ■ Provide help desk chat.
6.18 Arrange information consistent with its importance	■ Prioritize information. ■ Use tables when appropriate.

KNOWLEDGE

7.1 Organize content to match users' knowledge and understanding	■ Group, order, and label content in ways that are meaningful to *users*.
7.2 Use vocabulary familiar to your audience	■ Avoid technical jargon. ■ Spell words out.
7.3 Don't assume the user has a correct mental model of the device, app, or website	■ Design a simple, clear conceptual model. ■ Match users' mental model of navigation space.

7.4 Help users predict what buttons do and where links go	■ Make link labels descriptive.
7.5 Make instructions easy to understand	■ Be explicit. ■ If steps are to be executed in a certain sequence, number them.
7.6 Minimize the negative impact on users of new versions	■ Avoid needless change. ■ Change gradually. ■ Guide users from old to new.
7.7 Label interactive elements clearly	■ Label with text if possible. ■ Use easy-to-recognize icons.

SEARCH

8.1 Help users construct successful queries	■ Put the search box in upper right. ■ Show search terms in large font. ■ Make the search box long. ■ Make the search box "smart." ■ Anticipate likely searches.
8.2 Design search results to be friendly to users	■ Mark paid results. ■ Show search terms. ■ Mark already visited results.

ATTITUDE

9.1 Be flexible in how users can enter, save, and view data	■ Provide "smart" data input. ■ Put users in control.
9.2 Earn users' trust	■ Ask only what's necessary. ■ Mark ads clearly. ■ Don't make users log in.
9.3 Make your design appeal to all your users, including older adults	■ Understand older adults' values. ■ Don't talk down to older adults. ■ Don't assume users are young adults. ■ Don't blame users. ■ Don't be scary. ■ Don't rush users. ■ Don't skip steps.
9.4 Provide ready access to information users might want	■ Provide an easy way to contact you. ■ Provide a telephone alternative. ■ Show summary. ■ If you offer senior discounts, say so.

WORKING WITH OLDER ADULTS

10.1 Choose a study design or protocol suited to the population.	■ Make use of the advice offered by other age-related researchers. ■ Decide between individual or group designs. ■ Make sure the study situations are relevant to your participants. ■ Choose between concurrent and retrospective think-aloud protocols. ■ Avoid using user diaries. ■ Make it easy for participants to participate. ■ Avoid between-subjects experimental design.
10.2 Identify potential design or study participants.	■ Know your population. ■ Approach group living settings with caution.
10.3 Recruit and schedule participants.	■ Having a personal connection helps. ■ Select your contact method. ■ Recruit early, recruit extras. ■ Decide the desired diversity level in advance. ■ Plan to modify your screening tool. ■ Schedule your participants with their needs in mind, not yours. ■ Do yourself a favor: use reminders. ■ Take extra steps to increase participant attendance.
10.4 Plan the activity with extra attention to older-adult-centric details.	■ Be patient, be nice. ■ Be on the alert for any access issues. ■ Take control of the logistics and security. ■ Take the pressure off data collection.
10.5 Be especially mindful when conducting an activity with older adult participants.	■ Be polite, considerate and respectful. ■ Be as clear as possible. ■ Be patient. ■ Set expectations. ■ Warm up first.
10.6 Have an ethical "exit strategy" for your participants.	■ Wrap it up. ■ Teach your participants something new. ■ Return everything to its place. ■ Do no harm.

AARP, March 2014. You're old, I'm not: how Americans really feel about aging. AARP The Magazine 40–41. Retrieved from: pubs.aarp.org/aarptm/20140203_CA?pg=44#pg44.

Affonso de Lara, S.M., Massami Watanabe, W., Beletato dos Santos, E., Fortes, R.P.M., September 27–29, 2010. Improving WCAG for elderly web accessibility. In: Proceedings of SIGDOC '10, São Carlos, SP, Brazil.

Alexenko, T., Biondo, M., Banisakher, D., Skubic, M., March 19–22, 2013. Android-based speech processing for eldercare robotics. In: Proceedings of IUI '13 Companion, Santa Monica, CA, USA.

Almeida, N., Teixeira, A., Filipa Rosa, A., Braga, D., Freitas, J., Sales Dias, M., Silva, S., Avelar, J., Chesi, C., Saldanha, N., 2015. Giving voices to multimodal applications. In: Proceedings of the 17th International Conference on Human-Computer Interaction, HCI International 2015, Los Angeles, CA.

Anderson, M., October 29, 2015. Technology Device Ownership: 2015. The Pew Research Center. Retrieved from: www.pewinternet.org/files/2015/10/PI_2015-10-29_device-ownership_FINAL.pdf.

Arch, A., May 14, 2008. Web Accessibility for Older Users: A Literature Review. World Wide Web Consortium (W3C). Retrieved from: www.w3.org/TR/wai-age-literature/.

Arch, A., Abou-Zahra, S., September 2008. How web accessibility guidelines apply to design for the ageing population. In: Proceedings of the Accessible Design in a Digital World Conference, York, UK.

Arch, A., Abou-Zahra, S., Henry, S.L., 2009. Older Users Online: WAI Guidelines Address Older Users Web Experience. World Wide Web Consortium (W3C). Retrieved from: www.w3.org/WAI/posts/2009/older-users-online.

Bakaev, M., 2008. Fitts' law for older adults: considering a factor of age. In: Proceedings of the ACM Conference on Computer-Human Interaction, CHI '08, Porto Alegre, Brazil.

Bera, P., April 2016. How colors in business dashboards affect users' decision making. Communications of the ACM 59 (4), 50–57.

Besdine, R.W., n.d. Changes in the Body with Aging. Merck Manuals Consumer Version. Retrieved from: www.merckmanuals.com/home/older-people-s-health-issues/the-aging-body/changes-in-the-body-with-aging.

Blackwell, D.L., Lucas, J.W., Clarke, T.C., February 2014. Summary health statistics for U.S. Adults: National Health Interview Survey, 2012. Vital and Health Statistics 10 (260). Retrieved from: www.cdc.gov/nchs/data/series/sr_10/sr10_260.pdf.

Boechler, P., Watchorn, R., Dragon, K., Foth, D., May 2012. Older adults' vs. younger adults' web search: memory, performance and strategies. International Journal of Education and Ageing 2 (2), 125–128.

Bohan, M., Scarlett, D., February 11, 2003. Can expanding targets make object selection easier for older adults? Usability News (Software Usability Research Laboratory, Wichita State University) 5 (1), 5–7.

Bonilla-Warford, N., February 15, 2012. What to Do with 'New' Presbyopes. Review of Optometry. Retrieved from: www.reviewofoptometry.com/article/what-to-do-with-new-presbyopes.

Bowen, A., July 22, 2015. Why More Americans Would Choose to Stay at Age 50 than 20. Chicago Tribune. Retrieved from: www.chicagotribune.com/lifestyles/health/sc-hlth-afraid-aging-20150722-story.html.

Broady, T., Chan, A., Caputi, P., 2010. Comparison of older and younger adults' attitudes towards and abilities with computers: implications for training and learning. British Journal of Educational Technology 41 (3), 473–485.

Burns, P., Jones, S.C., Iverson, D., Caputi, P., 2013. Usability testing of AsthmaWise with older adults. Computers, Informatics, Nursing (CIN) 31 (5), 219–226.

Campbell, K.L., Shafto, M.A., Wright, P., Tsvetanov, K.A., Geerligs, L., Cusack, R., Tyler, L.K., November 2015. Idiosyncratic responding during movie-watching predicted by age differences in attentional control. Neurobiology of Aging 36 (11), 3045–3055. dx.doi.org/10.1016/j.neurobiolaging.2015.07.028.

Campbell, O., February 5, 2015. Designing for the elderly: ways older people use digital technology differently. Smashing Magazine. Retrieved from: www.smashingmagazine.com/2015/02/designing-digital-technology-for-the-elderly/.

Carmien, S., Garzo, A., June 22–27, 2014. Elders using smartphones: a set of research based heuristic guidelines for designers. In: Proceedings of the 8th International Conference, UAHCI '14, Held as Part of the HCI International 2014, Heraklion, Crete, Greece.

Cattell, R.B., 1987. Intelligence: Its Structure, Growth, and Action. Advances in Psychology, vol. 35. Elsevier Science Publishing Company, New York, NY.

Centers for Disease Control, December 1, 2015. Incidence of Diagnosed Diabetes per 1,000 Population Aged 18–79 Years, by Age, United States, 1980–2014. Centers for Disease Control and Prevention. Retrieved from: www.cdc.gov/diabetes/statistics/incidence/fig3.htm.

Charness, N., Boot, W.R., 2009. Aging and information technology use. Current Directions in Psychological Science 18 (5), 253–258.

Charness, N., Dijkstra, K., 1999. Age, luminance, and print legibility in homes, offices, and public places. Human Factors: The Journal of the Human Factors and Ergonomics Society 41 (2), 173–193.

Chisnell, D., February 28, 2011. Involving Older Adults in Design of the User Experience: Inclusive Design. Usability Works. Retrieved from: usabilityworks.com/involving-older-adults-in-design-of-the-user-experience-inclusive-design/.

Chisnell, D., Redish, J., December 14, 2004. Designing Web Sites for Older Adults: A Review of Recent Research. AARP. Retrieved from: assets.aarp.org/www.aarp.org_/articles/research/oww/AARP-LitReview2004.pdf.

Chisnell, D., Redish, J., February 1, 2005. Designing Web Sites for Older Adults: Expert Review of Usability for Older Adults at 50 Web Sites. AARP. Retrieved from: assets.aarp.org/www.aarp.org_/articles/research/oww/AARP-50Sites.pdf.

Chisnell, D., Redish, J., Lee, A., 2006. New heuristics for understanding older adults as web users. Technical Communication 53 (1), 39–59.

Cohen, S., 1994. Most comfortable listening level as a function of age. Ergonomics 37 (7), 1269–1274.

Coleman, G., Gibson, L., Hanson, V., Bobrowicz, A., McKay, A., August 16–20, 2010. Engaging the disengaged: how do we design technology for digitally excluded older adults? In: Proceedings of DIS '10, Aarhus, Denmark.

Cooper, A., 2004. The Inmates Are Running the Asylum: Why High Tech Products Drive Us Crazy and How to Restore the Sanity. Sams Publishing, Indianapolis, IN.

Cornish, K., Goodman-Deane, J., Ruggeri, K., Clarkson, P.J., September 2015. Visual accessibility in graphic design: a client-designer communication failure. Design Studies 40 (C), 176–195.

Correia de Barros, A., Leitão, R., September 2013. Young practitioners' challenges, experience and strategies in usability testing with older adults. In: Proceedings of the Assistive Technology Research Series, Vilamoura, Portugal.

Correia de Barros, A., Leitão, R., Ribeiro, J., 2014. Design and evaluation of a mobile user interface for older adults: navigation, interaction and visual design recommendations. In: Proceedings of the 5th International Conference on Software Development and Technologies for Enhancing Accessibility and Fighting Info-Exclusion, DSAI '13, Vigo, Spain.

Czaja, S.J., Lee, C.C., 2007. Information technology and older adults. In: Sears, A., Jacko, J.A. (Eds.), The Human-Computer Interaction Handbook: Fundamentals, Evolving Technologies and Emerging Applications, second ed. CRC Press, Boca Raton, FL, pp. 777–792.

Davidson, J., Jensen, C., October 21–23, 2013. What health topics older adults want to track: a participatory design study. In: Proceedings of ASSETS '13, Bellevue, WA.

Desjardins, J.L., Doherty, K.A., November–December 2014. Effect of hearing aid noise reduction on listening effort in hearing-impaired adults. Ear & Hearing 35 (6), 600–610.

Dickinson, A., Arnott, J., Prior, S., 2007. Methods for human-computer interaction research with older people. Behaviour & Information Technology 26 (4), 343–352.

Docampo Rama, M.H., de Ridder, H., Bouma, H., 2001. Technology generation and age in using layered user interfaces. Gerontechnology 1 (1), 25–40.

Dunn, T., February 1, 2006. Usability for Older Web Users. Webcredible. Retrieved from: www.webcredible.com/blog/usability-older-web-users/.

Durick, J., Robertson, T., Brereton, M., Vetere, F., Nansen, B., 2013. Dispelling ageing myths in technology design. In: Proceedings of the 25th Australian CHI Conference, OzCHI '13, Adelaide, Australia.

Eagleman, D., 2011. Incognito: The Secret Lives of the Brain. Pantheon Books, New York.

Fadeyev, D., September 24, 2009. 10 useful usability findings and guidelines. Smashing Magazine. Retrieved from: www.smashingmagazine.com/2009/09/10-useful-usability-findings-and-guidelines/.

Fairweather, P.G., October 12–15, 2008. How older and younger adults differ in their approach to problem solving on a complex website. In: Proceedings of the 10th ACM Conference on Computers and Accessibility, ASSETS '08, Halifax, Nova Scotia.

Family Caregiver Alliance, n.d. Caregiver Statistics. Family Caregiver Alliance. Retrieved from: www.caregiver.org/caregiver-statistics-demographics.

Finn, K., October 7, 2013. Designing User Interfaces for Older Adults: Myth Busters. UX Matters. Retrieved from: www.uxmatters.com/mt/archives/2013/10/designing-user-interfaces-for-older-adults-myth-busters.php.

Finn, K., Johnson, J., July 21–26, 2013. A usability study of websites for older travelers. In: Proceedings of the 7th International Conference, UAHCI '13, held as Part of the HCI International 2013, Las Vegas, NV.

Fisk, A.D., Rogers, W.A., Charness, N., Czaja, S.J., Sharit, J., 2009. Designing for Older Adults: Principles and Creative Human Factors Approaches. CRC Press, Boca, Raton, FL.

Franz, R., Mundane, C., Neves, B., Baecker, R., August 24–27, 2015. Time to retire old methodologies? Reflecting on conducting usability evaluations with older adults. In: Proceedings of MobileHCI '15, Copenhagen, Denmark.

Gao, Q., Sun, Q., August 2015. Examining the usability of touch screen gestures for older and younger adults. Human Factors: The Journal of the Human Factors and Ergonomics Society 57 (5), 835–863. dx.doi.org/10.1177/0018720815581293.

Gilbertson, T., 2014. Industry Attitudes and Behaviour towards Web Accessibility in General and Age-Related Change in Particular and the Validation of a Virtual Third-age Simulator for Web Accessibility Training for Students and Professionals (Unpublished doctoral dissertation). Loughborough University, England.

Gilbertson, T., 2015. Attitudes and behaviours towards web accessibility and ageing: results of an industry survey. Gerontechnology 13 (3), 337–344.

Goddard, N., Nicolle, C.A., 2012. What is good design in the eyes of older users? In: Langdon, P., Clarkson, J., Robinson, P., Lazar, J., Heylighen, A. (Eds.), Designing Inclusive Systems. Springer, London, pp. 175–184.

Graham, J., April 19, 2012. 'Elderly' No More. The New York Times: The New Old Age. Retrieved from: newoldage.blogs.nytimes.com/2012/04/19/elderly-no-more/.

Grindrod, K.A., Li, M., Gates, A., January–March 2014. Evaluating user perceptions of mobile medication management applications with older adults: a usability study. JMIR Mhealth Uhealth 2 (1).

GSMA Intelligence, 2015. The Mobile Economy 2015. GSMA. Retrieved from: www.gsmamobileeconomy.com/GSMA_Global_Mobile_Economy_Report_2015.pdf.

Habeskot, T., Vogel, A., Rostrup, E., Bundesen, C., Kyllingsbaek, S., Garde, E., Ryberg, C., Waldemar, G., April 2013. Visual processing speed in old age. Scandinavian Journal of Psychology 54 (2), 89–94. dx.doi.org/10.1111/sjop.12008..

Haddrill, M., Heiting, G., May 2014. Peripheral Vision Loss (Tunnel Vision). All about Vision. Retrieved from: www.allaboutvision.com/conditions/peripheral-vision.htm.

Hakobyan, L., Lumsden, J., O'Sullivan, D., 2015. Participatory Design: How to engage older adults in participatory design activities. International Journal of Mobile Human Computer Interaction (IJMHCI). Retrieved from: www.igi-global.com/article/participatory-design/128325.

Hanson, V., April 20–21, 2009. Age and web access: the next generation. In: Proceedings of the 2009 International Cross-Disciplinary Conference on Web Accessibililty, W4A '09, Madrid, Spain.

Hanson, V.L., Fairweather, P.G., Arditi, A., Brown, F., Crayne, S., Detweiler, S., 2001. Making the web accessible for seniors. In: Proceedings of International Conference on Aging (ICTA), Toronto, Canada.

Hanson, V.L., Gibson, L., Coleman, G.W., Bobrowicz, A., McKay, A., 2010. Engaging those who are disinterested: access for digitally excluded older adults. In: Presented at the Conference on Human Factors in Computing Systems, CHI '10, Atlanta, GA.

Hard, G., October 20, 2015. Car Reliability Is Hurt by Some New Technologies. Consumer Reports. Retrieved from: www.consumerreports.org/cars/car-reliability-is-hurt-by-some-new-technologies/.

Hart, T., Chaparro, B.S., Halcomb, C.G., 2008. Evaluating websites for older adults: adherence to "senior-friendly" guidelines and end-user performance. Behaviour & Information Technology 27 (3).

Hawkins, K., 2011. 6 Tips for Creating a Senior-Friendly Website. Quickbooks Resource Center. Retrieved from: quickbooks.intuit.com/r/marketing/6-tips-for-creating-a-senior-friendly-website/.

Hawthorn, D., 2006. Designing Effective Interfaces for Older Users (Doctoral thesis) The University of Waikato, NZ. Retrieved from: researchcommons.waikato.ac.nz/handle/10289/2538.

Heingartner, D., October 2, 2003. Now Hear This, Quickly. The New York Times.

Hill, R., Betts, L.R., Gardner, S.E., July 2015. Older adults' experiences and perceptions of digital technology: (Dis)empowerment, wellbeing, and inclusion. Computers in Human Behavior 48, 415–423.

Howe, N., Strauss, W., June 2007. The next 20 years: how customer and workforce attitudes will evolve. Harvard Business Review 85 (7–8), 41–52. Retrieved from: hbr.org/2007/07/the-next-20-years-how-customer-and-workforce-attitudes-will-evolve.

Jahn, G., Krems, J.F., 2013. Skill acquisition with text-entry interfaces: particularly older users benefit from minimized information-processing demands. Journal of Applied Gerontology 32 (5), 605–626.

Jarrett, C., 2003. Making web forms easy to fill in. In: Proceedings of the Business Forms Management Symposium, Baltimore, MD.

Johnson, J., 2007. GUI Bloopers 2.0: Common User Interface Design Don'ts and Dos, second ed. Morgan Kaufmann Publishers, Burlington, MA.

Johnson, J., 2014. Designing with the Mind in Mind: Simple Guide to Understanding User Interface Design Guidelines, second ed. Morgan Kaufmann Publishers, Waltham, MA.

Johnson, J., Henderson, A., 2011. Conceptual Models: Core to Good Design. Morgan & Claypool Publishers, San Rafael, CA.

Kahneman, D., 2011. Thinking Fast and Slow. Farrar, Straus and Giroux, New York, NY.

Kascak, L.R., Lee, S., Liu, E.Y., Sanford, J.A., August 2–7, 2015. Universal Design (UD) guidelines for interactive mobile voting interfaces for older adults. In: Proceedings of the 9th International Conference, UAHCI '15, held as Part of the HCI International 2015, Los Angeles, CA.

Kerber, N., 2012. Web Usability for Seniors: A Literature Review (Unpublished class paper) University of Baltimore. Retrieved from: www.nicolekerber.com.

Ketcham, C.J., Stelmach, G.E., 2002. Motor control of older adults. In: Ekerdt, D.J., Applebaum, R.A., Holden, K.C., Post, S.G., Rockwood, K., Schulz, R., Sprott, R.L., Uhlenberg, P. (Eds.), Encyclopedia of Aging. Macmillan Reference USA, New York, NY.

Kobayashi, M., Hiyama, A., Miura, T., Asakawa, C., Hirose, M., Ifukube, T., September 5–9, 2011. Elderly user evaluation of mobile touchscreen interactions. In: Proceedings of the 13th IFIP TC 13 International Conference, Lisbon, Portugal.

Komninos, A., Nicol, E., Dunlop, M., 2014. Reflections on design workshops with older adults for touchscreen mobile text entry. Interaction Design and Architecture(s) Journal (IxD&A) 20, 70–85.

Koyani, S., Bailey, R.W., Ahmadi, M., Changkit, M., Harley, K., 2002. Older Users and the Web. National Cancer Institute Technical Report.

Kurniawan, S., Zaphiris, P., October 9–12, 2005. Research-derived web design guidelines for older people. In: Proceedings of the 7th International ACM SIGACCESS Conference on Computers and Accessibility, ASSETS '05, Baltimore, MD.

Legge, G.E., Cheung, S.H., Yu, D., Chung, T.L., Lee, H.W., Owens, D., 2007. The case for the visual span as a sensory bottleneck in reading. Journal of Vision 7 (2), 1–15.

Leitão, R.A., October 2012. Creating Mobile Gesture-based Interaction Design Patterns for Older Adults: A Study of Tap and Swipe Gestures with Portuguese Seniors (Thesis, Master in Multimedia). Universidade do Porto, Portugal.

Leitão, R., Silva, P., October 19–21, 2012. Target and spacing sizes for smartphone user interfaces for older adults: design patterns based on an evaluation with users. In: Proceedings of the 19th Conference on Pattern Languages of Programs, PLoP '12, Tucson, AZ.

Leung, R., April 4–9, 2009. Improving the learnability of mobile device applications for older adults. In: Proceedings of the 2009 ACM Conference on Computer-Human Interaction (CHI '09), Boston, MA.

Leung, R., Findlater, L., McGrenere, J., Graf, P., Yang, J., 2010. Multi-layered interfaces to improve older adults' initial learnability of mobile applications. ACM Transactions on Accessible Computing 3 (1), 1–30.

Leung, R., Tang, C., Haddad, S., McGrenere, J., Graf, P., Ingriany, V., December 2012. How older adults learn to use mobile devices: survey and field investigations. ACM Transactions on Accessible Computing 4 (3) Article 11.

Ligons, F.M., Romagnoli, K.M., Browell, S., Hochheiser, H.S., Handler, S.M., October 22–26, 2011. Assessing the usability of a telemedicine-based Medication Delivery Unit for older adults through inspection methods. In: Proceedings of the AMIA Annual Symposium 2011, Washington, DC.

Lim, C., 2010. Designing inclusive ICT products for older users: taking into account the technology generation effect. Journal of Engineering Design 21 (2–3), 189–206.

Lim, C.S.C., Frohlich, D.M., Ahmed, A., 2012. The challenge of designing for diversity in older users. Gerontechnology 11 (2), 297.

Lin, F.R., Niparko, J.K., Ferrucci, L., November 14, 2011. Hearing loss prevalence in the US. Archives of Internal Medicine 171 (20), 1851–1852. Retrieved from: www.ncbi.nlm.nih.gov/pmc/articles/PMC3564588/.

Lindsay, S., Jackson, D., Schofield, G., Olivier, P., May 5–10, 2012. Engaging older people using participatory design. In: Proceedings of the 2012 ACM Conference on Computer-Human Interaction (CHI '12), Austin, TX.

Massimi, M., Baecker, R., September 17–21, 2006. Participatory design process with older users. In: Proceedings of the 8th International Conference on Ubiquitous Computing, UbiComp '06, Workshop on Future Networked Interactive Media Systems and Services for the New-Senior Communities, Orange County, CA.

McCreery, R.W., Venediktov, R.A., Coleman, J.J., Leech, H.M., December 2012. An evidence-based systematic review of directional microphones and digital noise reduction hearing aids in school-age children with hearing loss. American Journal of Audiology 21, 295–312.

Miño, G.S., 2013. Recommendations for Designing Interfaces for Seniors. Universidad del Desarrollo, Santiago, Chile (Publisher: Author).

Mitzner, T.L., Smart, C., Rogers, W.A., Fisk, A.D., 2015. Considering older adults' perceptual capabilities in the design process. In: Hoffman, R., Hancock, P.A., Scerbo, M.W., Prasuraman, R., Szalma, J.L. (Eds.), The Cambridge Handbook of Applied Perception Research. Cambridge Handbooks in Psychology, vol. 2. Cambridge University Press, Cambridge, England, pp. 1051–1079.

NASA Ames Research Center. n.d. NASA Ames Research Center, Color Usage Research Lab. Retrieved from: colorusage.arc.nasa.gov/guidelines_ov_design.php.

National Eye Institute (NIH), September 2015. Facts about Age-Related Macular Degeneration. National Eye Institute (NIH). Retrieved from: www.nei.nih.gov/health/maculardegen/armd_facts.

National Eye Institute (NIH). Age-related eye diseases. n.d. National Eye Institute (NIH). Retrieved from: nei.nih.gov/healthyeyes/aging_eye.

National Institute on Aging (NIH), March 2009. Making Your Website Senior Friendly: Tips from the National Institute on Aging and the National Library of Medicine. National Institute on Aging (NIA). Retrieved from: www.lgma.ca/assets/Programs-and-Events/Clerks-Forum/2013-Clerks-Forum/COMMUNICATIONS-Making-Your-Website-Senior-Friendly–Tip-Sheet.pdf.

Neves, B., Franz, R., Munteanu, C., Baecker, R., Ngo, M., April 18–23, 2015. "My hand doesn't listen to me!": adoption and evaluation of a communication technology for the 'oldest old'. In: Proceedings of the 2015 ACM Conference on Computer-Human Interaction (CHI '15), Seoul, Republic of Korea.

Newell, A.F., 2011. Design and the digital divide: insights from 40 years in computer support for older and disabled people. In: Baecker, R.M. (Ed.), Synthesis Lectures on Assistive, Rehabilitative, and Health-Preserving Technologies, first ed. Morgan & Claypool, San Rafael, CA.

Newell, A., Arnott, J., Carmichael, A., Morgan, M., July 22–27, 2007. Methodologies for involving older adults in the design process. In: Proceedings of the 2007 Human-Computer Interaction International Conference (HCII '07), Beijing, China.

Nielsen, J., January 1, 1995. 10 Usability Heuristics for User Interface Design. Nielsen Norman Group. Retrieved from: www.nngroup.com/articles/ten-usability-heuristics/.

Nielsen, J., May 28, 2013. Seniors as Web Users. Nielsen Norman Group. Retrieved from: www.nngroup.com/articles/usability-for-senior-citizens/.

Nunes, F., July 31, 2010. Healthcare TV Based User Interfaces for Older Adults (Thesis, Master in Informatics and Computing Engineering). Universidade do Porto, Portugal.

Nunes, F., Kerwin, M., Silva, P.A., October 22–24, 2012. Design recommendations for TV user interfaces for older adults: findings from the eCAALYX Project. In: Proceedings of the 14th International ACM SIGACCESS Conference on Computers and Accessibility, ASSETS '12, Boulder, CO.

O'Hara, K., 2004. "Curb Cuts" on the information highway: older adults and the internet. Technical Communication Quarterly 13 (4), 426–445. dx.doi.org/10.1207/s15427625tcq1304_4.

Olmsted-Hawala, E., Romano Bergstrom, J.C., Rogers, W.A., July 21–26, 2013. Age-related differences in search strategy and performance when using a data-rich web site. In: Proceedings of the 7th International Conference, UAHCI '13, Held as Part of the HCI International 2013, Las Vegas, NV.

Olmsted-Hawala, E., Romano Bergstrom, J., 2012. Think-aloud protocols: does age make a difference? STC Technical Communication Summit 12, 86–95.

Or, C., Tao, D., 2012. Usability study of a computer-based self-management system for older adults with chronic diseases. JMIR Research Protocols 1 (2). Retrieved from: www.researchprotocols. org/2012/2/e13/pdf.

Oregon State University, August 7, 2013. Cognitive Decline with Age Is Normal, Routine, but Not Inevitable. ScienceDaily. Retrieved from: www.sciencedaily.com/releases/2013/08/130807155352.htm.

Ostergren, M., Karras, B., November 10–14, 2007. ActiveOptions: leveraging existing knowledge and usability testing to develop a physical activity program website for older adults. In: Proceedings of the AMIA Annual Symposium 2007, Chicago, IL.

Owsley, C., Sakuler, R., Siemsen, D., 1983. Contrast sensitivity throughout adulthood. Vision Research 23 (7), 689–699.

OXO, n.d. Our roots. OXO. Retrieved from: www.oxo.com/our-roots.

Pak, R., October–December 2009. Age-sensitive design of online health information: comparative usability study. Journal of Medical Internet Research 11 (4), e45. www.jmir.org/2009/4/e45/.

Pak, R., McLaughlin, A., 2011. Designing Displays for Older Adults, second ed. CRC Press, Boca Raton, FL.

Patsoule, E., Koutsabasis, P., 2014. Redesigning websites for older adults: a case study. Behaviour & Information Technology 33 (6), 561–573. www.tandfonline.com/doi/abs/10.1080/0144929X. 2013.810777.

Pernice, K., Estes, J., Nielsen, J., 2013. Senior Citizens (Ages 65 and Older) on the Web. Nielsen Norman Group. Purchased from: www.nngroup.com/reports/senior-citizens-on-the-web/.

Perrin, A., Duggan, M., June 26, 2015. Americans' Internet Access: 2000–2015. Pew Research Center. Retrieved from: www.pewinternet.org/2015/06/26/americans-internet-access-2000-2015/.

Phiriyapokanon, T., 2011. Is a Big Button Interface Enough for Elderly Users? Towards User Interface Guidelines for Elderly Users (Thesis, Master of Computer Engineer). Mälardalen University, Sweden.

Plaza, I., Martín, L., Martin, S., Medrano, C., 2011. Mobile applications in an aging society: status and trends. Journal of Systems and Software 84 (11), 1977–1988 Elsevier Inc., Amsterdam, Netherlands.

Poushter, J., February 22, 2016. Smartphone Ownership and Internet Usage Continues to Climb in Emerging Economies. Pew Research Center. Retrieved from: www.pewglobal.org/2016/02/22/smartphone-ownership-and-internet-usage-continues-to-climb-in-emerging-economies/.

Practicology, 2016. Mobile Usability Report 2015/16: identifying the conversion blockers on the mobile websites of 15 UK retailers. Practicology. Retrieved from: www.practicology.com/files/5114/4543/6039/Practicology_WhatUsersDo_Mobile_Usability_Report_2015_Download. pdf.

Prensky, M., October 2001. Digital Natives, Digital Immigrants. On the Horizon, vol. 9 (5). MCB University Press, West Yorkshire, United Kingdom. Retrieved from: www.marcprensky. com/writing/Prensky%20-%20Digital%20Natives,%20Digital%20Immigrants%20-%20 Part1.pdf.

Quigley, H.A., Broman, A.T., 2006. The number of people with glaucoma worldwide in 2010 and 2020. British Journal of Ophthalmology 90 (3), 262–267. Retrieved from: www.ncbi.nlm.nih. gov/pmc/articles/PMC1856963.

Rae, A., 1989. What's in a name? International Rehabilitation Review. Retrieved from: disability-studies.leeds.ac.uk/files/library/Rae-Whatsname.pdf.

Raymundo, T.M., da Silva Santana, C., 2014. Fear and the use of technological devices by older people. Gerontechnology 13 (2), 260.

Reddy, G.R., Blackler, A., Popovic, V., Mahar, D., 2014. Adaptable interface model for intuitively learnable interfaces: an approach to address diversity in older users' capabilities. In: Proceedings of Design Research Society Conference 2014, 16–19 June 2014, Umea, Sweden.

Roberts, S., December 2009. The Fictions, Facts, and Future of Older People and Technology. International Longevity Centre, UK. Retrieved from: www.ilcuk.org.uk/images/uploads/publi-cation-pdfs/pdf_pdf_118-2.pdf.

Romano Bergstrom, J.C., Olmsted-Hawala, E.L., Jans, M.E., 2013. Age-related differences in eye tracking and usability performance: website usability for older adults. International Journal of Human-Computer Interaction 29, 541–548.

Russell, S., 2009. The Impact of Current Trends and Practices in Website Design on the Older Adult User in the Context of Internet Banking (PhD dissertation). Department of Computer Science, University College of Cork, Ireland. Retrieved from: dl.dropboxusercontent.com/u/600126/Thesis/Thesis.pdf.

Sackmann, R., Winkler, O., 2013. Technology generations revisited: the internet generation. Gerontechnology 11 (4), 493–503. dx.doi.org/10.4017/gt.2013.11.4.002.00.

Salthouse, T.A., Babcock, R.L., 1991. Decomposing adult age differences in working memory. Developmental Psychology 27 (5), 763–776.

Sanjay, J., Bailey, R.W., Nall, J.R., 2006. Research-Based Web Design and Usability Guidelines. U.S. Department of Health and Human Services. Retrieved from: www.usability.gov/sites/default/files/documents/guidelines_book.pdf.

Sapolsky, R., March 30, 1998. Open season. New Yorker 74 (6), 57–58 71–72.

Sayago, S., Blat, J., April 20–21, 2009. About the relevance of accessibility barriers in the everyday interactions of older people with the web. In: 2009 International Cross-Disciplinary Conference on Web Accessibility (W4A), W4A '09, Madrid, Spain.

Sayid, R., March 15, 2016. The REAL Age You Reach Old Age Is Revealed – and You Might Be Surprised. Mirror Online. Retrieved from: www.mirror.co.uk/news/uk-news/real-age-you-reach-old-7557520.

Shneiderman, B., Plaisant, C., Cohen, M., Jacobs, S.M., Elmqvist, N., Diakopoulos, N., 2016. Designing the User Interface, sixth ed. Pearson Education Ltd.

Siira, E., Heinonen, S., July 2015. Enabling mobility for the elderly: design and implementation of assistant navigation service. In: Proceedings of Transed 2015, Lisbon, Portugal.

Silva, P.A., Holden, K., Jordan, P., January 5–8, 2015. Towards a list of heuristics to evaluate smartphone apps targeted at older adults: a study with apps that aim at promoting health and well-being. In: Proceedings of the 48th Hawaii International Conference on System Sciences, HICSS '15, Kauai, HI.

Silva, P., Nunes, F., November 8–10, 2010. 3 x 7 usability testing guidelines for older adults. In: Proceedings of the 3rd Workshop on Human-Computer Interaction, MexIHC '10, San Luis Potosí, SLP, Méx.

Singh, R., Saxena, R., Varshney, S., 2008. Early detection of noise induced hearing loss by using ultra high frequency audiometry. The Internet Journal of Otorhinolaryngology 10 (2) Retrieved from: ispub.com/IJORL/10/2/4039.

Spencer, B., March 14, 2016. Old age? It starts at 85, say dynamic sixtysomethings: two thirds of those aged 60 to 69 plan to take up new hobbies or go travelling. The Daily Mail. Retrieved from: www.dailymail.co.uk/news/article-3492483/Old-age-starts-85-say-dynamic-sixtysomethings-Two-thirds-aged-60-69-plan-new-hobbies-travelling.html.

Spool, J., January 14, 2009. The $300 million button. User Interface Engineering. Retrieved from: articles.uie.com/three_hund_million_button.

Stevens, G., Flaxman, S., Brunskill, E., Mascarenhas, M., Mathers, C.D., Finucane, M., December 24, 2011. Global and regional hearing impairment prevalence: an analysis of 42 studies in 29 countries. The European Journal of Public Health 23 (1), 146–152. dx.doi.org/10.1093/eurpub/ckr176.

Stößel, C., July 3, 2012. Gestural Interfaces for Elderly Users: Help or Hindrance? (PhD thesis). Prometei Graduate School, Berlin Institute of Technology, Germany.

Strengers, J., October 16, 2012. Smartphone Interface Design Requirements for Seniors (Master's thesis) University of Amsterdam, Netherlands. Retrieved from: dare.uva.nl/document/460020.

Subasi, Ö., Leitner, M., Hoeller, N., Geven, A., Tscheligi, M., 2011. Designing accessible experiences for older users: user requirement analysis for a railway ticketing portal. Universal Access in the Information Society 10 (4), 391–402.

Tsui, B., August 21, 2015. The aging advantage. Pacific Standard Magazine. Retrieved from: www.psmag.com/health-and-behavior/the-aging-advantage.

Tullis, T., July 20, 2004. Tips for conducting usability studies with older adults. In: Proceedings of the Seminar on Older Users and the Web. GSA, & AARP, Washington, DC. Retrieved from: assets.aarp.org/www.aarp.org_/articles/research/oww/university/Tullis-Techniques.ppt.

United Nations Department of Economic and Social Affairs, Population Division, 2015a. World Population Prospects: The 2015 Revision, Key Findings and Advance Tables. Working Paper No. ESA/P/WP.241. United Nations, New York, NY. Retrieved from: esa.un.org/unpd/wpp/publications/files/key_findings_wpp_2015.pdf.

United Nations Department of Economic and Social Affairs, 2015b. Population Division: World Population Prospects, the 2015 Revision. United Nations Department of Economic and Social Affairs. Retrieved from: esa.un.org/unpd/wpp/DataQuery/.

United Nations Educational, Scientific and Cultural Organization (UNESCO), June 2013. Adult and Youth Literacy: National, Regional and Global Trends, 1985–2015. UNESCO Institute for Statistics, Montreal, Quebec, Canada. Retrieved from: www.uis.unesco.org/Education/Documents/literacy-statistics-trends-1985-2015.pdf.

Veiel, L.L., Storandt, M., Abrams, R.A., 2006. Visual search for change in older adults. Psychology and Aging 21 (4), 754–762.

Vines, J., Dunphy, P., Blythe, M., Lindsay, S., Monk, A., Oliver, P., February 11–15, 2012. The joy of cheques: trust, paper, and eighty somethings. In: Proceedings of the "Ethnography in the Very Wild Session", ACM Conference on Computer-Supported Collaborative Work, CSCW '12, Seattle, Washington.

Vipperla, R., 2011. Automatic Speech Recognition for Ageing Voices (PhD dissertation, Doctoral of Philosophy) Institute for Language, Cognition and Computation, School of Informatics, University of Edinburgh, Scotland. Retrieved from: homepages.inf.ed.ac.uk/srenals/pdf/ravi-thesis.pdf.

W3C-WAI-AGE Project (IST 035015), October 31, 2012. Web Accessibility Initiative: Ageing Education and Harmonisation (WAI-AGE). Retrieved from: www.w3.org/WAI/WAI-AGE/.

W3C-WAI-older-users, December 18, 2010. Web Accessibility and Older People: Meeting the Needs of Ageing Web Users. Retrieved from: www.w3.org/WAI/older-users/.

W3C-WCAG2.0, December 11, 2008. Web Content Accessibility Guidelines (WCAG) 2.0. Retrieved from www.w3.org/TR/WCAG20/.

Wahlman, A., April 20, 2015. Subaru Forester Lags with Terrible Infotainment System. TheStreet. Retrieved from: www.thestreet.com/story/13116864/1/subaru-forester-lags-with-terrible-infotainment-system.html.

Waycott, J., Vetere, F., Pedell, S., Kulik, L., Ozanne, E., Gruner, A., Downs, J., April 27–May 2, 2013. Older adults as digital content producers. In: Proceedings of the 2013 ACM Conference on Computer-Human Interaction (CHI '13), Paris, France.

Waycott, J., Morgans, A., Pedell, S., Ozanne, E., Vetere, F., Kulik, L., Davis, H., 2015. Ethics in evaluating a sociotechnical intervention with socially isolated older adults. Qualitative Health Research I-II 25 (11), 1518–1528. journals.sagepub.com/doi/full/10.1177/1049732315570136.

Weinschenk, S., 2011. 100 Things Every Designer Needs to Know about People. New Riders Publishing, San Francisco, CA.

Werner, C.A., U.S. Census Bureau, November 2011. The Older Population: 2010. Retrieved from: www.census.gov/prod/cen2010/briefs/c2010br-09.pdf.

Whiting, S., September 5, 2015. Eph Engleman, Violinist and Rheumatologist, Dies at Desk at 104. San Francisco Chronicle. Retrieved from: www.sfgate.com/art/article/Dr-Eph-Engleman-violinist-and-renowned-6485895.php.

Wilkinson, C., 2011. Evaluating the Role of Prior Experience in Inclusive Design (Thesis submitted for the Degree of Doctor of Philosophy). Cambridge University Engineering Department, Cambridge, UK.

Wilkinson, C., De Angeli, A., 2014. Applying user centered and participatory design approaches to commercial product development. Design Studies 35 (6), 614–631.

Wilkinson, C., Gandhi, D., February 2015. Future Proofing Tomorrow's Technology: UX for an Aging Population. User Experience: The Magazine of the User Experience Professionals Association. Retrieved from: uxpamagazine.org/future-proofing-tomorrows-technology/.

Williams, D., Alam, M.A.U., Ahamed, S.I., Chu, W., July 29–30, 2013. Considerations in designing human-computer interfaces for elderly people. In: Proceedings of the 13th International Conference on Quality Software (QSIC), Nanjing, China.

Wirtz, S., Jakobs, E., Ziefle, M., 2009. Age-specific usability issues of software interfaces. In: Proceedings of the 9th International Conference on Work with Computer Systems (WWCS), Beijing.

Worden, A., Walker, N., Bharat, K., Hudson, S., March 1997. Making computers easier for older adults to use: area cursors and sticky icons. In: CHI '97 Conference Proceedings. Proceedings of Human Factors in Computing Systems, Atlanta, Georgia. ACM, New York, NY, pp. 266–271.

World Health Organization, 2016. Global Health Observatory (GHO) data: Life Expectancy. World Health Organization. Retrieved from: www.who.int/gho/mortality_burden_disease/life_tables/situation_trends_text/en/.

Wroblewski, L., May 4, 2010. Touch Target Sizes [Web Log Post]. LukeW Ideation + Design. Retrieved from: www.lukew.com/ff/entry.asp?1085.

Youmans, R.J., Bellows, B., Gonzalez, C.A., Sarbonne, B., Figueroa, I.J., July 21–26, 2013. Designing for the wisdom of elders: age related differences in online search strategies. In: Proceedings of the 7th International Conference, UAHCI '13, held as Part of the HCI International 2013, Las Vegas, NV.

Zajicek, M., May 22–25, 2001. Interface design for older adults. In: Proceedings of the EC/NSF Workshop on Universal Accessibility of Ubiquitous Computing: Providing for the Elderly, WUAUC '01, Alcecer do Sal, Portugal, pp. 60–65.

Zeitchik, S., July 18, 2015. Ian McKellen's Not Slowing Down, Taking 'Mr. Holmes' on a Thoughtful Journey. Los Angeles Times. Retrieved from: www.latimes.com/entertainment/movies/la-et-mn-ian-mckellen-mr-holmes-20150718-story.html#page=1.

Zickuhr, K., 2013. Who's Not Online and Why. Pew Research Center. Retrieved from: www.pewinternet.org/files/old-media//Files/Reports/2013/PIP_Offline%20adults_092513_PDF.pdf.

Ziefle, M., Bay, S., 2005. How older adults meet complexity: aging effects on the usability of different mobile phones. Behaviour & Information Technology 24 (5), 375–389.

Index